FAMILY GROUP CONFERENCES IN SOCIAL WORK

Involving families in social care decision making

Edited by Deanna Edwards and Kate Parkinson

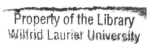

First published in Great Britain in 2018 by

Policy Press
University of Bristol
1-9 Old Park Hill
Bristol
BS2 8BB
UK
t: +44 (0)117 954 5940
pp-info@bristol.ac.uk
www.policypress.co.uk

North America office:
Policy Press
c/o The University of Chicago Press
1427 East 60th Street
Chicago, IL 60637, USA
t: +1 773 702 7700
f: +1 773-702-9756
sales@press.uchicago.edu
www.press.uchicago.edu

British Library Cataloguing in Publication Data
A catalogue record for this book is available from the British Library

Library of Congress Cataloging-in-Publication Data
A catalog record for this book has been requested

978-1-4473-3580-1 hardback
978-1-4473-3582-5 paperback
978-1-4473-3581-8 ePdf
978-1-4473-3583-2 ePub
978-1-4473-3584-9 Mobi

Cover design by Hayes Design
Front cover image kindly supplied by Anya Humphrey
Printed and bound in Great Britain by CPI Group (UK) Ltd, Croydon, CR0 4YY
Policy Press uses environmentally responsible print partners

Kate:
For Ruby, Sam and Scarlett – may
you be who you want to be.

Deanna:
In memory of Bridget Lindley who inspired so many
and fought so hard for justice for families.

For Anya whose love, kindness and passion for life
demonstrate to me daily the true meaning of family.

Contents

Glossary of terms

Anti-discriminatory practice
Practice that seeks to counter and challenge the impact of discrimination of people, as a result of gender, race and ethnicity, sexual orientation, disability, religion or belief and socio-economic status (see definition of discrimination).

Anti-oppressive practice
Practice that seeks to counter and challenge the oppression of others (see above). See also 'oppression'.

CAMHS (Child and Adolescent Mental Health Service)
A NHS service that assesses and supports young people with mental health difficulties.

Care order
An order is made by the court under Section 31 of the Children Act 1989 which places a child in the care of the local authority, with parental responsibility being shared between the parents and the local authority. A care order lasts until a child turns 18, unless someone applies for it to end earlier under Section 39, 'Discharge of a care order'.

Care proceedings
Care proceedings are court proceedings issued by the Social Services department of the local authority where an application is made for a 'care order' or 'supervision order' in respect of a child.

Children in need
'Children in need' is the term used in the Children Act 1989 to describe children who need services that will allow them to be brought up within their families, and that local authorities have powers and duties to provide. Section 17, Children Act 1989, states that a child in need is a child who is unlikely to achieve or maintain a reasonable level of health or development, or their health and development is likely to be significantly impaired or further impaired, without the provision of services. This definition does not apply in Wales from April 2016 when the Social Services and Well-being (Wales) Act 2014 was implemented.

Child protection conference

A meeting that is convened when a child is assessed as being at risk of or experiencing significant harm (see 'significant harm'), under the Children Act 1989. The meeting is chaired by an independent chair and attended by social workers and other professionals with the aim of determining the risks to children and considering how to minimise identified risks. The conference will result in a child protection plan, which will identify the responsibilities of family members, professionals and services in addressing the risks identified, with the aim of keeping children safe from harm.

Collectivist cultural systems

A system that values the needs of a group over those of the individual.

Community conferences

Conferences that involve members of a particular community including residents and other stakeholders such as public servants, business owners to address particular questions, problems or issues faced by the community. Community Conferences are facilitated by and independent coordinator.

Cultural competence

Being able to understand a broad spectrum of varying cultures and having a developed understanding of the important and influential beliefs related to specific cultures. A culturally competent social worker will better understand how culture and diversity may impact on how services are delivered and what interventions could produce better outcomes for those people receiving services.

Discrimination

Discrimination is the practice of treating one person or group of people less fairly or less well than other people or groups on the basis of gender, race and ethnicity, sexual orientation, disability, religion or belief and socio-economic status.

Ecological systems theory/Ecological social work theory

A theory of social work that seeks to understand the impact of environmental factors on individuals, families and communities and the complex interactions between an individual and their environment.

Empowerment
The process of granting an individual person or a group of people power and status within a particular context or situation.

Harmful sexual behaviour (children and young people)
Calder (2002) suggests the following definition for harmful sexual behaviour in young people:

> Young people (below the age of 18 yrs) who engage in any form of sexual activity with another individual that they have powers over by virtue of age, emotional maturity, gender, physical strength, or intellect and where the victim in this relationship has suffered a sexual exploitation and betrayal of trust. Sexual activity includes sexual intercourse, sexual touching, exposure of sexual organs, showing pornographic material, exhibitionism, voyeurism, obscene communication (frottage), fetishism and talking in a sexualised way. We should also include any form of sexual activity with an animal, and where a young person sexually abuses an adult. (adapted from Palmer, 1995)

HCPC (Health and Care Professions Council)
The HCPC is an independent regulator which regulates 16 health and care professions including social work. Social Workers and other professions are registered to the HCPC. Professionals can be de-registered if they practice in a manner which contravenes the HCPC standards for practice.

Looked-after child
'Looked after' is a legal status for a child or young person which creates specific rights for the child and powers and duties for the local authority. The child may be looked after by the local authority either because (1) their parents have agreed to this under s 76 Social Services and Well-being (Wales) Act 2014) or Section 20 Children Act (1989) or because (2) there has been a court order giving the local authority a share in parental responsibility. These court orders are section 31 (care order) and section 38 (interim care order). Looked-after children are often referred to as 'in care'.

Munro review
A systems analysis of child protection policies and practices in the UK undertaken by Professor Eileen Munro in 2010, with 15 recommendations for improvements to the child protection system.

Neoliberal
Neoliberalism is a political philosophy of competitive individualism that calls for minimal state involvement in social and economic regulation. Associated with the emergence of the New Right in the 1980s (Reagan and Thatcher). Associated with high levels of social and economic inequality between social groups, with extremes of great wealth and poverty.

Oppression
The cruel or unfair treatment of a particular group of people on the grounds of gender, race and ethnicity, sexual orientation, disability, religion or belief and socio-economic status.

Pedagogic
Pedagogy is the theory of teaching and learning.

Person-centred practice
Practice which ensures that an individual is at the heart of decision making about their lives and the care and support that they receive.

Pre-proceedings process
Part of the Public Law Outline (PLO) (see definition) under which a local authority formally notifies a parent that a care application is being considered. It involves a letter before proceedings and a pre-proceedings meeting.

Psychodynamic approaches
An approach to social work practice that locates adult problems and difficulties in their childhood experiences. This approach is criticised for failing to address the impact of environmental factors and the social origins of problems and difficulties.

Public Law Outline (PLO)
Procedures that local authorities have to follow when care proceedings are to be initiated. The PLO governs the local authority at every stage of the process, including pre-proceedings (see above) and mandates

for care proceedings to be completed within 26 weeks (unless there are exceptional circumstances).

Quasi-experimental treatment group

A quasi-experimental study is a study which evaluates the effectiveness of interventions but where randomisation is not possible. Such studies do not have a control group. A quasi-experimental treatment group will be a group of people who have been involved in a particular intervention which is being tested.

'Rape myth culture'

Rape myths are stereotypical or prejudicial beliefs to explain sexual assault and rape. These myths are influenced by various cultural factors such as traditional gender roles, attitudes towards interpersonal violence and misunderstandings around the nature of sexual assault.

Referral order

A **referral order** is an **order** available for young offenders who plead guilty to an offence whereby the young offender is referred to a panel of two trained community volunteers and a member of the youth offending team. It can be for a minimum of three months and a maximum of twelve months.

Restorative practice

Restorative practice is a term used to describe practice which helps to build and maintain healthy relationships, resolve difficulties and repair harm where there has been conflict. It is an umbrella term which covers a range of approaches including restorative justice and FGCs.

Safeguarding adults

Safeguarding means protecting people's health, wellbeing and human rights, and enabling them to live free from harm, abuse and neglect. Safeguarding adults includes:

- Protecting their rights to live in safety, free from abuse and neglect.
- People and organisations working together to prevent the risk of abuse or neglect, and to stop them from happening.
- Making sure people's wellbeing is promoted, taking their views, wishes, feelings and beliefs into account.

Safeguarding children

Safeguarding means protecting people's health, wellbeing and human rights, and enabling them to live free from harm, abuse and neglect. Safeguarding children and promoting their welfare includes:

- Protecting them from maltreatment or things that are bad for their health or development.
- Making sure they grow up in circumstances that allow safe and effective care.

Significant harm

The Children Act 1989 introduced the concept of 'Significant Harm' as the threshold that justifies compulsory intervention in family life in the best interests of children and gives local authorities a duty to make enquiries to decide whether they should take action to safeguard or promote the welfare of a child who is suffering, or is likely to suffer significant harm.

There are no absolute criteria to rely on when judging what constitutes Significant Harm. Whether the harm or likely harm suffered by the child is significant is determined by comparing the child's health or development with that which could reasonably be expected of a similar child. Professionals must also take account of the child's reactions, and his/her perceptions and wishes and feelings, according to their age and understanding.

Signs of safety

An approach to social work created by Turnell and Edwards (1999) in which workers consider family strengths that can be built upon and risks that they seek to minimise.

Solution-focused practice

An approach that involves working collaboratively to identify solutions to identified problems and difficulties. It is a future orientated approach and one which builds upon the strengths of individuals and families.

Strengths-based approaches

An umbrella term for practice which recognises and seeks to identify and build upon the existing strengths and resources of individuals, families and communities. The underlying philosophy of these approaches is that every individual has strengths that can be built upon. Includes FGCs, signs of safety restorative conferences and solution focused approaches.

Task centred theory

A theory of social work practice which places strong emphasis on solving problems considered to be important to the service user themselves by completing a series of small tasks.

Triangulated randomised control group

A study in which a number of similar people are randomly assigned to two (or more) groups to test a specific drug, treatment or other intervention. One group (the experimental group) has the intervention being tested, the other (the comparison or control group) has an alternative intervention, a dummy intervention (placebo) or no intervention at all. The groups are followed up to see how effective the experimental intervention was. Outcomes are measured at specific times and any difference in response between the groups is assessed statistically. This method is also used to reduce bias.

Youth offending service

A team of professionals who support young people who have been involved in criminal activity. The focus of the team is to divert young people away from offending.

References

Calder, M.C. (ed.) (2002) *Young people who sexually abuse – building the evidence base for your practice*, Lyme Regis: Russell House Publishing.

Criminal Justice and Courts Bill: Referral orders. https://www.gov.uk/government/uploads/system/uploads/attachment_data/file/322209/fact-sheet-youth-referral-orders.pdf.

Munro, E. (2011) *Munro review of child protection: a child-centred system.* London: Department of Education.

National Institute for Health and Clinical Excellence (NICE), *NICE Glossary*, https://www.nice.org.uk/glossary

Pierson, J. and Thomas, M. (2006) *Collins Dictionary of Social Work*, Glasgow: Collins.

Practice direction 12a – care, supervision and other Part 4 proceedings: guide to case management. https://www.justice.gov.uk/courts/procedure-rules/family/practice_directions/pd_part_12a.

Turnell, A. and Edwards, S. (1999) *Signs of safety: a safety and solution oriented approach to child protection casework*, New York: WW Norton.

Webber, M. (ed.) (2015) *Applying Research Evidence in Social Work Practice*, London: Palgrave Macmillan.

Yeates, N. (ed.) (2014) *Understanding Global Social Policy, 2nd edn*, Bristol: Policy Press.

Notes on contributors

Monique Anderson is currently undertaking a PhD at the University of Leuven (Belgium). Her research examines the justice interests of young people who have been sexually harmed by another young person from within their family circle. The study seeks to understand whether such knowledge could be used to enhance restorative justice processes. Prior to starting her PhD, Monique held the position of Executive Officer at the European Forum for Restorative Justice. Before relocating to Belgium in 2011, Monique worked in the criminal justice system in London (UK). Previous roles include: Neighbourhood Crime and Justice Coordinator (for the Home Office Neighbourhood Crime and Justice Unit), Community Safety Coordinator (Barking and Dagenham Community Safety Team), various roles within Youth Offending Teams and serving as a Prisoner Officer at HMP Wormwood Scrubs. Monique holds a Master of Criminology degree from KU Leuven (Belgium), a postgraduate diploma in Forensic and Legal Psychology from the University of Leicester (UK) and a Bachelor of Science degree in Psychological Sciences from the University of Westminster (UK).

Dr Louise Brown is an Associate Professor of Social Work at the University of Bath, England. She is a qualified social worker with a background in child protection practice. Dr Brown has over 15 years' experience as a social work educator and researcher. A key area of her research expertise is the development, implementation and evaluation of family group conferencing as it moves between countries. In recent years she has been involved in supporting the transfer of the FGC model to China, where she has been examining the importance of cultural adaptation and the role of evidence in the movement and transfer of social work practice internationally.

Jonny Cohen currently works for Leeds Youth Offending Service (YOS) as a ReConnect coordinator. (ReConnect is the FGC service of Leeds YOS). Jonny has been in this role since January 2012, setting the service up from scratch. Jonny is a qualified Social Worker, with a Social Work Masters qualification from the University of York. His career has included stints as a Generic Area Social Worker (1996–1999), a Social Worker specialising in adolescent casework (1999–2000), YOS case manager (2000–2006 and 2008–2009), parenting programme coordinator and practitioner (2006–2008), and a strategic role in developing parenting programme provision across Leeds (2009–2011).

Deanna Edwards is a lecturer in Social Work at the University of Salford with a keen interest and practice background in Family Group Conferences. She has been involved in FGCs since 1998 and has been a coordinator and has set up and managed a FGC service. She has previously worked as a FGC policy adviser for Family Rights Group and is an experienced trainer and FGC consultant. She has an interest in service user participation particularly with reference to children and young people.

Dr Iyabo Ayodele Fatimilehin is a Consultant Clinical Psychologist and director of Just Psychology CIC, a social enterprise she founded in 2011 to address the psychological and mental health needs of black and minority ethnic (BME) children, families and communities. Previously, she worked in the NHS for over 20 years and was service lead for a specialist CAMH service for BME children and families that delivered Family Group Conferences for several years. She works as a trainer, therapist, and consultant and provides expert witness assessments for the courts. Iyabo's skills and experience include service development and management, facilitation of community participation and community development, research, evaluation. She has published journal articles and book chapters on issues of race, culture and ethnicity in relation to working with BME children and families. Iyabo is an Associate Fellow of the British Psychological Society, has chartered status, and is a registered practitioner psychologist with the Health and Care Professions Council.

Tim Fisher has been involved in Family Group Conferencing for more than ten years as an advocate, coordinator and manager of FGC projects in Cardiff, Essex and Camden. Tim is a former chair of the All Wales FGC Network and a current member of the national accreditation of FGC projects development group. A qualified social worker with MA research on direct payments and time spent working with the NSPCC, Welsh Government and Research in Practice for Adults. He has developed his ideas on Family Group Conferencing; blogging and writing various articles in places such as Community Care, Research in Practice and the Centre for Family Potential.

Nick Frost is Professor of Social Work (Childhood, children and families), at the School of Health and Community, Leeds Beckett

University. Nick has published widely in the fields of child welfare: most recently, 'Family Support' (Polity, 2015, with Abbott and Race). 'Developing Multi-professional Teamwork for Integrated Children's Services' (McGraw Hill, 2016, with Robinson) the 'Routledge Handbook of Global Child Welfare' (2017, with Dolan). Nick is a registered social worker, and practiced in local authority social work settings for 15 years before commencing his academic career. He has experience of chairing two Local Safeguarding Children Boards.

Bernie Jackson is one of the Team Managers of Leeds Family Group Conference Service. She was seconded to set up and deliver a FGC service in South Leeds in 2008 and became the manager in 2010 when it expanded to become a city wide service. Bernie holds a BA (Hons) in Social Policy and Administration and qualified as a Social Worker in 1984, initially working in Kirklees, and has worked with all client groups, including working as an Approved Social Worker under the Mental Health Act. She joined Leeds Children's Services in 1991 working in a children and families team and in 1999 became a specialist in child protection, undertaking complex assessments with families, mentoring newly qualified social workers, chairing child protection conferences and delivering multi agency child protection training. Bernie is interested in service user involvement and leads the FGC Adult Service User Group in Leeds.

Dr Jie Lei is the Associate Professor in Social Work as well as the Deputy Director of the Centre for Social Work Education and Research at Sun Yat-sen University, China. Dr Lei's research areas are professionalisation of social work, social assistance and child protection in China. He has published research articles in the *British Journal of Social Work*, *Critical Social Policy*, *International Social Work* and *Social Policy and Society*.

Beth Mooney became interested in restorative principles whilst studying Sociology at the LSE (London School of Economics and Political Sciences). She focused her undergraduate dissertation on the topic and has since pursued this interest through Family Group Conferencing in the social work space. She is set to return to further study in October 2017 with an MPhil in Criminology at the University of Cambridge.

Dave Norton currently works for Leeds Youth Offending Service (YOS) as a ReConnect coordinator. (ReConnect is the FGC service of Leeds YOS). Dave has been in this role since October 2012. Dave's career in social care began in 1994 as a Care Officer in an all-female children's home in Leeds. From 1998–2006 Dave worked at a Secure Children's Home in Leeds as a Senior Care Officer, and latterly as an Assistant Team Leader. Dave started with Leeds YOS in 2006 and was a case manager through to 2012 when he joined ReConnect. During this period Dave attained a Foundation Degree in Youth Justice from Open University.

Andrew Papworth became a social worker in the early 1970s working with a wide spectrum of people and communities. He was constantly aware of the lack of trust between 'clients' and the agencies. In 1989/91, now working with only children and families he saw the introduction of the 1989 Children Act, with its emphasis on working in partnership. It was apparent that this change did not mean very much to the people he worked with. In 1995 he became aware of FGCs and then – with great joy – he realised that they were not only a good idea, but that they worked and were valued by families. He started working as an independent co-coordinator and helped several London authorities to develop their FGC provision, including Camden, which he managed from 2003–6. He then started looking at the potential for using FGCs with adults. He knows that there remains enormous potential for this participatory model.

Kate Parkinson is a lecturer in Social Work at the University of Salford. She has a background in children and families social work and has managed a FGC service in the Midlands. Her research interests include FGCs and restorative approaches to social work, domestic abuse and the relationship between poverty and social work. Kate is a passionate advocate for FGCs and considers that FGCs should form the basis for an alternative child protection system.

Michaela Rogers is a Lecturer in Social Work at the University of Salford, UK. She is a registered social worker and has a professional and academic background in social work and social care. Previously her work in the statutory and voluntary sectors has involved working with different groups of vulnerable people (including young people, women and children escaping domestic abuse). Michaela's research has centred on the needs of vulnerable and marginalised communities (including trans people and people with mental health difficulties) in relation to social care and social work, and this extended to homelessness in her PhD research, which explored trans people's experiences of domestic abuse and the service response in terms of social care and housing-related support. Michaela is a member of the Sustainable Housing and Urban Studies Unit and the Children and Young People Research Group at the University of Salford.

Marilyn Taylor is the co-founder and CEO of Daybreak Family Group Conferences (FGC). She has worked in social work and probation, as a practitioner, manager and trainer, in both the statutory and voluntary sectors, in England and in Canada. Daybreak remains the only charity in England to focus entirely on FGC. It values innovative and reflective practice, including using FGC to address issues for vulnerable adults and domestic violence. She leads Daybreak's provision of a FGC social franchise as well as expanding its training and consultancy programmes. Marilyn has presented at a range of national and international conferences.

Acknowledgements

We would like to thank the following people:

Our friends and colleagues at the University of Salford including Ian Cummins, Donna Peach and Sarah Pollock; staff at Family Rights Group; our friends and family for their support and encouragement especially Stuart, Paul and Anya; the families we have worked with; Salford University students past and present; contributing authors; Anya Humphrey for the cover art.

This book has been a labour of love and we feel privileged to be writing about FGCs. It would however not have been possible without your support.

Note

A number of case studies appear throughout this book. All of these are based on real cases. Names and identifying details have been changed unless otherwise stated.

Foreword

In 1995 Family Rights Group published the first UK book[1] on family group conferences (FGCs). Contributors to the book addressed questions as to whether FGCs can bring families together, whether families will make decisions and how best to implement the FGC approach.

In 2006 we published the Family Group Conference Toolkit and in 2007 a book, *Family group conferencing – Where next?: Policies and practices for the future*, with commentaries analysing the development of FGCs in this country.

I'm delighted that this book by Deanna Edwards and Kate Parkinson builds upon those publications by examining innovations in the field, and the challenges, constraints and opportunities facing those committed to the FGC approach.

There have been notable domestic successes in the last ten years. FGCs are now promoted in English Government statutory pre-proceedings guidance, and in Scotland new legislation similarly promotes family decision making. Family Rights Group has developed the first post-qualifying FGC award, and together with the national FGC Network, drew up an accreditation scheme for FGC services to help ensure FGCs operated to consistent high-quality standards and consistent values. Twenty-six local FGC services have now been accredited, with a further six in the process. Internationally, FGCs have been introduced as a child welfare approach in countries as diverse as Sri Lanka, Bulgaria and France.

Seventy-six percent[2] of English local authorities now have some form of FGC service, compared to thirty-eight percent in 2001.[3] There is also renewed interest in FGCs by local authorities in Scotland. Leeds City Council has shown that FGCs can become a core part of the state's offer in how it works with families, utilising families' capacities and strengths to protect and support children to live safely within their family network, where possible. FGCs are also being increasingly used creatively to address a range of situations affecting families, as several chapters describe. One new area of development that Family Rights Group is embarking on is Lifelong Links for children in care. The Lifelong Links operational model draws upon the US family-finding model, learning from a pilot in Edinburgh and the input of young people in care, care leavers, social workers and families. It involves tools and techniques for professionals to use to search for and find family members (known or unknown to the child) and other adults (such as former foster carers or teachers) who care about the child. This network is then brought together in a FGC to make a life-long support plan with, and for, the young person. This should then become part of their care and pathway plan. It is being trialled initially in seven English and two Scottish authorities and will be independently evaluated.

Yet, despite the good news, there's still a huge task ahead. Care proceedings are at record levels within England, many FGC services are small scale and only a minority are accredited. Most families are not offered an FGC prior to their child entering the care system. Nor in most authorities are the values of FGC reflected consistently in how child welfare services work with families.

So, there is plenty to do. But it is striking that while practice, services and research have all substantially developed and grown, the core FGC principles have remained the same. Family Rights Group has a critical role in continuing to work with partners to ensure agencies that are using FGCs hold on to the integrity of the approach.

Family Rights Group is proud to support the development of FGCs and I am sure that this book will play a significant role in influencing the future development of child welfare policy and practice.

Cathy Ashley, Chief Executive, Family Rights Group

Notes

[1] Morris, Kate and Tunnard, Jo (1995) *Family Group Conferences: Messages from UK Practice & Research*, London: Family Rights Group.

[2] Family Rights Group survey conducted in 2015 (unpublished).

[3] Brown, L. (2002) *Follow up survey of Family Group Conference Use Across England and Wales*, Bath: University of Bath Research Summary.

Part One
Introducing Family Group Conferences

ONE

Introduction

Deanna Edwards

This book presents a set of chapters which explore the application of Family Group Conferences (hereafter often referred to as FGCs) as a family-led decision-making model in the social care field. The first three chapters provide a context for FGCs. Chapter Two explores the legislative and policy context for FGCs within the UK. Chapter Three provides a detailed description of FGCs and emphasises the distinction between the model and other decision-making processes. Chapter Four examines the theoretical context of FGCs and locates the model within social work and sociological theory frameworks. Subsequent chapters explore the application of Family Group Conferences in particular areas of social care practice: child protection, youth justice, young people who display harmful sexual behaviour and adult social care. Other chapters discuss the relevance of Family Group Conferences as a culturally competent method of social work practice and demonstrate the cross-cultural application of the model, as a global model of decision making. The book aims to provide a detailed overview of FGCs for a wide audience of interested readers. These may include social workers and social work students, FGC practitioners and family members who have had, or are considering, an FGC. The book provides a multi-disciplinary approach with contributing authors from a range of backgrounds. This includes family members who have experienced an FGC, practitioners and academics. Inevitably this leads to a varied approach to chapters which aims to add to the wide appeal of the book. A glossary is provided for those not familiar with social work terminology. Since there are a range of authors this will encompass a range of views on the FGC process which encompasses both an enthusiastic endorsement and a more critical perspective.

History and development

Family Group Conferences are welfare decision-making meetings which originated in New Zealand in the 1980s. They emerged in response to concerns in New Zealand (Aotearoa) about the outcomes for Maori children and young people involved with social care services. This resulted in the 1988 Puao te ata tu report (Ministerial Advisory Committee, 1988) which was the result of extensive consultation with Maori communities. The report recommended the development of participatory decision making when working with the Maori community and a requirement to respect Maori culture and tradition. This was enshrined in legislation as part of the 1989 Children, Young Persons and their Families Act as a requirement to offer families a Family Group Conference. The CYPF Act remains the primary legislation in governing child welfare and youth justice in New Zealand and, as Maxwell and Morris (2006) have observed, the Act defends the rights and needs of the indigenous population and makes families central to decision making. This means that, wherever possible, the family should participate in decisions that affect the child or young person and consideration should be given to the wishes of that child or young person. The Act gives licence to use FGCs in both child welfare and youth justice cases.

FGCs were introduced to the UK in 1992 by Family Rights Group, a UK charity which focuses on supporting families involved with social care services. Family Rights Group assisted the development of six FGC pilot projects in England and Wales. Subsequently two of these services dropped out leaving three English and one Welsh project. These were in Hampshire, Wandsworth, Hereford and Worcester, and Gwynedd, North Wales. The first UK based FGC was held in Wales in 1993 coordinated by the Cwlwm project. An evaluation of the projects was conducted by the University of Sheffield (Crow and Marsh, 1997, Marsh and Crow, 1998) in tandem with local evaluation and research (Edwards, 2007). Since then there has been a growth of empirical research on FGCs in the UK, and this theme will be explored in later chapters.

The introduction of FGCs into the UK fitted the agenda drives for children's social care at that time, including the recent introduction of the 1989 Children Act, which places emphasis on partnership working and the growing understanding of the family as expert. The introduction of FGCs also coincided with an increasing belief that 'protection is best achieved by building on the existing strengths of the child's living environment rather than expecting miracles from isolated and spasmodic interventions' (Department of Health, 1995).

The current context

Since then FGCs have grown gradually in the UK and exist worldwide. They are used in all areas of child welfare. Family Rights Group (2015) state that 76% of local authorities across England and Wales had a child welfare-based FGC service. FGCs are also being increasingly used in adult social care services, particularly in mental healthcare, learning disability and the care of older people (see Chapter 12 for a detailed discussion of FGCs with adults). More recently child welfare FGCs have been influenced by the Public Law Outline (known as the PLO and since 2014 as Practice Direction 12A). The PLO recommends the use of FGCs in identifying and planning for family and friends' care and support in the pre-proceedings stage of public law proceedings. Statutory guidance (Children Act 1989, Court Orders 2014 and Children Act 1989, Department for Education, 2011a) recommends the use of FGCs if there is a possibility that a child or children may not be able to remain with parents. The majority of FGCs in England and Wales use FGCs in pre-proceedings and proceedings cases. The PLO does not apply to Scotland and Northern Ireland, where FGCs are being used across the spectrum of child welfare services and not just at the pre-care stage.

The UK Government's response to the Family Justice Review highlights FGCs and their use at the pre-proceedings stage, arguing that 'the benefits of Family Group Conferences should be more widely recognised and their use should be considered before proceedings' (Ministry of Justice, 2012: 58).

In terms of cost effectiveness, it can be argued that FGCs are cost effective if they prevent proceedings, prevent children and young people entering the care system or enable children and young people to return home. Of course, as with any social care intervention it is difficult to prove beyond doubt a cause and effect relationship between the FGC and the outcome. Nevertheless a number of Local Authorities have attempted to evidence where FGCs have contributed to a significant cost saving. One example of this is Coventry FGC service, who in 2013 estimated savings of between £477,000 and £879,000 in fostering, contact, daycare and respite costs and an additional saving of £53,231 in family support worker hours (Coventry Council, 2013).

Key principles and values of the model

A detailed account of the FGC model will be presented in Chapter Three with a guide to preparing and convening an FGC, so for the purposes of this introductory chapter a brief guide to the model will be presented alongside a summary of the underlying principles. Several of these principles make FGCs distinctive from other social care interventions. The first of these is the use of an independent coordinator or facilitator to convene the meeting. This person, although often employed directly by the local authority, is not a decision maker for the family in question, and is there only to convene the FGC. As Chapter Three highlights, there is often an attempt to 'match' this person to the family in terms of ethnicity, culture and language although for smaller projects this may be an unachievable ideal. The second distinctive key principle is the provision of 'private family time'. This is an unlimited amount of time during the meeting when the family are left alone without the presence of any social care professionals to formulate a family plan. Careful preparation to enable the family to effectively and safely make use of this planning time is essential to the success of FGCs and private planning time ensures that the family are the architects of the plan. FGCs therefore begin with the appointment of an FGC coordinator who facilitates the process. He or she will meet with the family and prepare them for their FGC. The FGC will take place at a time and place convenient for all those attending and a key principle of the process is that the family decide who to invite to the meeting and can define 'family' as widely as they choose. This means that families will often choose to invite friends and other supporters to their FGC. They may choose to invite people who work with them such as family support workers, teachers etc., although those who attend the meeting in a professional capacity will not be invited to participate in private family time.

A further key principle is that the family children's services social worker (or referrer if the referral doesn't come from a social worker) will attend the meeting and will be the person who approves the plan. They will provide a report for the meeting which will include strengths of the family, key concerns, questions that need addressing and the 'bottom line'.

The central principle of FGCs is that the family devise and agree a plan during private family time. This plan will be agreed by the referrer if it addresses concerns and the bottom line and it is safe and legal. The difference between this and other decision-making meetings is that in an FGC the family decide the plan in consultation with social care professionals, while in other social care decision-making meetings social care professionals make decisions in consultation with the family.

The value base of FGCs is one of empowerment and it comes from the strengths-based tradition (Saleebey, 2002) of social work interventions which holds the core belief that all individuals have strengths and resources (Laursen, 2003) and therefore focuses on a person's skills and support systems (Nissen et al., 2005). An FGC should therefore seek to build upon family strengths and minimise concerns. This is discussed further in Chapter Two.

The FGC model begins with a **referral**. Reasons for referral will depend upon the criteria of the agency but the referral question or questions should be clear and direct. Once a referral is accepted an FGC **coordinator** is appointed. As we have seen the coordinator needs to be independent and is the person who will prepare and convene the meeting. The FGC coordinator will work with the family to decide who attends the meeting and when and where the meeting will take place. Once preparation is complete the FGC will take place. Meetings take place in neutral venues chosen by the family – often community and family centres. Coordinators will help the family to decide a suitable venue.

The meeting takes place in three distinct stages – information sharing; private family time; and agreeing a plan. Information sharing involves those at the meeting in a professional capacity outlining the information they have, what needs addressing at the meeting and what the 'bottom line' is – that is, what won't be agreed to in a family plan. Once this is established the family can go into private family time, where they discuss and agree a plan. Once this is done they will call the coordinator and others back into the meeting to discuss their plan and to determine if it has addressed concerns and is safe and legal. If so, the plan will be agreed. Once the plan is clarified and agreed the coordinator will set a date for it to be **reviewed** and the meeting will be closed. A full and detailed discussion of the stages and process of an FGC will be presented in Chapter Three.

FGC research: a brief overview

FGC research in the UK began with an evaluation of the original pilot projects started by Family Rights Group in 1992. This evaluation was conducted by Crow and Marsh and was published in 1997. Future chapters will present more detailed analysis of some of the FGC research. It is worth noting, though, that Marsh (2009) has argued that FGCs have been more widely researched than any other areas of social work practice, which makes comparisons difficult. Research in the UK has tended to focus on outcomes for children involved in child protection processes. Research has been mixed in terms of the efficacy of FGCs but there is some consensus (Ashley (ed.),

2006; Ashley and Nixon (eds), 2007; Huntsman, 2006) that FGCs can result in:

- significantly fewer children entering state care/significantly more children remaining in the care of their families;
- improved contact arrangements between children in care and their families;
- families developing safe plans for their children;
- children and families being more engaged than in traditional child protection processes.

It is important to note that much of the research on the efficacy of FGCs has tended to be small scale in nature, focusing on small geographical areas (Fox, 2008). Furthermore, there have been no comparative studies undertaken in the UK of any significance that have compared the outcomes from FGCs with traditional approaches to child protection decision-making (Frost, Abram and Burgess, 2014b). Much of the UK research on FGCs also dates back to the 1990s and there is clear need for up-to-date and larger scale UK-based research to be conducted. There does, however, exist some more recent UK-based research which substantiates the success of FGCs. For example, Morris (2007), in her evaluation of the Camden FGC service, found a significant reduction in the use of formal child protection proceedings and an increase in the number of children being looked after by their family following an FGC. Frost and Elmer (2008) also concluded in his evaluation of the South Leeds FGC service that acceptable plans were agreed at all of the FGCs in the evaluation. Furthermore a good deal of the UK research has focused upon the participation and engagement of families in the FGC process and suggests that families feel increasingly empowered by FGCs and are positive about them, and children and young people felt they had more say over decision making about their lives (Bell and Wilson, 2006: Holland et al., 2005; Holland and O'Neill, 2006; Marsh and Walsh, 2007; Frost and Elmer, 2008; Percy-Smith and Thomas, 2010).

Current developments in FGCs

We have seen earlier in the chapter how FGCs have developed as a recommendation in current legislative practice and how their growth has steadily increased from their UK inception in the 1990s. A consequence of the growth of FGCs is that Family Rights Group has emerged as the UK champion of FGCs and is seen by many as both the originator and guardian of FGC practice nationally. It has developed both a national and international reputation for FGC expertise and offers training in a range of FGC related fields, including coordinator training and FGC consultancy. Family Rights Group has for many years provided the National FGC Network, a network that UK-based FGC projects, practitioners and family members can join to keep up-to-date with current FGC practice, policy and legislation. Alongside their members, Family Rights Group has lobbied continuously for a voice for families involved with social care services, as part of which it has advocated passionately for FGC practice. For many years it has provided guidance for projects and practitioners and produced its first set of practice guidance in 2002, written in partnership with Barnardos and NCH (National Children's Home [now known as Action for Children]). Family Rights Group provides quarterly FGC Network meetings for FGC practitioners and projects, and has been among the first UK organisations to provide accreditation for both FGC practitioners and FGC projects and services. The process of accreditation for both is still voluntary – neither coordinators nor services are required to have an accredited qualification or kitemark. An increasing number of coordinators are becoming accredited, however, either through the Family Rights Group/University of Chester (and latterly University of Salford) Post-Graduate Certificate in FGCs, or through Netcare, who also provide an FGC qualification. A number of FGC services are now asking for coordinators to have an FGC qualification, or at least to have completed accredited training.

In 2011, Family Rights Group was commissioned by the Department for Education to pilot an accreditation scheme for projects. Individual coordinator accreditation was already underway and a growing number of FGC services with an increased FGC profile and a potential for variation in standards has led to pressure to both provide guidance for good practice and to measure minimum standards that projects should reach. This pressure has not only come from projects, but also from judges seeking to recommend FGCs, from successive governments recommending them as good practice and from families demanding an equitable service.

The pilot accreditation scheme was evaluated by Brown (2013). At this time 15 services had taken part in the pilot, citing their reasons as being to reflect on their practice, to secure funding and to improve their practice. Since then, the project roll-out has aimed to accredit a further 40 services (Family Rights Group, 2016). While services have found this process useful, it needs to be stressed that at present most services are not accredited and there is currently no requirement for accreditation. This inevitably leads to variation in practice standards, and we recognise that during the current climate of austerity there is pressure to cut the time taken to prepare and convene FGCs and other key principles that make FGCs successful. It is therefore essential to promote minimum FGC standards, such as those developed by Family Rights Group.

FGC practice standards: a summary

Family Rights Group, in consultation with the national FGC network of England and Wales, agreed seven FGC standards. The aim of these is to '[assist] families as well as professionals to understand what a Family Group Conference is and what to expect if involved in one' (Family Group Conference project accreditation, 2016: 2).

These standards are as follows:

1. The FGC coordinator is independent.
2. The FGC should respect the family's consent to proceed.
3. The FGC should be family-led, and include 'private time' for the family to make a plan in response to concerns.
4. The central focus should be the child or adult who is the subject of the FGC, and they should be offered support in their involvement including an advocate.
5. The FGC service should ensure that the family has all necessary resources, including adequate preparation, relevant information and a safe and appropriate environment to make its plan.
6. The FGC should respect the family's privacy and right to confidentiality.
7. The FGC should be sensitive to the family's culture, taking account of ethnicity, language and religion.

These standards are further divided into a number of sub-standards (Family Rights Group, n.d.b).

FGC coordinator training

As stated in the previous section, on 'Current developments in FGCs', there is currently no requirement for FGC practitioners to hold a qualification in FGCs or a related field in order to practice as an FGC coordinator. Similarly, in the UK, there is no absolute requirement for FGC coordinators to undertake training, although most employers will require some evidence of expertise in FGCs which usually includes a requirement to have undergone some form of FGC training. FGC training has grown organically over the years and this growth has been led, again, by Family Rights Group and a number of large providers of FGCs such as Daybreak, Barnardos and Action for Children. It is now almost universally standard practice in the UK to offer a minimum of three days basic training for FGC coordinators. This tends to take place over three consecutive days and both Netcare and the University of Salford have built this training into their FGC qualification. Training will include information on the model, legal issues, how to engage and prepare families and children and young people and how to work with resistance. Typical FGC training will include a mix of information, group work and role play exercises.

An FGC case study

All case studies presented in this book are based on real cases. Names and identifying details have been changed unless otherwise stated.

Carla had been referred for a family group conference by a hospital social worker following concerns about her mental health and an attempted suicide. This suicide attempt followed the recent death of her mother. Carla, 14, and her brother Jacob, 12, had been living with her mother and step-father and had had little contact with their birth father for several years. Following their mother's death they remained in the care of their step-father but their relationship with him had deteriorated and he had moved his 16-year-old son Stephen in with them. Carla and Jacob did not get on well with Stephen and had made claims that both Stephen and their step-father had physically chastised them. Carla had started to self harm and her attendance at school became sporadic. She was briefly admitted to hospital following an overdose and was allocated a social worker following her discharge. The social worker referred the family to the local FGC service; both Carla and Jacob engaged well with the FGC coordinator. Their step-father was also keen to improve the home situation and was willing to be involved in an FGC. The questions set for the FGC were 'where will Carla and Jacob live following the death of their mother?' and 'who in the family will help to support Carla and Jacob following the death of their mother?'.

Carla and Jacob were involved in all aspects of the FGC, including who to invite to the meeting. Their invitation list included their step-father and Stephen, their birth father, paternal grandparents, maternal grandparents, paternal aunt and uncle, and their maternal aunt and cousin. Carla also wanted to invite her CAMHS (child and adolescent mental health service) worker and a school teacher, both of whom she felt had been very supportive following her bereavement. Neither Carla nor Jacob felt they required advocacy support for the meeting, though this was offered.

The meeting was held in a local family centre on a weekday evening. All invited participants attended the meeting. Both Carla and Jacob provided 'wishes and feelings' which were read out during the information sharing stage of the meeting. The plan produced at the meeting included the following:

- Carla and Jacob to start to have regular contact with birth father and paternal grandparents with a view to re-establishing relationships and possibly living with them in the future.
- Carla to move temporarily in with maternal grandparents to give both her and her step-father a break.
- Stephen to spend weekends with his mum to give the step-father a break and to try and improve his relationship with Carla and Jacob.
- Maternal aunt and cousin to offer respite when required and support for the family, and aunt to take Carla to school while she is with grandparents.

Carla remained permanently with maternal grandparents and Jacob moved in with his father once they had re-established a relationship. Carla and Jacob maintained regular contact.

Conclusion

This chapter has introduced the reader to the use and current status of FGCs in the UK. FGCs have been used in the UK since the early 1990s and are now used worldwide following their inception in New Zealand in the 1980s. FGCs belong to an area of social work practice often known as 'strengths based approaches' because they seek to utilise the existing and developing strengths of the family and reduce or eliminate concerns. They are used in a wide range of social care child welfare situations from early intervention onwards, but recent use has focused upon their use in child protection, pre-proceedings and proceedings cases. They seek to empower families: their key principles include the family as primary decision maker, the use of private family time and the independence of the FGC coordinator.

FGCs remain a voluntary process in the UK and are not part of statutory provision. They are, however, part of recommended practice in a number of recent Government policies and are seen as key to early engagement of families in the pre-proceedings stage of public law. FGC standards also remain a voluntary process. These standards exist in relation to both individual coordinators and FGC services, but while we would recommend them as good practice there is currently no compulsory training or qualification for coordinators or accreditation process for projects or services. Future chapters in this text will explore some of the issues presented in this chapter in more depth, starting with a detailed exploration of the theoretical context for Family Group Conferences in Chapter Two.

TWO

The theoretical context for FGCs

Kate Parkinson

FGCs have been written about extensively, as a global model of social work practice and decision making (Ashley and Nixon, (eds) 2007; Barnsdale and Walker, 2007; Frost, Abram and Burgess 2014a,b). The cultural origins of the model are rooted in the traditions and cultural practices of the Maori people, something which is well documented (Barn and Das, 2016; Burford and Hudson (eds) 2000; Pakura, 2003). Little, however, has been written about the theoretical underpinnings of the FGC model (Metze, Abma and Kwekkeboom, 2013). References are made in the literature to FGCs as a strengths-based approach and a model based upon the empowerment of families. It appears, however, that most writing on FGCs does not involve a comprehensive analysis of the theoretical underpinnings of the model.

The FGC model is a social work process and is used within approximately 76% of local authorities within England and Wales as well as in several countries across the globe to address issues that social workers are facing (Family Rights Group, 2015). It is therefore important that social workers understand the model in relation to the theoretical framework of the profession. This chapter contextualises the FGC model in relation to key social work and sociological theories. It aims to create a framework for social work students, social work practitioners and educators to understand the model and where it fits into contemporary social work theory and practice.

Key social work theories will be taken in turn and applied to the FGC approach. It is important to note that one chapter cannot address each theory in great depth and that each theory could have a chapter in its own right. Thus, relevant reading will be provided at the end of the chapter for those who wish to explore the theoretical context of FGCs further.

This chapter can be linked to Chapters One and Three, which identify and address the key values of FGCs, and Chapter Nine, which examines FGCs and their application to marginalised communities.

Throughout the chapter, examples of FGC services have been applied to demonstrate theoretical perspectives in practice. Much of this information is from the author's own practice knowledge of FGC services and is not published or documented. Indeed there is a wealth of knowledge and practice wisdom within the field of FGCs, which is purely anecdotal and is undocumented.

The strengths-based approach

Much has been written about the FGC model as a strengths-based approach, with the underlying philosophy being that all individuals, families and communities have strengths and that they are the 'experts' on their own difficulties and issues (Ashley and Nixon (eds) 2007; Barnsdale and Walker, 2007; Metze, Abma and Kwekkeboom, 2013). Moreover, the strengths-based approach to practice is widely viewed as best practice in social work by academics, policy makers and practitioners (Care Act, 2014; Department for Education, 2015c; Munro, 2011; SCIE, 2015). Eileen Munro (2011) in her review of child protection processes in the UK advocates for a strengths-based approach to managing child protection cases prompting several local authorities to adopt the Signs of Safety Approach (Turnell and Edwards, 1999), a strengths-based model of child protection, originating in Australia (Signs of Safety, n.d.). Furthermore, within the field of adult social care, the Care Act 2014 states that:

> The Care Act 2014 requires local authorities to 'consider the person's own strengths and capabilities, and what support might be available from their wider support network or within the community to help' in considering 'what else other than the provision of care and support might assist the person in meeting the outcomes they want to achieve'. In order to do this the assessor 'should lead to an approach that looks at a person's life holistically, considering their needs in the context of their skills, ambitions, and priorities'. (Care Act, 2014)

Subsequent practice guidance (2015) recommends the use of strengths-based approaches to social work in adult social care, promoting some local authorities, such as Tower Hamlets, to develop a 'signs of safety' approach to safeguarding adults (Stanley, 2016).

Similarly, in practice within mental health social work, the strengths-based approach aligns itself with the Recovery Model, which emphasises a paradigm shift in mental health practice (Jacob, 2015). The Recovery Model focuses on resilience and supporting service users to take control over their lives, rather than pathologising their illness using a medicalised approach. This model is also applied in practice with those misusing drugs and alcohol (Jacob, 2015).

Practice within the field of youth justice across the globe also embodies a strengths-based approach, with restorative approaches to youth offending (see Chapter Eleven) being well established in New Zealand, Australia, the US, Canada and Europe (van Ness, 2005).

The strengths-based approach offers an alternative to traditional, deficit models of social work (Early and GlenMaye, 2000; Saleebey, 1996; Simmons and Lehmann, 2013). The approach is concerned with the capacity of individuals, families and groups to harness their strengths and resources to address difficulties, issues and concerns. The fundamental philosophy is that strengths exist within all individual, families and communities and that professionals can offer support to enable these strengths to be harnessed (Pattoni, 2012). The approach is not about ignoring risk, rather it is about recognising that need and risk are inextricably linked and that by meeting the needs of service users, risk will be reduced (Pattoni, 2012). The approach recognises that while people often need support to address issues, difficulties and concerns, if this support does not complement their existing strengths and resources, it can undermine a person's ability to learn and develop and be self-determining (Rapp, Saleebey and Sullivan, 2008).

Rapp, Saleebey and Sullivan (2008) offer six standards for judging what constitutes a strengths-based approach.

1. Goal orientation: Strengths-based practice is goal oriented. The central and most crucial element of any approach is the extent to which people themselves set goals they would like to achieve in their lives.
2. Strengths assessment: The primary focus is not on problems or deficits, and the individual is supported to recognise the inherent resources they have at their disposal which they can use to counteract any difficulty or condition.
3. Resources from the environment: Strengths proponents believe that in every environment there are individuals, associations, groups and institutions, all of whom have something to give, that others may find useful, and that it may be the practitioner's role to enable links to these resources.

4. Explicit methods are used for identifying client and environmental strengths for goal attainment: These methods will be different for each of the strengths-based approaches. For example, in solution-focused therapy clients will be assisted to set goals before the identification of strengths, whilst in strengths-based case management, individuals will go through a specific 'strengths assessment'.

5. The relationship is hope-inducing: A strengths-based approach aims to increase the hopefulness of the client. Further, hope can be realised through strengthened relationships with people, communities and culture.

6. Meaningful choice: Strengths proponents highlight a collaborative stance where people are experts in their own lives and the practitioner's role is to increase and explain choices and encourage people to make their own decisions and informed choices. (Rapp, Saleebey and Sullivan, 2008: 81)

If one refers to the six standards listed above, it is clear that FGCs are an embodiment of the strengths-based model. They are goal orientated, in that a family are asked to develop a plan to meet identified needs, issues and concerns and to set goals for their family to meet in addressing these issues. The philosophy of FGCs is based upon the fundamental belief that there are strengths in all families, individuals and communities that can be mobilised to meet identified need. The basis of an FGC is one of hope – that a family will be able to develop a safe plan. Furthermore, the process is a collaborative one in the sense that an FGC is a family-led rather than a professionally led meeting. Finally, families have a choice as to whether to engage with the FGC process or not (Ashley and Nixon (eds), 2007; Barnsdale and Walker, 2007; Fox, 2008).

Some FGC services, such as Edinburgh and Essex, have incorporated a Signs of Safety approach into their FGC model, with the professional report for the FGC using the Signs of Safety format: that is, 'what are we worried about?', 'what is working well?', 'what needs to happen?' (Bunn, 2013). This is clearly similar to the traditional language of FGC reports which focuses on strengths, concerns and the bottom line. Furthermore some FGC services, such as Blackburn, use the Three Houses Tool which is a Signs of Safety approach to ascertaining the wishes and feelings of children, to prepare children for their FGC and to enable them to meaningfully contribute.

Solution-focused practice

Solution-focused practice is acknowledged as being aligned to the strengths-based approach to practice, sharing many of the same assumptions and underlying principles (Healy, 2014). While the solution-focused approach does not have its origins in a particular theoretical framework, having being developed by practitioners trying to develop their practice and understand 'what works' in helping others (Shennan, 2014), the solution-focused approach is underpinned by a set of theoretical principles (Healy, 2014). These principles are that all individuals have the capacity to change and that they, not the professionals are the 'experts' on their situation; and that change occurs by focusing on solutions and not problems and building on the positive elements in any given situation (Myers, 2007: 5–10).

It is these theoretical principles that can be related to the FGC model. It could be argued that the FGC approach is based upon 'change' in that there is a recognition that a family need to work together to develop a plan which addresses the risks in a given situation. The belief is that a family can develop a safe plan that addresses the risks and, in this sense, have the capacity to change. Furthermore, while the risks are not ignored, there is a focus on the positive aspects of a situation and this message is clear in reports for FGCs, in which the strengths of the family are clearly highlighted (Ashley (ed.), 2006). Barnsley FGC Service have incorporated a solution-focused approach into their FGC model, using the language and tools of solution-focused practice in all stages of the FGC process (Preferred Futures, n.d.). The name of their FGC service, Preferred Futures, embodies this language, as one of the key elements of the solution-focused approach is encouraging people to think about their preferred futures and how they might get there (Shennan, 2014). Furthermore, key solution-focused tools, such as scaling and the miracle question are used to support families to develop a plan for the future safety and well-being of their children (de Shazer, 1988).

Task-centred theory

Gambrill (1994) defines task-centred practice as, '...a short-term problem-solving approach in which the focus is on tasks that clients and practitioners carry out to resolve problems that clients have agreed to work on'. (p. 578).

Like other future-focused approaches, the emphasis is on goal-setting to facilitate change and it very much emphasises the importance of the social worker in facilitating this change. The model suggests an individual-focused intervention, rather than a group decision-making process, as the focus is on individuals setting goals which are particular to their situation (Healy, 2014). Despite this, however, it can be argued that task centred theory can be applied to the FGC model. Indeed Healy (2014: 142–3) outlines eight practice principles of the task centred approach and six of these principles can be applied to FGCs, as outlined below.

Seek mutual clarity with service users

Under the task-centred approach, developing mutual clarity with service users on the issues to address and how to achieve these is considered to be a necessary feature of developing a constructive working relationship between professionals and service users. This is indeed the case in the FGC process. Obtaining the agreement and the co-operation of a family in the FGC process very much relies on a family agreeing to the identified issues and concerns and to their involvement in addressing these issues and concerns. Prior to an FGC taking place, the social worker's report is shared with the family and mutual agreement reached about the purpose of the FGC. For an FGC to be successful, a family need to be fully engaged with the process and committed to addressing the identified issues – they are after all the key decision makers (Connolly and Morris, 2011).

Aim for small achievements rather than large changes

The focus of many FGCs is on large decisions and changes, for example, who is going to look after a child or young person that cannot be cared for within their immediate family (Barnsdale and Walker, 2007). Therefore, this principle, arguably, does not apply to the FGC approach, as the focus is on small changes. One of the fundamental principles of the FGC approach, however, is that families and communities can work together to support each other to achieve change. Thus the contribution and changes that each individual is making could potentially be quite small in the wider scheme of things, but when each individual's contribution is combined together in a family plan, the overall result can be significant. Furthermore, from experience of encountering hundreds of FGC plans, many plans are intricate and very detailed, with a number of people taking individual responsibility for seemingly very small tasks and activities, the outcome being that the 'big' issues are addressed by the minutiae.

Focus on the here and now

The task-centred approach is not concerned with the historical context of problems, difficulties and issues, unlike psychodynamic approaches to social work. In fact advocates for the task-centred approach consider that focusing on the past can impede an individual's capacity to address their current issues (Healey, 2014). So, too, are FGCs focused on the here and now. The independent coordinator for an FGC does not have historical information about the family that they are supporting. Furthermore, the social worker's report for the FGC does not include a chronology of past events or provide a historical context, as reports for other social work meetings tend to (Ashley (ed.), 2006). Instead the report focuses on the current situation, issues and risks and what needs to change to keep children or vulnerable adults safe. In doing so, the aim is to keep the family future-focused and facilitate change, rather than creating a situation where families get stuck in the past and are not able to move on. Social work should be about facilitating change, not maintaining the status quo, and both task-centred approaches and FGCs are rooted in this belief.

Promote collaboration between worker and service user

The task-centred model is based upon a collaborative partnership between service user and the social worker, with both parties playing an active role in the change process. The role of the social worker is to facilitate, assist and advise and the service user is expected to undertake the changes identified and be accountable for doing so. This process mirrors the relationship between FGC coordinator and a kinship/family group. The role of the FGC coordinator is to support a family through the FGC process. Their role is to ensure that a family understand the practice of an FGC and what will be expected of them at an FGC, to ensure that a family understand the issues and concerns to be addressed, to negotiate between family members if required, to support a family to agree their family plan and to support them in presenting their plan to professionals (Ashley (ed.), 2006; Barnsdale and Walker, 2007). This is, in effect, a facilitation and advisory role. Families on the other hand are expected to develop a safe plan and be accountable for this plan, engaging with a review process if necessary.

The success of an FGC depends upon a collaborative relationship between the FGC coordinator and the family. The independence of the coordinator from decision-making processes emphasises the collaborative nature of the relationship between both parties, as an attempt to redress the balance of power between service users and professionals (Frost, Abram and Burgess, 2014b).

Build client capacities for action

The task-centred approach is focused on supporting service users to build their capacity to address the issues, problems or difficulties in their lives. Healy (2014) states that the task-centred approach does not ignore the fact that an individual's problems may be connected to psychological issues or structural factors and inequalities (one of the criticisms often applied to the approach – see, for example, Oak and Campling, 2008), rather it encourages the service user to focus on using their own strengths, capacities and resources to address their issues, recognising the structural and psychological issues are beyond the scope of an individual's problem-solving capacity. Indeed, one potential criticism of the FGC approach is that by encouraging families to take responsibility for their own issues, difficulties and concerns, this ignores the impact of structural factors, such as poverty, inequality, oppression and discrimination and in a neo-liberal context, could locate the focus of 'blame' onto family members. Furthermore, there is a danger of professionals placing all of the responsibility to address issues with the family and the resources they have between them, rather than providing professional advice and support. Indeed, research has suggested that in situations where family plans fail, in many cases this is due to a local authority not providing resources promised to a family and sufficient support (Crampton, 2007; Kanyi, 2013; Weigensberg, Barth and Guo, 2009).

It is indeed the case that an FGC can neither address the structural factors that have impacted upon a family's current situation nor can it address the psychological issues that may be present as a result of past trauma. What an FGC does do is support a family to identify the strengths and resources that they already have, and to build and capitalise on these to address problems and concerns in their family plan (Barnsdale and Walker 2007; (Ashley (ed.), 2006); Frost, Abram and Burgess, 2014b). It is the role of the independent coordinator to support a family through the FGC process, with the aim of enabling them to identify what strengths and resources they already have within their family (Barn and Das, 2016; Barnsdale and Walker, 2007; (Ashley (ed.), 2006); Frost, Abram and Burgess, 2014a). Furthermore, it is the role of the social worker to identify resources which may enable a family to build upon these strengths (Olson, 2009).

Planned brevity

Task-centred practice is focused on planned, short term interventions, which is considered to benefit both service users and welfare agencies. Reid and Epstein (1972) argue that having timescales motivates service users and that short, less resource intensive interventions benefit cash strapped local authorities (in Healy, 2014). While the FGC approach is a decision-making process, rather than a social work intervention, the principle of planned brevity to a large extent applies to the approach. The FGC process is, in itself, not time limited, unless it has to fit into statutory processes, such as child protection procedures. The principle of minimum social work intervention and families utilising their own resources to meet assessed need and address risk, however, rather than having social care services involved with their family, is fundamental to the FGC process. After all, FGCs were born out of inappropriate and punitive state responses and the belief that the family and communities could address the failings of the state (Umbreit and Peterson Armour, 2011). Furthermore, just as Reid and Epstein (1972) highlighted the dual benefit of task-centred approaches for both service users and welfare providers, research into FGCs has highlighted these benefits too. There is a large body of established research on the potential benefits of FGCs for families and newly emerging research that has highlighted the cost benefits to local authorities. For example, recent figures from Coventry City Council (2013) estimated that the city's FGC service made an annual cost saving of between £651,000 and £1,230,000 (Coventry City Council, 2013).

Empowerment theory

Empowerment can be defined as 'a process, a mechanism by which people... gain mastery over their lives' (Rosenfield in Tilley and Pollock, 1999: 47). Tengland states that for empowerment to be apparent, the professional needs to '... retreat[s] as much as possible from her paternalistic position, and that there is a reduction of the power, control, influence, or decision-making, of the professional and at the same time an increase in power in the individual or group supported' (Tengland, 2008, quoted in Metze, Abma and Kwekkeboom, 2013: 91). Empowerment is a central feature of social work practice and it is embedded in the language of legislation and policy (Pease, 2002; Braye and Preston-Shoot, 2011).

FGCs have often been related to empowerment; this is a specific goal of the FGC process (Metze, Abma and Kwekkeboom, 2013).

The notion that FGCs empower those involved in the process has long been a discourse surrounding FGCs. Much has been written about the FGC process redressing a balance of power between professionals and service users, that is, shifting decision-making powers from professionals to family members (Adams and Chandler, 2004; Hayes and Houston, 2007; Holland et al., 2005). While it is widely acknowledged that families are the decision makers at an FGC, some argue that the application of the FGC model to existing social care structures, which are bureaucratic, risk averse and professionally led, can create tensions (Adams and Chandler; 2004; Holland et al., 2005; Merkel-Holguin, 2004). Holland et al. (2005: 65) introduced the concept of 'imposed empowerment' to the use of FGCs in the field of child protection. They raise a question about whether an FGC can truly be an empowering process when families are expected to engage and comply with child protection process and that the local authority and/or the courts make the ultimate decision about the welfare of children. Indeed, it is an embedded part of FGC discourse that families have the choice whether to participate in an FGC (Barnardos, NCH and Family Rights Group, 2002). The notion of choice becomes questionable, however, when families are faced with the prospect of 'losing' their children and may feel pressured to engage in the FGC approach. Despite these concerns, Holland et al. (2005) conclude that even within the 'punitive' world of child protection, FGCs offer the potential for a more balanced relationship between family members and the state, and that an FGC ensures more 'democracy' for family members.

Traditionally the factors that contribute to the empowerment process have been divided into emotional, behavioural and cognitive factors, although it has been difficult to pinpoint what empowerment really means and how it can be measured (Healey, 2014; Metze, Abma and Kwekkeboom, 2013). Christens (2011) adds another factor to this list, that of social and interpersonal relationships, that is, relational empowerment. It is this element of empowerment that Metze, Abma and Kwekkeboom (2013) argue has meaning for the FGC process. Relational empowerment links empowerment to human relationships. Given that the process of the FGC is that of a social network working together to develop a plan for the care and/or protection of a vulnerable member of their group, relational empowerment becomes an appropriate lens through which to understand the empowering nature of the FGC process.

There appears to be no concrete definition of relational empowerment and some writers assert the view that a person cannot be empowered by others; they can only empower themselves (Metze, Abma and Kwekkeboom, 2013). Furthermore, empowerment has become synonymous with the concept of autonomy, that is, people being independent and having self-determination in decision making (Braye and Preston-Shoot, 2011). On the other hand, it is widely acknowledged that a key component of feeling empowered is the availability of social support and that although empowerment is about an individual feeling autonomous, people still need the support of others (Barringer et al., 2016). This has been referred to as relational autonomy, that is, being able to make decisions independently but being able to draw on the support of others if needed (Christman, 2004). Metze, Abma and Kwekkeboom (2013) argue that relational autonomy is at the centre of the FGC process and couple this with the psychological concept of 'resilience' to create a theoretical framework for FGCs.

Metze, Abma and Kwekkeboom (2013) argue that at an FGC the shared decision making undertaken by a social group is underpinned by relational autonomy. Everyone participating in an FGC has the opportunity to express their autonomy and have their say (being supported to do so if necessary by an advocate) while at the same time drawing on the support of the rest of the group and engaging in a collaborative process to agree a plan and share the responsibility for it.

Luthar and Cicchetti (2000) define resilience as, 'a dynamic process wherein individuals display positive adaptation despite experiences of significant adversity or trauma' (p. 858).

In other words, resilience is about the capacity of individuals to cope and manage with difficult situations in their lives and to 'bounce back' from these circumstances, thus potentially growing stronger. In this sense resilience has been related to empowerment and the feeling of being in control over one's own life (Brodsky and Cattaneo, 2013). Several 'resilience factors' have been identified, that contribute to the development of resilience (Rutter, 1980: 316). One of these factors is that an individual has a positive support network (Ozbay et al., 2008). Metze, Abma and Kwekkeboom (2013) argue that the FGC, in mobilising an individual's support network to develop a package of care and support for them, can enhance an individual's resilience and their feeling of being in control. They argue that the FGC has the potential to increase an individual's self-esteem, in recognising that others value them enough to contribute to supporting them at the FGC. This, coupled with emotional support that others may provide at the FGC when discussing potentially difficult issues and circumstances, can ensure that an individual feels valued and worthy of support. The sense of control that an individual might feel can thus lead to a feeling of being empowered.

Hence, the FGC process can be an empowering one, by its very nature. Furthermore, while questions remain about the tensions that exist between the FGC approach and traditional case-planning approaches in social work, and how empowering an FGC can be when it is part of a statutory process, it can be argued that the relational nature of the FGC encourages a sense of autonomy, enhances resilience and creates conditions necessary for empowerment to occur.

Culturally competent social work practice

Social work practice in recent years has become concerned with the concept of culturally competent practice. For decades, the profession has been concerned with the provision of anti-discriminatory practice (ADP) and anti-oppressive practice (AOP), which recognises and challenges the impact of structural discrimination and oppression of minority groups (Thompson, 2016). Linked with empowerment theory, theories of ADP and AOP are conceptualised as being necessary to support and enable disempowered and disenfranchised groups of people to have equality of opportunity and to claim power and control over their lives, having been marginalised by oppressive societal structures, organisations and popular ideologies (Dominelli, 2002; Thompson, 2016). It is well known that FGCs were created in response to the structural racism towards the Maori community in New Zealand, and is shaped by Maori cultural practices. In this sense, the FGC model embodies an anti-discriminatory approach to social work practice. It was born out of a recognition that traditional approaches to managing child welfare concerns and youth justice in New Zealand had been shaped by the context of European colonisation and white control. Thus, service responses to both were culturally inappropriate for the indigenous population. Furthermore, in acknowledging that individuals, families and communities, rather than institutions and organisations, are best placed to address difficulties, issues and concerns in family/community life because individuals, families and communities are wonderfully diverse, the FGC model potentially reduces the potential for discrimination and oppression. It is the family who are the decision makers at an FGC not professionals with their own cultural norms, values, attitudes and prejudices, potentially influencing the decision-making process.

The concept of culturally competent social work practice is well established in the US and is becoming embedded in social work discourse in the UK (Barn and Das, 2016). Cultural competence can be defined as 'the ability of professionals to function successfully with people from different cultural backgrounds including, but not limited to, race, ethnicity, culture, class, gender, sexual orientation, religion, physical or mental ability, age, and national origin' (Council of Social Work Education, in Kohli, Huber and Faul, 2010: 257). Weaver (2004) argues that a culturally competent social worker is one who can effectively apply social work skills within a context of knowledge and respect for a service user's culture. Furthermore, it is acknowledged that a culturally competent social worker needs to have an awareness of their own attitudes, values and beliefs and be accepting to 'truths' that may differ from their own (Kohli, Huber and Faul, 2010). In other words, a culturally competent social worker needs to work hard at not allowing their own attitudes, values and beliefs to impact one their ability to work in a respectful way with others. Weaver (1997) highlights three areas of understanding that a social worker should have to enable culturally competent social work:

- knowledge of the service user's cultural context including history;
- knowledge of internal group contemporary issues and world views;
- appropriate values and skills.

(from Barn and Das, 2016: 945)

It can be argued that FGCs are an embodiment of culturally competent practice. Not only do they have their origins in the attempt to develop cultural appropriate child welfare and youth offending services in New Zealand, they have developed as a global model of social work decision making, being used in several different countries across the globe including the UK, the US, Canada, Russia, China, Sri Lanka, Eastern Europe, Western Europe and Australasia (Barn and Das, 2016; Barnsdale and Walker, 2007; Fox, 2008; Frost, Abram and Burgess, 2014b).

Barn and Das (2016) in their research into the use of FGCs in five London boroughs attempt to understand the FGC process as a form of culturally appropriate social work decision making. They argue that while FGCs are acknowledged as being a model of culturally competent practice, their use appears to have been limited with BME communities in Western Europe (Haresnape, 2009) and within BME communities in the UK (O'Shaughnessy, Fatimilehin and Collins, 2010) although in recent years projects focusing on BME communities have started to emerge in the UK (Ashley and Nixon (eds), 2007). Furthermore, evidence suggests that BME communities are under-represented in referrals to FGC services in the UK (Family Rights Group, 2005; Chand, 2008; Haresnape, 2009) and little has been written regarding developing an understanding of what cultural competence means for the delivery of FGCs with diverse communities. Citing Waites et al. (2004), Barn and Das (2016) identify five key areas in FGC practice that are significant when considering cultural competence:

- the importance of a culturally appropriate location for the FGC;
- recognition of cultural traditions;
- identification with the community including language considerations;
- the role of family elders in hosting and convening the FGC;
- community education and awareness. (947–9)

Furthermore, they emphasise that the dominant theme that emerges from the literature on FGCs with regards to ethnicity, is the importance of a family being allocated an FGC coordinator who understands a family's specific cultural context and who will work sensitively within this context. This view is endorsed in the UK national standards for FGC services (2002) which states that, '[where] possible, coordinators should reflect the local community and families will be offered a coordinator who speaks their language and who has an understanding of the way religious beliefs, cultural traditions and other lifestyle issues influence how the family operates' (Principle 2a, Barnardos, Family Rights Group and NCH, 2002: 7).

The issue of cultural competence is addressed in Chapter Nine with reference to using FGCs with marginalised communities.

Ecosystems theory

FGCs are rooted in ecosystems approaches, with the underlying principle being that the family or community can understand and assume responsibility for the care, protection and behaviours of its members (Harawitz, 2006). Ecosystems theory is concerned with the interaction between an individual and their social environment and the principle that an individual can be understood within the context of these interactions. The role of the social worker is to understand the 'transaction' between a person and their environment and to promote change in these 'transactions' (Healy, 2014: 118). Bronfenbrenner (1979) developed a concentric model to understand the social environment of an individual, using the terms microsystem, mesosystem and macrosystem to understand the different types of systems that impact on service user's lives.

The microsystem refers to informal systems such as home, family and community; the mesosystem refers to formal systems that have a direct impact on an individual's life such as schools and social services; the macrosystem refers to society as a whole and the large social institutions of government and business (Healy, 2014). It is the micro- and mesosystems that are relevant to the FGC model. As a family decision-making model, the FGC approach is inevitably concerned with the microsystem of the family. The role of the independent coordinator is to support the family to work together to develop a plan; an inevitable consequence of this is the possibility for improved communication and relationships within the family (Frost and Elmer, 2008; Holland et al., 2005; Litchfield, Gatowski and Dobbin, 2003; Pennell and Burford, 2000). Furthermore, in placing responsibility on the family to pool their resources to care for or support a child or vulnerable adult in their family, this inevitably has an impact on the individual's transactions with their family, as support for them is potentially increased or provided by another family member. For example, if another family member agrees to care for a child who cannot return to the care of their immediate family, due to levels of risk, the transaction between the child and this family member changes. The child's transaction with their family system is thus improved, as they are now, it is hoped, safely cared for within the family system.

The FGC approach can have an impact on an individual's interaction with their mesosystem. If we consider FGCs that take place within a social care, educational or youth justice context, the FGC offers an alternative decision-making paradigm which shifts the balance of power from professional to family-led decision making and arguably improving an individual's transactions with those systems. Some evaluations of FGC services reflect that family members have reported improved relationships with social workers and other professionals, as a result of being involved in an FGC and of feeling listened to and heard (Pennell and Burford, 2000; Litchfield, Gatowski and Dobbin, 2003). The outcomes from FGCs often result in a changed and improved transaction between family members and mesosystems. For example, research suggests that FGCs have the potential to lead to more children being cared for within their families and not entering state care (Laws and Kirby, 2008; Sawyer and Lohrbach, 2008; Titcomb and LeCroy, 2003); FGCs in educational settings lead to improved attendance of young people, when the purpose of the FGC is to address non-school attendance (Crow, Marsh and Holton, 2004; Hayden, 2009; McMorris et al., 2013); and outcomes from youth justice FGCs have shown the potential for a reduction in offending among young people and a decrease in custodial sentences (Barnsdale and Walker, 2007; Fox, 2008; MacFarlane and Anglem, 2014). All of these examples represent significant change and improvement with an individual's interaction with the mesosystem.

Ecosystems theory has tended to have been located in the process of social work assessment and understanding an individual's situation to inform subsequent service interventions. It is clear, however, that it can also be applied to social welfare decision-making processes and provide a framework for understanding family-led decision making.

FGCs and sociological theory

So far this chapter has looked at FGCs through the lens of social work theory, as it is important that social workers and social work students understand FGCs as a social work model of decision making. Two sociological concepts, those of agency and social capital can, however, be introduced into the discourse and provide a context for understanding the theoretical foundations of the FGC model.

It is important to note that this discussion is not designed to be an in-depth analysis of social capital and agency, rather a discussion on how these two concepts relate to FGCs.

Agency can be described as

> The idea that individuals are equipped with the ability to understand and control their own actions, regardless of the circumstances of their lives.... We exercise agency, for example when we indicate our intention to vote one way or the other, or make choices about what to eat from a restaurant menu. (Webb, Schirato and Danaher, 2002: ix)

Bourdieu (1977) theorised that an individual's agency is determined by objective social structures, such as those relating to class, ethnicity and gender, for example. In other words, the higher the social class, the more agency an individual has. It is widely acknowledged that the bulk of service users of social care services are people who are poor, marginalised and disenfranchised (Backworth, 2015), that is, using a Bourdieusian analysis, they have little agency. Research has emphasised the disempowering nature of social care processes and how individuals can feel powerless and disenfranchised within these processes, feeling that their voice gets lost within the bureaucracy (Adams, 2008; Eassom et al., 2014; Featherstone, White and Morris, 2014; Fook, 2008; Meunch, Diaz and Wright, 2016). For example, Meunch, Diaz and Wright (2016) in their study of child and parental involvement at child protection conferences found that in most cases, the involvement of children was minimal, parents felt unsupported and both felt that their views were not taken into consideration. Further research by Eassom et al. (2014) about the involvement of family members in mental health decision-making processes found many organisational and procedural barriers to the involvement of family members and their ability to exercise their agency.

FGCs, on the other hand, as a family-led decision-making process can be conceptualised as a model for encouraging the agency of the families involved, encouraging individuals to express their opinions and contribute to the development of a family plan through a collective decision-making process. The notion of a collective decision-making process can be linked to another sociological concept mentioned earlier, that of social capital.

There are many different interpretations of social capital which can lead to some confusion in understanding the meaning of the concept (Robinson, Schmid and Siles, 2002). There is, however, a general consensus within the social science field that it relates to the role of networks and civic norms and that the key indicators of social capital include social relations, formal and informal social networks, group membership, trust, reciprocity and civic engagement (Office for National Statistics, 2001).

Coleman (cited in Edwards, Franklin and Holland 2003: 302) describes social capital as, 'a... "by-product" that "inheres in the structure of relations between persons and among persons", and that its value lies in facilitating both the actions of individuals to realise their interests, as well as in "the provision of public goods...which are not in the interest of any individual to produce alone, but...are of benefit to many"' (Edwards, Franklin and Holland, 2003: 393).

In Coleman's definition of social capital (as cited in Edwards, Franklin and Holland, 2003) the family are at the centre. Coleman identifies that the relationships between parents and their children and among siblings are a source of social capital which has the potential to enable individuals within the family to realise their interests and potential. Coleman further focuses on extra-familial relationships as being a source of social capital, identifying the support that social networks can provide to individuals within families and to the family as a whole to enable the family to function effectively.

The FGC model is based upon the belief that all families have strengths which can be drawn upon to support a vulnerable child or adult in that family and to develop and contribute to a plan for their care and protection (Metze, Abma and Kwekkeboom, 2013). Furthermore, the definition of 'family' within the FGC approach is a broad one and refers to social networks and extra-familial relationships (Ashley (ed.), 2006). Social capital is thus at the core of FGCs, as FGCs are based on the supportive relationships between individuals and groups within a family, the strengths that are derived from these relationships and the collective responsibility of the family group to ensure an outcome that is beneficial to the family as a whole.

Conclusion

This chapter has brought together the core theoretical concepts that relate to FGCs. It has provided an overview of key social work theory and some sociological concepts in relation to FGCs. The chapter provides an overview of the theoretical concepts. For a more in-depth understanding of each area of theory, it is advised that readers undertake some further reading.

Social work has, in recent years moved towards an evidence based approach to practice (Howard, McMillen and Polio, 2003). Social work theory has long shaped the practice of the profession (Coulshed and Orme, 2012; Fook, 2008; Healy, 2014) but it is only in recent years that social workers are being asked to evidence the theoretical basis to their interventions, in assessment and court reports (Turney et al., 2012). FGCs are widely used in social work practice across the globe, so it is crucial that social workers understand the theoretical basis to the model.

For independent coordinators of FGCs, some of whom are social work qualified and many of whom are not (Burford and Hudson (eds) 2000; Family Rights Group, 2009; Skaale Havnen and Christiansen, 2014), it is crucial that these practitioners understand the theoretical basis to their work and for them to be recognised as skilled and research informed practitioners in their own right, given the evidence-based practice landscape of social care.

For policy makers, having an understanding of the theoretical underpinnings of the FGC model and the relationship between FGCs and what is considered to be good social work practice is significant. The theoretical framework ensures that the model is given credibility and offers the potential for it to become a viable alternative to existing processes.

Further reading

Barn, R. and Das, C. (2016) 'Family group conferences and cultural competence in social work', *British Journal of Social Work*, 46(4): 942–59.

Healy, K. (2014) (2nd edn) *Social work theories in context*, Basingstoke: Palgrave Macmillan.

Metze, R.N., Abma, T.A. and Kwekkeboom, R.H. (2013) 'Family group conferencing: a theoretical underpinning', *Health Care Analysis,* 23(2): 165–80.

Office for National Statistics (2001) 'Social capital: a review of the literature', Social Analysis and Reporting Division Office for National Statistics, October 2001, London: ONS.

Shennan, G. (2014) *Solution focused practice: effective communication to facilitate change*, Basingstoke: Palgrave Macmillan.

Webb, J., Schirato, T. and Danaher, G. (2002) *Understanding Bourdieu*, London: SAGE.

THREE

A guide to convening a FGC

Deanna Edwards

This chapter will build upon information presented in Chapter One and aims to provide guidance for convening a Family Group Conference. It should however be noted that it does not replace FGC training and it is recommended that anyone wishing to convene an FGC completes, as a minimum, three days of training such as that offered by Family Rights Group, and spends time shadowing experienced practitioners. The information presented in this chapter is based on my own experience of coordinating FGCs and managing FGC practitioners and an FGC service.

The FGC process

Figure 3.1 outlines the basic FGC process. Each stage will be covered in detail. This chapter will focus upon child welfare FGCs but the process of convening an adult FGC will be broadly similar. Differences will be highlighted in Chapter Twelve.

The referral process

Referral criteria will be dependent upon the FGC agency with agencies often having significantly different referral pathways. Some FGC services accept multi-agency referrals but Family Rights Group (see Further Reading) state that in most areas the referrer is likely to be a social worker. In theory, however, FGCs can be and indeed have been used for a wide variety of child welfare concerns. Referrals should be specific in that FGCs are designed to allow the family to plan in response to a question or set of questions asked of them by the referrer. Therefore the referral should make reference to this question. It should also set the parameters for the answering of this question by defining the boundaries of decision making. Therefore the referral should make clear anything that the family would not be permitted to include in their plan. This is often known as the **bottom line**

Figure 3.1: An outline of the basic FGC process

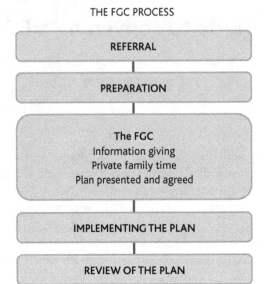

THE FGC PROCESS

REFERRAL

PREPARATION

The FGC
Information giving
Private family time
Plan presented and agreed

IMPLEMENTING THE PLAN

REVIEW OF THE PLAN

and needs to be made clear to the family from the outset. Once the question and bottom line are established the referrer needs to be clear about both the **strengths** of the family and what **concerns** they have regarding the family alongside any health and safety information that the coordinator needs to know. Referrers usually complete a referral form which will be seen and signed by someone in the family who has parental responsibility for the child. Asking family members to sign a referral form ensures that they are aware of what information is being passed on to the FGC service. It can also act as a consent form to allow this information to be shared with the wider family although coordinators should also always check that they have permission to do this prior to doing so. It is also essential that referrers make families aware of the voluntary nature of FGCs prior to a referral being made and explain clearly the FGC process to the family.

Once a referral is received it will go through a process of approval set by the FGC project. This may involve a suitability panel or it may be overseen by the FGC service manager. Once the referral has been approved, an **independent coordinator** is appointed. Independence in this context means that the role of the FGC coordinator is only to convene the FGC; they are not decision makers and they do not have any other role with the family. Families may be offered a choice of coordinator but the parameters of this will be set by the project and are often resource dependent. Smaller projects may offer little or no choice while larger ones may offer families choice in terms of gender, cultural background or languages spoken. It is worth noting here a word of caution about offering families a coordinator from a similar cultural background. Barn and Das (2016) point out that some families may not wish to be matched with a coordinator from their own culture for various reasons which may include fear that their privacy will not respected within their community, and therefore coordinators should always be mindful of the need to ask families what their preferences are. Once a coordinator has been appointed to facilitate the FGC then they will begin the process of preparing the family for their meeting.

Preparation

Arguably preparation is the most important stage of the FGC process and good preparation is essential to the success of the meeting. Preparation is carried out by the independent coordinator who will often start the process by contacting the referrer. This serves several purposes which include: gathering any additional information, including health and safety, finding out what the referrer's knowledge and experience of FGCs is, helping the referrer to plan their report for the FGC and preparing them for the meeting. If it is not evident from the referral form, the referrer needs to be clear about when they are available to attend an FGC. This involves being honest and open to the possibility of out of hours meetings which should be explored early on in the process. Not all referrers will be familiar with the model and in these instances the coordinator will need to be clear about what an FGC is and the roles and responsibilities of all involved in the process. It must be made clear that referrers need to attend the FGC. For social work referrals they remain the case holder and normal social work processes continue alongside preparation for the FGC. It is *never* the coordinator's responsibility to case-hold or to take on social work tasks with the family during the FGC process.

One of the essential tasks of working with the referrer during the preparation stage is to prepare them for the FGC. Coordinators need to recognise that referrers may well be unsure what to expect and nervous of attending an FGC especially if they perceive family members to be hostile towards them. The coordinator therefore has a duty to ensure that the referrer is prepared to attend, has strategies for managing any issues they may encounter and feels confident and informed about their role in the meeting.

Referrer preparation: a case study

Lucy, an experienced social worker had just made her first referral to the FGC project and was meeting with the FGC coordinator to prepare for the process. The referral was about Carol, a single mother of three children, who had significant problems with alcohol which impacted on her ability to care for the children. Lucy had a difficult relationship with Carol but Carol had responded well to the FGC referral and their relationship had somewhat improved. Lucy was concerned, however, that the family would invite Carol's brother Dan. He had been very hostile in the past towards Lucy and had made several phone calls to her where he had been angry and abusive. Lucy recognised that he had an important role to play in the FGC but was worried about how he would react to her in the meeting. The coordinator listened to Lucy's concerns and helped her to develop a strategy for managing any potential conflict. They agreed that the coordinator would work with Dan during the preparation stage, agreeing acceptable behaviour ground rules and emphasising the future focus of the meeting in order to minimise possible conflict. They also agreed on what Lucy would do if Dan became verbally aggressive towards her. The day of the meeting came and despite the work of the coordinator Dan verbally attacked Lucy while she was giving her report during the information sharing stage. Lucy calmly informed him that if he continued this behaviour she would leave the meeting. Dan continued to be rude and hostile and Lucy left the meeting. The family became quite anxious at this point fearing that the meeting would go awry without the social worker. They therefore insisted that Dan had to apologise to her and curb his behaviour. They reminded him that the meeting was intended to focus on the future. Dan apologised to Lucy and asked if she would return to the meeting. She agreed but asked him not to re-join the meeting until private family time. Dan agreed and the meeting progressed without further incident and the family were able to agree an acceptable plan.

Writing the report for the FGC

Another important task for coordinators to help referrers with is the task of writing the report for the meeting. Information which forms the basis of the report may be in the referral form which can just be updated prior to the meeting. The advantages of this are that the family will have already seen it and signed to agree to it being shared. It is important that the report addresses family strengths as well as concerns, has a clear bottom line and clear and answerable questions to address at the meeting. It needs to be clear and jargon-free and adhere to the FGC principle of '**no new news**', that is, that the family should not be given any new information at their FGC.

Family preparation

Once the referrer has been briefed, the coordinator will continue their preparation with the family. This will start with the person or people with parental responsibility and (if appropriate) children and young people. The coordinator will need to establish if they have understood and consented to an FGC, whether children understand the process and whether it is appropriate to involve them. The next step of the process is to start to help the family to develop an invitation list for the FGC which can include any supporters – family or friends. It may also include any service providers the family wish to invite in addition to the referrer who should always attend.

The coordinator will proceed to contact, invite, visit and prepare all these people to attend the meeting. This will involve sharing information (with family consent), explaining the process and purpose of the FGC, discussing dates, times and venues for the FGC as well as practical arrangements for their attendance. They will also discuss how family members might manage the meeting, including the drawing up of ground rules for the meeting, ensuring family members know who else in the family is attending and helping them to think about how they will manage any difficulties that may arise in the meeting. This may include dealing with difficult or dominant family members who may have been invited. The coordinator will help them to think about what they may realistically be able to contribute to the family plan that will be discussed at the meeting.

Ground rules

Many people who attend FGCs like to have ground rules established which cover general expectations of the meeting. Coordinators will usually work with family members prior to the meeting to draw up and agree a set of ground rules. These rules may include ensuring the meeting remains focused on the future not the past, giving everyone an equal voice, and having no time limits to the meeting, for example. Family members often want to add specific ground rules. Common ones include rules about not blaming, not shouting and taking it in turns to speak.

Advocacy

It is accepted generally in social care services and specifically in FGCs that sometimes a family member may feel or be vulnerable in a meeting. Reasons for this are numerous but may include age: children and young people are often considered vulnerable at FGCs as are older people; people with learning disabilities or mental health conditions. In these situations we need to ensure that these vulnerable family members have access to advocacy. This advocacy can come from family members, from those service providers already involved with the family or from trained advocates provided by the FGC service. Clearly each option has advantages and disadvantages and for a summary of these see Laws and Kirby's (2008) evaluation of the Brighton and Hove FGC service. To summarise, one might argue that the advantages of a family member advocate is that they can be present during private family time without compromising it and they know the family and the issues. Questions could be raised, however, about how competent they are at representing a vulnerable family member's voice, and whether they might try to persuade or bias the family member they are advocating for. Therefore a professional already working with the family may be more appropriate. This may be the case particularly for those family members who already have significant service involvement in their lives and have a trusted person that they already work with. This can work well, providing that the advocate is not the coordinator or the decision maker at the FGC. Alternatively many FGC Services are able to provide a professional advocate for the meeting. Clearly there are advantages and disadvantages of using professional advocates. Advantages may include the fact that professional advocates are trained advocates, they are neutral, that is, not from the family or agencies involved with a family and that they will have no emotional involvement with the family. Disadvantages can include the fact that their presence in private family time could dilute and change the process and it ceases to be 'private' if a professional advocate is present. Hence one could argue that advocates should only be present at the very beginning of private family time in order to present the wishes and feelings of the person they are advocating for. They should then arrange time at the end of private family time to discuss the family plan with the person they are advocating for (Laws and Kirby, 2008).

Preparing children and young people for FGCs

Children and young people need special consideration at FGCs if they are to have a real voice in the process (Connolly and Masson, 2014). Horan and Dalrymple (2003) have argued that children and young people often do not feel heard at FGCs and that they all too often can become adult-orientated decision-making processes. Conversely, when preparation of children and young people is undertaken effectively they can feel that they have been involved more fully than they have in any other decision-making process that they have experienced (Bell and Wilson, 2006). Young people from Torbay's FGC 'young people's group' and other FGC young people's groups have testified at many events about how powerful the process can be for young people if preparation is effective (Tapsfield, 2003).

It is important from the outset for all involved to have discussions about whether it is appropriate for children to attend the FGC meeting. While children and young people should be directly involved as often as possible there are some situations where it may not be appropriate to directly involve them. These may include FGCs where abuse is being discussed, particularly where there are quite young children involved. Services may have a direct policy regarding the involvement of children and young people in cases where there has been significant abuse. Laws and Kirby (2008) have argued, furthermore, that it may be useful to build in some adult-only time to the FGC. This does not however mean that children are unable to have a voice at the FGC. There are many different ways of involving children and young people in their FGC if they are unable to be directly involved.

Children's voices: an FGC case study

A FGC was held for a family where there has been significant domestic abuse. The father was serving a prison sentence for violence perpetrated against his partner (mother to the children). The children, aged seven and nine, were living with their mother. Their father was soon to be released from prison and the focus of the FGC was 'how can the children be kept safe when their dad comes out of prison'. The social worker's 'bottom line' was that the father could not return to the family home to live with the children. The referrer and family decided that due to the nature of the referral and the issues likely to be discussed at the FGC that the children should not be present in the meeting. The FGC coordinator contacted them and helped them instead to write letters and develop a 'wishes and feelings' list to be presented at the meeting. The letters outlined the devastating effect the domestic abuse had had on their lives and their wishes and feelings outlined their wish that they could have safe contact with their father but that they did not want to live with him; in fact that they were afraid of living with him again and they were afraid for their mother. The letters and wishes were read out during the meeting and had a profound impact on their family. No-one in the family had recognised the effect the domestic abuse had had on the children and no-one had realised how much the children had seen and heard. As a result of this realisation the family became aware that they needed to prioritise the children's well-being and devise a plan that would keep them safe and help them feel secure once their father came out of prison. They agreed that the children's father would go to live with his parents who would supervise all contact between him and the children. The children would continue to live with their mother.

Children's wishes and feelings

In a child-welfare FGC, children and young people's participation and perspectives are central to the process and an effective FGC should allow young people to participate fully in the process. This means engaging them from the beginning of the process and involving them in all aspects of the meeting. This could include who to invite, when and where the meeting is held, what food to have at the meeting, where people sit at the meeting and what decisions need to be made. Inclusive and creative ways of involving young people may include them helping to plan the menu, writing ground rules, food shopping and preparation, room layout and asking them if they would like to do the invitations for the meeting. Young people should be consulted about the social workers report which should be clear and easy for them to understand. The report should also be clear about what question/s need addressing at the FGC and what the 'bottom line' is. The FGC process should be explained and young people should be asked for their wishes and feelings which are then presented at the meeting. This may take several meetings with the young person particularly if the issues to be discussed and decisions to be made are complex and life changing. Coordinators and advocates should always make it clear that young people do not need to be present at the meeting to have a voice and are not required to stay for the duration of the meeting if they do not wish to. This should be made clear at the outset so the young person can make an informed choice about whether and how they want to be involved. Children and young people should be offered an advocate to help them present their wishes and feelings if they want one. The coordinator, and the advocate if involved, will support the young person to develop their list of wishes and feelings for the meeting and will need to support them to make decisions about what is safe and appropriate to share at the meeting. The scope and limits of confidentiality also needs to be made clear, and, given the central FGC principle of 'no new news', any important and significant wishes and feelings the young person wants to state at the meeting will need to be shared prior to the meeting.

Coordinators and advocates often use creative approaches to engage with children and young people, such as the Three Houses tool (Weld and Greening, 2004) or the Fairy/Wizard tool (designed by Vania de Paz, Department of Child Protection, Western Australia; Turnell and Edwards, 1999) to look at what they are worried about, what are the good things in their life and what they wish to gain from the meeting. This fits with a central tenet of FGCs which is that both strengths and concerns of the family are presented at the meeting. Children and young people should have a choice at the meeting about when to present their wishes and feelings and who will do this. Often young people will want to present their own but if they do not wish to do so, a family member, coordinator or advocate can do this for them. Coordinators and advocates also have a role at the meeting to ensure that wishes and feelings are heard and that they are incorporated into the plan made at the meeting. As part of this role they have a responsibility to ensure that the young person understands the plan made at the meeting and is in agreement with it.

Addressing cultural issues in FGCs

FGCs originate from the perspective of an oppressed cultural group who wished to maintain their cultural traditions when working with child protection services (Te Awatea Violence Research Centre, 2014) and so created a process which respects cultural traditions (Connolly, 2006). This will be explored more fully in Chapter Nine but it is worth stating here a little about how FGC services may strive to ensure that cultural issues are addressed in preparation and in the meeting. FGCs are family led and therefore the family are at liberty to decide where and when the meeting should be held. Unlike formal social care led meetings in which generally families are allocated a time and place within traditional office hours, families having an FGC can decide when to have the meeting thus avoiding or choosing days, dates or times that have cultural or other significance for them. Families can often also choose the venue for their FGC and can choose venues that have personal or cultural significance. In addition they can choose or avoid food at the meeting that suits their cultural or dietary needs. Finally, families can run FGCs in a way that suits their needs and so therefore can add worship time to their meeting and can invite any important community members that they wish to. The FRG Family Group Conference toolkit (Ashley (ed.), 2006) and subsequent good practice guidance recommends that wherever possible the FGC should be held in the preferred language of the family with a choice of coordinator if available (p 84). This may, of course, involve the use of interpreters for the service providers attending the FGC.

The FGC meeting

As previously stated, the FGC meeting will be held in a neutral venue at a time and place that suits all those attending. Venues should be appropriate with a suitable meeting room and a breakout room, facilities to make drinks and preferably a kitchen area to prepare and serve refreshments. The venue needs to be suitable from a health and safety perspective. Coordinators should familiarise themselves with the building prior to the meeting, ensuring that they know where fire escapes are and that there are suitable facilities for all attending. This includes ensuring that the venue is suitable for anyone attending who has a disability and the venue is suitably private and confidential and has a flexible arrangement for the end time of the meeting. This allows space for the FGC to take as long as necessary.

Information sharing stage

The FGC coordinator will informally chair the meeting and start with welcome and introductions. The coordinator may be the only person who knows everyone so this is an important stage and is also useful for everyone to state what their relationship is to the child or children who are the subject of the meeting. Once this is established, the coordinator should outline the purpose and process of the meeting and discuss and agree any ground rules. At this stage the children's wishes or feelings may be introduced but this will be dependent upon when and how young people have stated they want these wishes and feelings presented.

The coordinator will ask the referrer to present their report to the meeting. As previously stated, referrer's reports should be shared with the family prior to the meeting so that the meeting contains no surprises. After listening to the report the family should be given the opportunity to ask questions and to clarify anything they wish to. If the family have invited other service providers to their meeting this is also time for them to present their information to the meeting. As with the social work report, this may also contain information about resources they can offer to the family. Again the opportunity should be given for the family to ask any questions or to clarify anything they wish to clarify. This stage of the meeting is known as the **information sharing** stage because it is the family's opportunity to gather information on the issues to be addressed and the resources available to help them to address them. Once the family have heard all this information they are ready to go into private planning time. The coordinator needs to check that they are ready and they know what is expected of them and have everything they need to help them plan. Good coordinators will ensure that families have been well prepared for this stage of the meeting and that they are aware of the following: that the referrer, coordinator or any other information giver can be called back into private family time if the family need them to, that private time is not time-limited, and that family members can take breaks when they choose to (either individually or together). They also need to identify someone in the family who will take responsibility for asking the coordinator to return to the meeting and someone to record the plan.

Private family time

This is unlimited time in which the family are together to make a plan which they agree and record. No service providers are in the room during this time unless invited back in by the family. If service providers are invited in, for example to answer family members' questions, they should do so and then leave the meeting once again. This ensures that the plan made at the meeting is that of the family and not one influenced by those attending the meeting in a professional capacity. Advocates may be in private family time at the beginning and end to represent the views of those they are advocating for. Private family time is fundamental to the FGC process. It is what makes it a distinctive process and ensures that the meeting is family-led and the decisions made are family decisions (Ashley (ed.), 2006).

Once the family have agreed a plan they are asked to call everyone back together for the third and final stage of the meeting where the plan is discussed and agreed.

Agreeing a plan

This is the final stage of the FGC in which the plan made by the family is discussed and, if appropriate, agreed by all present. The process starts with the coordinator asking the family if they have agreed a plan and, if so, asking them to share it. The coordinator and those at the meeting in a professional capacity may ask for clarification of parts of the plan and the coordinator will help the family to add some detail to the plan where necessary. For example, if the family have decided that the child will be spending weekends with grandparents the coordinator may ask for clarity regarding when this will start from, what constitutes a weekend, what for the plan would be for when the grandparents go on holiday, and so on. In this way they are helping the family where necessary to 'flesh out' the plan so it is sufficiently detailed to be understood by everyone who might read it. This may include people who are not present at the meeting to whom the family want the plan to be sent, social workers, judges in cases that are in the court process and others involved with the family. The plan therefore needs to be clear and transparent with the name of the person who is responsible for monitoring each item on the plan. For example, if as part of the family plan the family have agreed that the parents would benefit from parenting classes, the coordinator needs to establish who will be responsible for making this referral, when it will be made and what the timescales are likely to be. It is also possible that some elements of the family plan are not able to be agreed on the day, for example if the referrer needs to go and check if a resource is available, so in these instances referrers are asked to give an estimate of when they will have a decision by. This 'fleshing out' is done by the coordinator and each point will be checked back with the family to ensure that they are in agreement. While doing this it is important that both the essence and the wording of the family plan is kept when it is written up and clarified. To this end the coordinator should keep the original wording of the family plan as much as possible and make it clear where they have added to the plan.

Once the plan has been finalised and discussed, the coordinator will ensure that the family are all in agreement with this final version of the plan. The coordinator will then ensure that the referrer agrees the plan. It is important to note that to fit with the ethos of the FGC and its philosophy of being a family-led decision-making process referrers are asked to agree plans, subject to them being safe, legal and addressing all the concerns that were stated in the referrer's report. If the referrer is not satisfied that the plan meets these criteria they need to be clear about how and why this is the case, thus giving the family the opportunity to address and rectify and shortcomings the plan may have. If the family are not able to agree a safe plan the referrer will need to be clear about what the next steps are. There will also be circumstances where plans cannot be agreed by referrers, for example, when a family are in court proceedings, in which case plans would need to be agreed by the court. In these circumstances families need to be made aware of this.

Once the plan is finalised and agreed, the final task of the coordinator is to ascertain if a family wish to review their plan. Review dates are decided by the family in consultation with the referrer but may be influenced by other meeting dates or important events such as court dates, the birth of a baby or planning meeting dates. Whenever possible, coordinators should try to agree a review date at the original meeting while all the family are together so that this date can be included in the plan. Once this is done the FGC is over and the meeting will end.

After the FGC

After the FGC the coordinator will arrange for the plan to be written up and distributed to the family. This should be done as soon as possible after the meeting and many services have a deadline of a week (for example, Hertfordshire, Stockport, Surrey, Lancashire).

A fictional example of an FGC plan

1. Sheila (gran) will have both of the children to stay on Saturday nights. *This will happen from 12th November 2016. Bob will pick the children up at 5.30 after Sophie finishes football. He will return them around 10 am on Sunday.*

2. Aunty Jan will nip in every morning on her way to school to pick up Sophie and Lewis. *If Jan is unable to do this any morning she will let Pat know as early as possible.*

3. Bob will take Pat to her hospital appointment next week. He will wait for her so he can take her home.

4. Sheila and Bob will look after the kids when Pat goes into hospital. Jan will take them both to school and also pick them up from school every evening.

5. Suzi will help with childcare during school holidays. If Pat takes them round in the mornings she will have them in the mornings to give Pat a break and return them in the evening.

6. Social worker to make a referral for family support worker to help out while Pat is still ill and to refer for respite at weekends. *Social worker will make these referrals on Monday and will let Pat know of the outcome.*

7. Jamie and Colin will come round next weekend and repair Pat's door and decorate Sophie's bedroom.

The main points in this plan would have been written by the family with the points in italics added in the final stage of the meeting when the plan is discussed by all present. When the plan is typed up for distribution the wording used by the family is adhered to as much as possible. The plan will be distributed to everyone present at the meeting and anyone else the family would like it to go to, for example members who weren't able to attend. The plan is usually accompanied by a covering letter which will include details of the date, time and place of the proposed review meeting agreed at the FGC. This date can be changed if either family members or the referrer identifies the need to do so. This may be because the plan is not working well and needs revising. Conversely, sometimes reviews are cancelled or delayed because the plan is working well and there is nothing that needs reviewing at present. In these instances it is often useful to go ahead with a planned review nonetheless, simply to clarify that the plan is progressing well and to plan future social care involvement.

Following the sending out of the plan FGC projects may have arrangements to evaluate the service and often this process begins at the point that plans are sent out or soon after.

The FGC review process

FGC coordinators have little contact with families in the period between the FGC meeting and planning for the review. It is *never* their responsibility to monitor the plan. This will be done jointly by the referrer and the family and the plan should make it clear who is responsible for monitoring which part of the plan. Therefore the coordinator does not usually have reason to be in contact with the family until they start to plan for the review. Coordinators will typically want to check in with the family and the referrer a week or two prior to the review to make sure that the date, time and place are still convenient and that there is 'no new news' that needs to be shared prior to the review. They will often meet with children and young people or with anyone who was vulnerable or anxious at the initial meeting (or indeed an advocate may take on this role). The coordinator may undertake more preparation than this if the plan is not working well and the family need to devise a new plan. In this instance, the review may be treated in a similar manner to a new referral. Otherwise the review will require less work than the original referral, and it will simply be a case of checking that everyone can still attend and has transport and other such details.

In terms of chairing the FGC review, the coordinator usually starts with any necessary introductions, purpose and structure of the meeting and a restating of the ground rules. They will usually ask for an update from the family and from the referrer about the progress of the plan and a discussion of the plan may follow this. Families should always be given the option of private family time and indeed if a significant reworking of the plan is required private family time is certainly desirable and should be encouraged. If families are merely making minor alterations to the plan, then private family time may be superfluous and they may decide to do this with the referrer and coordinator present. As always with FGCs, coordinators should be asking families to lead on these decisions. As with the original FGC the adjusted plan should be agreed by referrers if it is safe, legal and addresses concerns. It should be typed up and sent out to those present at the meeting and anyone else the family would like it to be sent to. Once the review is completed, it is usual to close the FGC referral unless there are exceptional circumstances that require a further review.

Record keeping

FGC services should develop clear policy, procedures and guidance on record keeping. This is likely to be different from that required for other social care services, as FGC coordinators, unlike social workers, will not be recording in detail their conversations with family members, unless they need to breach the confidentiality of the family for safeguarding reasons. Guidance on record keeping is available from Family Rights Group (see Further Reading at the end of the chapter).

Conclusion

The FGC process is a complex and time-consuming piece of work and should be undertaken by a skilled and well trained and supported coordinator. Ongoing training and support for coordinators is crucial and should include full FGC training, safeguarding training and shadowing opportunities. As with all social care professionals, coordinators should be offered individual supervision by a manager who is knowledgeable and experienced in FGCs. Where possible, group supervision can also be useful.

The FGC process is designed to be family-led and empowering. As much of the decision making as possible should therefore be undertaken by the family, including decisions about the practicalities of the meeting. It is also important to consider the role that advocates can play in ensuing that the views of vulnerable family members are represented. An FGC can only be an empowering process for families if individuals are enabled to express their views.

Further reading

Ashley, C., Hilton, L., Horan, H. and Wiffin, J. (2006) *The family group conference toolkit*, London: Department for Education and Skills; Cardiff: The Welsh assembly and London: Family Rights Group.

Family Rights Group (n.d.a) www.frg.org.uk/involving-families/ family-group-conferences, London: Family Rights Group.

Zehr, H., McRae, A., and Pranis K. and Stutzman Amstutz, L. (2015) *The big book of Restorative Justice: four classic Justice & Peacebuilding books in one volume (Justice and Peacebuilding)*, Brattleboro, Vermont: Good Books Publishing.

FOUR

The policy and legislative context

Deanna Edwards, Kate Parkinson and Marilyn Taylor

Children's social care

> Getting everybody in one room at the same time is helpful, getting them to thrash it out and think about it, because otherwise we often get to court and then suddenly people pop up (and) put themselves forward...if everyone was put in the same room at the same time that might be less likely to happen.

The above statement is a comment from a participant at a Family Group Conference which reflects that FGCs are often used to circumvent court processes and to advise court about family wishes. This chapter will explore the interface between the law and FGCs using case studies to illustrate this relationship and tell stories of those experiencing their impact and outcomes.

The legal framework for FGCs varies between countries. In New Zealand, Family Group Conferencing is underpinned by legislation in the Children, Young People and their Families Act 1989. The principle of participative social work practice is fully embodied in the law. As this book explores elsewhere the legislation was implemented following complaints from the Maori community about the way in which their children and young people were being treated by the welfare and juvenile justice systems. This initiated a consultation with the Maori community and the subsequent seminal report Puao-te-ata-tu meaning 'daybreak' (Ministerial Advisory Committee on a Maori perspective for the Department of Social Welfare in New Zealand, 1990).

In the Netherlands the Child and Youth Act (2015) gave citizens the right to develop their own action plans in cases that require intervention from 2015 (Hilverdink, Daamen and Vink, 2015). Family Group Conferences are seen as a way of implementing this law (Eigen

Kracht, n.d.). This law promotes a citizen's rights approach to the model.

In England and Wales FGC practice is underpinned by the philosophy evident in the Children Act, 1989. Guidance on the Act (Department for Education and Skills, 2006) emphasised the importance of working in partnership with families and the welfare of the child. It emphasised consultation with children and young people (Department for Children, Skills and Families, 2010). The Act for the first time also mentions giving due consideration to race, religion, culture, language and disability. Evans (2011) reminds us that the Children Act 1989 also states that children are best brought up within their families and that local authorities are also expected to support children's contact with families and to reunite families wherever possible. Following the Act a number of messages from research emerged that reinforced the concept of partnership working and perceived the family as 'expert'. This included the messages from research (Department of Health, 1995) which emphasised developing an appropriate balance of power between service users and social workers. This report articulated that 'family members know more about their family than any professional can possibly know'. It stated that families have a 'unique knowledge and understanding' and that 'protection is best achieved by building on the existing strengths of the child's living environment, rather than expecting miracles from isolated and spasmodic interventions' (Department of Health, 1995: 52).

In the same year as the Children Act 1989, Article 12 of the UN Convention on the Rights of the Child (UN General Convention, 1989) also emphasised the rights of children and young people to express their views in matters affecting them. Ten years later, Working Together to Safeguard Children guidelines were first published (Department of Health, 1999). This also identified the need to involve children and young people in decision making. It stressed the desirability of involving parents in planning for children and that involving wider family protects children better. In addition to this the Human Rights Act (1998) states that children and families have a right to family life and that there should be no discrimination in exercising this right.

This policy and legislation provides the backdrop to the introduction of FGCs to England and Wales in 1992. The ethos of the Children Act and a 'permissive legislative framework' (Ashley and Nixon, 2007: 14) is the basis on which FGCs have been developed.

More recently the Public Law Outline (PLO) (Ministry of Justice, 2008, updated 2014) was introduced. This legislation came into effect in April 2008, following a pilot which involved FGC provision (Family Rights Group, 2009). The PLO provides a tool for the implementation of care and supervision orders under Section 31 of the Children Act 1989. The PLO outlines the stages that the local authority is required to follow in order to seek a Care or Supervision Order. In the pre-proceedings stage of the PLO the local authority has a duty to send a letter before proceedings to parents and others with parental responsibility. This letter outlines the local authority concerns and should invite parents, or those with parental responsibility, to a pre-proceedings meeting to agree proposals for addressing concerns (Ministry of Justice, 2008). If an agreement is not reached at this meeting the local authority will need to notify the court and the parents or those with responsibility that they are pursuing a Section 31 care order. While FGCs are not a legal requirement at this (or any) stage, statutory guidance (Department for Education, 2014: 16) recommends them as a useful tool in considering wider family and friends prior to the issue of proceedings (paragraph 3.8, 3.24). Further to this Practice Direction 36c on case management for courts (Ministry of Justice, 2010) states that a record of discussions with wider family are part of the court's checklist documents and that alternative dispute resolution procedures should be considered to be pre-proceedings. Family Group Conferences are recommended as a way forward for many families. Furthermore, Court Orders and Pre-proceedings Statutory Guidance 2014 (Department for Education, 2014) states that:

> local authorities should consider referring the family to an FGC if they believe there is a possibility the child may not be able to remain with their parents, or in any event before a child becomes looked after unless this would be a risk to a child. (Department for Education, 2014: 16)

In practice this means that FGCs can be useful in the pre-proceedings stage both as an attempt to avoid proceedings and (if this is not possible) to provide families with an opportunity to provide a robust plan to present to court which will include where possible alternative plans for the care of the child. Evans (2011) also argues that review FGCs can also be useful in supporting families to organise contact and can therefore be useful at different stages throughout the court process.

Smith and Hennessey (1998) found that FGCs prevented 47% of cases from going to court and more recent research (Morris, 2007;

Sawyer and Lohrbach, 2008; Walker, 2005) also found a significant reduction in the number of proceedings following an FGC.

The UK Government's response to the Family Justice Review (Ministry of Justice, 2012) highlights FGCs and their use at the pre-proceedings stage arguing that the 'benefits of Family Group Conferences should be more widely recognised and their use should be considered before proceedings' (p. 58). In this response, the Government also called for more research into FGCs, how best they might be used and their 'benefits' and 'costs' (Ministry of Justice and Department for Education, February, 2012: 58).

The 2011 Munro review also makes reference to the potential benefits of FGCs and other similar approaches: 'These evidence-based programmes are expensive to set up but there is increasing evidence that by avoiding the need for looked-after children to move to more intensive and expensive placements they not only provide better outcomes for children and young people but are cost effective' (p. 95).

Therefore it is evident that while no legal mandate exists for FGCs in the UK the model is regarded as key to early engagement with families in the pre-proceedings process.

Statutory guidance on Family and Friends Care (Department for Education, 2011a) makes further reference to FGCs and recommends the use and local availability of FGCs alongside a range of other support for family and friends carers.

The Public Law Outline emphasises assessments being undertaken in the pre-proceedings stage in order to (wherever possible) prevent cases going to court, which is why FGCs in this stage can be so useful. Following the Children and Families Act (2014), however, in those cases which go to court a 26-week time limit is imposed to try to minimise delays for children (section 14(2)) and a timetable is drawn up at the beginning of proceedings to this effect. This is congruent with the Children Act 1989 principle of delay being likely to prejudice the welfare of the child. Although there is provision for this timetable to be revised if necessary, this is only in exceptional circumstances if the court considers that the extension is 'necessary to enable the court to resolve the proceedings justly' (Section 32(8)). This makes it difficult to justify the use of FGCs during proceedings since potentially FGCs may lead to a delay, making it more important to ensure that FGCs are used in the pre-proceedings stage. Family Rights Group cites written evidence from the judges of the Family Division (CFB 55) which appears to support FGCs prior to the introduction of the Children and Families Act (2014):

Amongst issues that need to be addressed to prepare for the introduction of the 26 week timetable, we would identify... the quality and context of local authority pre-proceedings work with the family, in particular the examination of family placement options (through Family Group Conferences or otherwise) and assessments. (Children and Families Act, 2014)

In 2009, with funding from the Family Justice Council, Family Rights Group surveyed the provision of pre-proceedings FGCs following the introduction of the PLO and found a 'significant increase' (Family Rights Group in association with University of Birmingham: 4) in both the number of FGC referrals and the size of projects following its introduction. Projects responded that they thought the PLO had led to an increase in referrals and a shift in the nature of referrals. Some services also stated that there had been a change in their funding since the introduction of the PLO, with more funding targeted at 'PLO cases' (2009: 31). Unfortunately some projects also argued that families can sometimes feel coerced into an FGC and that it was now sometimes less of a voluntary process. A number of local authorities, however, collected data that evidenced that FGC plans had led to care proceedings being avoided.

The recent Special Guardianship Review (Department for Education, 2015b) also makes mention of FGCs. Several respondents commented on the importance of early work to reduce the number of individuals being introduced late and five respondents also commented that FGCs should be mandated or at least recommended. It is possible that local mandates could be developed which would require local authorities to refer to an FGC at the point of the letter before proceedings.

Evans (2011) points out that while there are advantages to using FGCs in the PLO process we must also acknowledge the limitations. These may include a number of 'bottom line' stipulations that make truly family-led plans difficult. She also states that if the social worker or court do not agree the plan, this can be seen as disempowering for the family. Despite these concerns, however, the FGC process ensures that families at the very least will have had a voice in the process.

In addition to pre-proceedings and proceedings work FGCs can be used in a wide variety of statutory processes. For example, Edinburgh City Council uses an FGC approach in pre-birth assessments. Hodson (2011) recognises that research on pre-birth assessments is scarce and that to complete a good assessment it is important to make use of the pregnancy time to work with both the family and the professional network. The aims of the FGC approach in pre-birth assessment in Edinburgh are to, whenever possible, keep babies at home with support from wider family, identify kinship placements and, where no family options are available, to inform permanency[1]. The project was set up in 2014 (Malone and Banks, 2016).

A number of innovative services such as this exist in which FGCs are being utilised with specific service user groups, in order to prevent care and increase family support. Questions remain, though, about how FGCs can be applied when children and young people are already in the care system and where family alternatives to care have already been explored or exhausted. An approach called 'Family Finding' (Campbell and Borgeson, 2016) is being used in Edinburgh and piloted in a number of local authorities by Family Rights Group with the aim of locating and developing relationships between extended family members and children and young people living in care, using an FGC approach to facilitate this process. The Family Rights Group have established a pilot service, 'lifelong links', with funding from the Department of Education Innovation programme in seven English authorities. It will include using online tools to search for relatives and convening an FGC with those who are able to commit to developing relationships with the child or young person.

Edwards et al. (2007) found higher rates of reunification for children whose families participated in an FGC, and FGCs can also be a useful tool in planning for permanency. According to McKillop (n.d.) FGCs provide considerable benefits including improving communication and giving children a sense of identity. Wang et al. (2012) found that FGCs increased the odds of reunification with family or of placement with relatives and did not make a significant difference in the time taken to achieve permanency.

It is clear that FGCs are regularly used and can be helpful when care is being considered, when children and young people are in care and when families are in public law proceedings. Consideration therefore needs to be given to the implications that this may have for FGC coordinators and projects involved in court processes. FGCs remain a voluntary process and cannot be directed by court. Family Rights Group guidance 'Family Group Conferences in the court arena' (2011a), developed in consultation with CAFCASS and endorsed by the Family Justice Council is clear on this point. The document is also clear that FGCs are not minuted meetings and that the only document to come out of an FGC is the family plan which can be presented at court as one of the checklist documents (Family Rights Group, 2011a). Coordinators are not case-holders, nor are they always social workers, and it is never appropriate for them to make judgements or assessments of family members for the purposes of court; these assessments should be directed back to social workers.

The above discussion has referred to public law in child welfare but FGCs are also applicable to private law proceedings. On 6 April 2011 *Practice Direction 3a – Pre-Action Protocol for Mediation* came into effect. The Practice Direction requires that any couple 'considering applying' for an order in the family courts must attend a 'Mediation Information and Assessment Meeting' (MIAM) about 'family mediation and other forms of alternative dispute resolution'. Subsequent guidance by Family Rights Group in partnership with CAFCASS (Family Rights Group, 2011a) on the use of FGCs in court proceedings suggests that FGCs can be directed by the court as an 'alternative dispute resolution' beyond the first hearing in private law proceedings.

Forward4Families, an FGC service based in Ealing, London, provide FGCs for families in private law proceedings, referring to them as 'Collaborative Decision Making'. FGCs are used to address the following issues:

- where children will live;
- the arrangements that will be made for them to spend time with each parent, grandparents and other close relatives;
- special provisions, if any, which might need to be made about such matters as education, religion, health and travel;
- any other support that is required to meet their needs. (Forward 4 Families, n.d.)

It appears that the use of FGCs in private law proceedings is yet to become an established form of FGC practice, however, and most services that offer FGCs in the court arena do so in relation to the Public Law Outline in public care proceedings (Family Rights Group, 2009).

The legislative context for adult FGCs

So far, this chapter has referred only to FGCs in the context of child protection. The use of FGCs to plan for vulnerable adults, however, is becoming more prevalent across the UK.

Current legislation in adult social care, while not providing a mandate for FGCs, does lend itself to the use of FGCs in decision making for vulnerable adults, including adult safeguarding situations. The Care Act 2014 requires local authorities to 'consider the person's own strengths and capabilities, and what support might be available from their wider support network or within the community to help' in considering 'what else other than the provision of care and support might assist the person in meeting the outcomes they want to achieve'. In order to do this the assessor 'should lead to an approach that looks at a person's life holistically, considering their needs in the context of their skills, ambitions, and priorities' (Care Act, 2014).

Furthermore, the statutory guidance states that all safeguarding partners should take a broad community approach to establishing safeguarding arrangements. It is vital that all organisations recognise that adult safeguarding arrangements are there to protect individuals. We all have different preferences, histories, circumstances and life-styles, so it is unhelpful to prescribe a process that must be followed whenever a concern is raised. Safeguarding should be person-led and outcome-focused. It engages the person in a conversation about how best to respond to their safeguarding situation in a way that enhances involvement, choice and control as well as improving quality of life, wellbeing and safety (Local Government Association, 2015).

Indeed FGCs are suggested as good practice in addressing adult safeguarding concerns in *Making safeguarding personal* (Ogilvie and Williams, 2010). There are some FGC services that implement FGCs to address adult safeguarding concerns. The Daybreak Service in Hampshire has been using FGCs to develop adult safeguarding plans since 2007 (Tapper, 2010), Kent FGC Service has been doing so since 2006 (Marsh and Walsh, 2007) and Camden, since 2013 (Fisher, 2016). Following the introduction of the Care Act 2014 and the related adult safeguarding procedures, it appears there has been an increased interest in FGCs for adults.

FGCs also lend themselves to meeting the principles of the Mental Capacity Act (2005) which aims to ensure that people without capacity are empowered to make decisions about their own lives (SCIE, 2012a. Indeed Hobbs and Alonzi (2013) state that the inclusive approach of FGCs has the potential to enable those without capacity to be supported by their family/kinship network to participate in and contribute to decision-making processes.

For a detailed discussion on adult FGCs, please refer to Chapter Twelve.

The impact of devolution

So far in this chapter, the authors have discussed the legislative context in relation to the UK as a whole and have not made distinctions between the four nations of the UK. It is important to acknowledge that the Children Act 1989 and the Public Law Outline (Ministry of Justice, 2008), for example, cover only England and Wales and that Scotland and Northern Ireland have their own separate, albeit similar pieces of legislation. In addition to this The Care Act 2014 only covers England, although Scotland and Wales have similar pieces of legislation.

Therefore, it would be remiss not to discuss the legislative context for FGCs in Scotland and Northern Ireland and highlight some of the legislative and policy differences.

In Scotland, legislation in both adult and children's social care lends itself to the FGC approach. The Children (Scotland) Act 1995 and the subsequent policy guidance (The National Guidance for Child Protection in Scotland, 2010) mirrors the Children Act 1989, with the principles of partnership with families and children's views informing decision making underpinning the legislation. Furthermore, the Getting it Right for Every Child (Scottish Government, 2016) guidance, following the Children and Young People (Scotland) Act 2014 advocates the national use of FGCs to support families experiencing difficulties and to prevent children from becoming looked after by the local authority. Scotland introduced a set of national FGC standards in 2015, with many Scottish local authorities having an FGC service (Barnsdale and Walker, 2007; Children 1st, 2007; Children 1st, n.d.; Family Rights Group, 2015).

It appears that Scotland is also at the forefront of innovative practice in the use of FGCs. The example of the Edinburgh FGC service using FGCs alongside pre-birth assessments has already been highlighted above. Furthermore, FGC services in Dumfries and Galloway have been among the first to offer FGCs to support adults with dementia (FGC European Network, 2014). Indeed the Social Care (Self Directed Support) (Scotland) Act 2013 with the emphasis on individuals making decisions about what support would best meet their needs clearly lends itself to family-led decision-making processes (Scottish Government, 2014).

Despite previously stating that a legislative mandate for FGCs does not exist in the UK, Doolan (1999) argues that a legislative mandate for FGCs does exist in Northern Ireland in the form of the Justice (Northern Ireland) Act 2002. This piece of legislation introduced a restorative framework for youth justice, with restorative conferences used to address offending in young people. The Act embodies the aim of the Good Friday agreement to bridge the gap between the state and the people of Northern Ireland (Barnsdale and Walker, 2007;

Payne et al., 2009). Since then, community conferences to address religious divides and conflict have been introduced and restorative approaches are embedded in education and care provision for young people. Indeed, Northern Ireland has become a world leader in the field of restorative approaches (Payne et al., 2009). Perhaps not surprisingly, then, the use of FGCs as a restorative approach to decision making is widespread, with four out of the six health board trust areas having well established and embedded FGC Services, focusing on child protection and child welfare (Family Group Conference, Northern Ireland, n.d.). The child protection legislative context lends itself to the FGC approach. The Children (Northern Ireland) Order 1995 underpins the same principles as the Children Act 1989 and subsequent legislation relating the children and young people has tended to mirror that of England and Wales (Department of Health, Social Services and Public Safety, Northern Ireland, 2004).

Legislation and policy in adult social care in Northern Ireland also mirrors that of England and Wales. For example the Adult Safeguarding Prevention and Protection in Partnership (Department of Health, Social Services and Public Safety and Department of Justice, 2015) emphasises empowering people to make their own decisions about their lives, with a person centred theme running through the document. There appears to be very little written about the use of FGCs to address the needs of vulnerable adults in Northern Ireland. The fact that the national standards for FGCs refers to FGCs for vulnerable adults (Family Rights Group, n.d.b) and that Northern Ireland has embodied a restorative approach suggests, however, that FGCs are being used in this way. Indeed, a recent conference in Northern Ireland, 'Innovation in FGC Practice' (2016) explored the use of adult FGCs.

The legislative context of FGCs globally

Very few countries have a legislative mandate for FGCs. In addition to New Zealand, which has a legislative mandate for their use in both child protection and youth justice fields, FGCs are legislated for in The Republic of Ireland, the Netherlands and in certain states and territories in Australia (2007). The legislative context for each country is explored in greater detail in Chapter Seven, which explores the implementation of FGCs internationally.

In the absence of a legislative mandate for most countries who implement FGCs, Doolan's (2002) typology of levels of FGC implementation provides a framework for understanding the statutory use of FGCs. Doolan's typology refers to three levels of implementation:

- a legal mandate, where a requirement to use FGC is enshrined in law;
- a procedural mandate, where authorities adopt the use of FGC as policy;
- a best practice mandate, where professionals who are convinced of the value of the model are able to set up conferences within their local system. (p. 14)

An example of a country that applies a procedural mandate is the US, where several states have implemented FGCs as a state-wide approach in the child protection field, following the introduction of the Adoption and Safe Families Act, 1997, recognising that FGCs are an ideal method of meeting the key principles of the Act (Adams and Chandler, 2004; Barnsdale and Walker, 2007; Department of Human Services, Hawai'i, 2012). In Hawai'i, for example, despite the absence of federal or state legislation for FGCs, FGCs are embedded in child protection procedures, ensuring that FGCs are the principle decision-making process. Between the implementation of the model in 1996 and 2012 there were 13,500 O'hana conferences across the state. Since 2006, there have been more than 1,000 conferences each year (Department of Human Services, State of Hawai'i, 2012).

As demonstrated earlier in the chapter, the UK is an example of a country where FGCs are implemented using the best practice mandate. FGCs are recommended as best practice within legislation and subsequent policy guidelines but local authorities do not have a statutory duty to implement them. The most recent figures estimate that 76% of local authorities have an FGC service (Family Rights Group, 2015). Services tend not to be embedded in child protection procedures, however, and are regarded as an 'add on' service used at the discretion of individual social workers in individual cases (Ashley and Nixon (eds), 2007). Despite this, there are several areas within the UK, where FGCs have become an embedded part of policy and practice, such as in Hull, Stockport, Leeds, Kent and some London boroughs (Leibmann and McGeorge, 2015; Morris, 2007. Last accessed 22/02/2017; Marsh and Walsh, 2007). Indeed Leeds, Hull and Stockport are 'restorative cities' where FGCs are implemented as part of a culture of restorative practice in education, youth justice and social care services (Liebman, 2015).

For a more detailed critical discussion on the benefits and pitfalls of each of the above mandates, please refer to Chapter Seven.

Case studies for FGCs in a legislative context

Emma

This case study concerns Emma, and will demonstrate the impact of an FGC before care proceedings in diverting children away from permanent local authority care.

Emma was 14 at the time of the referral, and was resident in local authority secure accommodation, under Section 25 of the Children Act 1989. Emma was due to be discharged from the secure unit but her social worker still had concerns about risks posed to Emma by an adult male, aged 30 years, whom Emma perceived to be her boyfriend. Emma's social worker had been trying to engage with Emma on ways of keeping herself safe but Emma refused to speak to her. The local authority was considering applying for an Interim Care Order for Emma to become looked after by the local authority. Under the PLO (Ministry of Justice, 2008) the social worker made a referral for an FGC, the purpose of which was for the family to consider family alternatives to local authority care. The FGC coordinator, Jenny, visited Emma in the secure accommodation. Emma agreed to see Jenny, and after some discussion, she seemed interested in the idea of a Family Group Conference. This was the first time she had agreed to be seen by another professional.

The FGC:
Emma's parents, her maternal grandparents, and her paternal uncle John came to the meeting. The professionals who attended included her social worker, her key worker, and the coordinator. Jenny had made contact with a cousin of Emma, who was a lawyer. She was unable to be away from work on the day of the meeting, but sent her views to the coordinator by email. Jenny read this out at the meeting, and left it with the family during the private family time.

Emma's little brother, Sam, age eight, was unable to come to the Meeting. Emma had 'used' her brother to provoke her parents in the past, and the ensuing violence had raised concerns about his own protection. The secure unit was a distance from the family home, which was another factor in the decision that he should not be involved.

Despite fears that she might disrupt or refuse to participate in the meeting, Emma stayed in the meeting for the full duration, and gave her views in the first stage.

The questions to be addressed:
- What needs to happen for Emma to return home?
- Who can provide emotional support to her?
- Who can support Emma and her parents if and when she returns home?

The information presented by the social worker included reference to the risk posed to Emma but the key worker was able to balance this by sharing that the school attached to the unit reported positively on Emma's attitude and achievements.

Outcomes of the FGC:
Emma remained for the second part of the meeting, the private family time. This seemed to be an empowering experience for her, as she took control of writing up the plan to be presented in stage three. Emma's action points were broad and encompassed many areas including:

- She would see her grandparents and help them with the cooking and shopping, and gradually move to stay overnight. Emma recognised that her grandparents were rather frail, and needed support themselves from her. She agreed to phone her parents for a lift home by 10.30 pm.
- The social worker agreed for the first time in months that Emma could visit her grandparents. This was arranged to happen three weeks after the meeting.
- Emma would meet her uncle at weekends, and this was agreed.
- Emma wanted to stay overnight with her parents, but the social worker agreed that this should happen in stages, building up trust during this time. She would first visit for the day, and then the social worker would discuss with both her parents and with Emma how this had gone. If everyone thought this had gone well, then there would be a move to some overnight stays. Again, progress would be monitored.
- It was agreed that Emma could ring her parents, grandparents and her cousin from the secure unit.
- It was recognised that Emma would need to find a new school where she could be happy. She was embarrassed to go back to her old school because of her previous pattern of truanting and bad behaviour.
- Her father said he would redecorate her bedroom.
- It was agreed that Emma would start looking for a part time job when home permanently.
- Emma would try to stop smoking, and would start to think about this straight away.

- All of her family agreed to work together to look for activities to distract Emma from risky behaviour.
- Emma wanted a new phone, but it was agreed she would have to work towards this, by helping her mother, for instance, walking the dog, and spending more time with her little brother, Sam.

There was a review meeting eight weeks later. The social worker reported that the plan was working well. She was behaving well in the secure unit, and in the associated school. The visits home had gone well from everyone's perspective. They shared that some family therapy for everyone was planned to start soon, to improve relationships with everyone in the family. This had been discussed at the first meeting, but of course was not a viable option while Emma was in the secure unit. Emma's relationship with Sam was also beginning to improve.

It was agreed that Emma could go home in five weeks. Various conditions were agreed that ensured monitoring of her behaviour and safety.

Hayley and George

This case study concerns Hayley and her son George and it exemplifies the use of an FGC following an interim care order and an application by the local authority for a full care order, with a view to seeking the adoption of George. This case study shows that when an FGC is instructed by the court, the local authority only has the power to agree a family's plan in principle, and the court makes the final decision about whether the plan is agreeable.

The referral:
At the time of referral, George, age 14 months, was living with a local authority foster carer. This was following an earlier FGC which had been offered to the father, Dan, but to which George's mother had not been invited. The social worker suggested that Hayley had a personality disorder and, on these grounds, was not able to care properly for her son. Following this earlier FGC, George had been taken into care under an Interim Care Order.

On application for a Full Care Order, the judge reviewed the case and drew attention to evidence from the GP showing that Hayley's mental health difficulties were less severe than claimed (mild depression). The judge also drew attention to the fact the Hayley had not been offered an FGC previously.

The judge gave three weeks for Hayley's family to produce a Family Action Plan for the possibility of the child returning to the mother's care.

It was agreed that because of the tight timescale, contact with the Hayley should be made straight away. The FGC Meeting date was arranged within four working days of receiving the referral and was planned to take place a further four working days later.

Questions for the FGC:
- What practical and emotional support can Hayley's family and friends offer to her?
- How can Hayley's family and friends support her wellbeing and if needed, recognise and respond to any possible relapse in her wellbeing?
- How will Hayley manage supervised contact with George's father and paternal family, enabling George to be kept safe during this contact?
- How can the contact between George and Dan progress and be supportive of his mother in the Primary Caring Role?

The FGC plan:
The FGC was a valuable opportunity for family to be updated and ask questions together as a group.

Family and friends used the private family time constructively and presented a comprehensive support plan for Hayley if George returned into her care.

Outcome of the FGC:
The local authority agreed to support the family's plan for George to return to the care of Hayley, under a supervision order.

The court agreed to this plan, hence preventing George becoming looked after by the local authority and subsequently adopted. The FGC ensured that George's right to remain in the care of his family was protected (UN General Assembly, 1989; Human Rights Act, 1998).

For a case study on the use of FGCs within an adult safeguarding context, please see Chapter Twelve.

Conclusion

This chapter has explored the legislative context for FGCs in both the UK and across the globe. While FGCs do not have a legislative mandate in the UK, with the exception of Northern Ireland, legislation and subsequent policy lends itself to the FGC approach and indeed in some cases recommends the use of FGCs as best practice. Very few countries across the globe have a legislative mandate for FGCs and most countries implement what Doolan (2002) refers to as a policy or a practice mandate. There is some debate about which mandate is the most effective and a detailed discussion on this debate can be found in Chapter Seven.

What is clear, particularly from the field of children's social care is that FGCs have been effectively applied in a legislative context to divert children away from care proceedings and/or from local authority care. Furthermore, service evaluations for those FGC services that are using FGCs in an adult social care context have highlighted that FGCs have been an effective tool for decision making and planning for vulnerable adults, including adult safeguarding cases.

The case studies demonstrate how FGCs have been applied to legislation in the field of children's social care, in the UK and emphasise the benefits of applying the FGC approach in a legislative context.

Note

[1.] To decide where a child will live permanently.

Further Reading

Evans C.A. (2011) 'The Public Law Outline and family group conferences in childcare practice', *Child Care in Practice*, 11 (1): 3–15.

Family Rights Group and University of Birmingham (2009) *Report on the impact of the Public Law Outline on Family Group Conference services in England and Wales*, London: Family Rights Group.

Hobbs, A. and Alonzi, A. (2014) 'Mediation and family group conferences in adult safeguarding', *The Journal of Adult Protection*, 15(2): 69–84.

Tapper, L. (2010) 'Using family group conferences in safeguarding adults', *The Journal of Adult Protection*, 12(1): 27–31.

FIVE

Research, policy and practice

Nick Frost and Bernie Jackson

Introduction

Family Group Conferences (FGCs) are a restorative child-welfare practice that have the goal of enabling families to develop and apply their own solutions to any child welfare challenges they may be facing. FGCs, known as Family Group Decision Making (FGDMs) in North America, are characterised by being a family-led, strengths-based, solution-focused process which is able to mobilise informal support mechanisms.

The basis of a restorative approach is that people can be more productive, creative and cooperative and make positive choices when professionals do things *with* them, rather than *to* them or *for* them. A restorative approach requires a shift in thinking on the part of the referrer demonstrating a willingness to share power and responsibility with a family, during the process and following the making of a family plan.

Family Group Conferences can be used in any situation where plans and decisions need to be made about a child or children, in the main where there are safeguarding or child welfare concerns. A case study is provided below that demonstrates how FGCs can be used in safeguarding situations. This case study will be linked with the evidence outlined throughout this chapter.

For professionals working with FGCs there is therefore a value commitment to FGCs – they believe in working with, empowering and enabling families to resolve the challenges they face. This chapter is, however, primarily concerned with the research evidence that underpins FGCs – it asks 'what evidence is there for the effectiveness of FGCs in terms of both process and outcomes?' The chapter will conclude by exploring some implications that follow from the evidence for policy and practice and will suggest some future directions for research.

Family Group Conferences: evidence and outcomes

There is now an extensive literature relating to FGCs and FGDMs, but there are relatively few studies that report outcomes: in particular there are not many longitudinal studies, which can therefore report outcomes over a period of time. The process-based literature is, however, more extensive. By outcomes we refer to 'what changes as a result' of the FGC, by process we refer to how FGCs 'are experienced'. Both elements, outcomes and process, are outlined in the discussion of five key research projects which illustrate key findings in relation to FGC research.

One of the earliest studies evaluated the Newfoundland and Labrador Family Group Decision Making Project (see Pennell and Burford, 2000). Local advisory committees provided oversight and guidance to the project and staff were hired to coordinate the conferences and collect the research data which was then analysed by the research team. The sample of 32 families were involved in a total of 37 conferences, 32 being first time conferences. While the sample of 32 families is relatively small there were in total 472 participants at the FGCs of which 384 were family members and 88 were professionals.

The research project aimed to assess outcomes using follow-up interviews with family group members (known as 'progress reports') and by reviewing the Child Protection Services (CPS) files for the presence of indicators of child abuse (known as 'child protection events'). The progress reports were compiled from interviews with 115 of the 472 participants, drawn from 28 of the 32 project families. The research team explored the number of child protection events one year before the conference and one year after, a process also carried out for a comparison group of 31 families. The researchers used the median date of the conferences to divide the comparison group into pre-conference and post-conference periods. Both groups were matched in terms of length of CPS involvement, ages of children and types of problem. It is noteworthy that the CPS workers had been asked to select difficult cases for the FGDM project and this was reflected in the higher number of child protection events a year prior to the conference compared with the comparison group. A similar positive outcome is outlined in the case study towards the end of this chapter.

The progress report interviews found that two thirds of interviewees felt the conference had been beneficial. Those who reported that the family plan had not been carried out in full reflected that the process had nevertheless been beneficial, with some of the participants noting that the process brought families closer and strengthened ties. As can be seen in the case study below the plan can have many action points. One participating mother in the Pennell and Burford study noted improvement in her self esteem saying that, "'I feel more secure and more confident with myself'" (2000: 149). The grandmother in this case added that the FGC had given her daughter "'a new and more positive outlook. She appreciates her children much more and offers the most positive parenting she can'" (Pennell and Burford, 2000, 149). This evidence supports the claim that the FGC process can empower parents by increasing self esteem which is also demonstrated in our case study.

Another issue explored by Pennell and Burford related to levels of safety for the children in project families, as compared to the control group. Both the progress reports and the child protection events demonstrated that there was a greater level of safety for those children, compared to control families, during a period of one year following the conference. While the case study used in this chapter is short term this is illustrated as well. The project families began with more child protection events a year prior to the conference than the comparison group; a year after the conference they had fewer than the comparison group. The study demonstrated that the child protection events for the project families reduced from 233 to 117 whereas child protection events for the comparison group rose from 129 to 165. This was supported by a comparison of CPS activity and substantiations of abuse and neglect. Analysis of these showed that both fell for the project families following the conference; substantiations halved for the project group but nearly doubled for comparison families. These findings were triangulated by interviews which suggested project families were suffering less abuse following conference and parents were providing better care than the comparison group. Pennell and Burford conclude their findings as follows:

> The conference should be viewed not simply as an end itself but as a step in an ongoing process of collaboration and empowerment in which families are invited, and supported, to take an active role in developing their potentials. (2000: 153)

A second study will now be explored which looked predominantly at diverting children away from the care system and maintaining placements within the family. Crampton and Jackson (2007) analysed data from a Michigan study that explored 96 referrals that were served by FGDM, comparing them with referrals that were worked with by mainstream care services. The study does not use randomised assignment to a control group therefore cannot prove or disprove the effectiveness of FGDM. The researchers' findings suggest that children placed through the FGDMs were less likely to be placed in an institutional setting and more likely to remain placed with extended family, they moved less between temporary homes and they had less additional contact with CPS, in particular less contact leading to substantiated claims of abuse or maltreatment.

The positive outcome findings from Crampton and Jackson contrast with a third study: this is a Swedish study which concluded that their data did not support the view that the FGC is more effective than traditional models in preventing future maltreatment. Sundell and Vinnerljung (2004) compared 97 children served by an FGC, with 142 children served by a traditional child services approach. They followed the children for three years and compared future child maltreatment events reported to child services between the two groups. After controlling for the child's age, gender, family background, and type and severity of problem, they found the FGC group had more re-referrals to child services (for abuse but not neglect), they were longer in out-of-home placements but over time had less intrusive support from child services. The researchers note that the FGC group were often re-referred by their extended family, another point illustrated in the case study presented in this chapter, which could be a result of the FGC making the extended family more aware of the situation and therefore more alert to any future abuse. The researchers report that many proposed plans involved extensive and intrusive support from extended family members which includes reporting parents to child services if they reverted to their former drug use. Sundell and Vinnerljung emphasise that the impact of the FGC accounted for less than 7% of the variance in the outcome variables and as such demonstrated limited positive impact. Sundell and Vinnerljung also report positive process events: the FGCs had high family attendance (75% of all extended family members invited and 67% of all children invited). In all the cases the family were able to agree on a plan and 65 out of 66 were immediately accepted by social services. In 86% of the plans, extended family members had offered some form of support and researchers found 72 examples of addressed issues in plans that were not initially raised by professionals. They also reported high levels of participant satisfaction with regards to being well informed about the FGC, having their views listened to by everyone and respected by professionals. 89% were satisfied with the plan at the end and 86% favoured the FGC as a child protection method. This is again illustrated in the chapter case study. Sundell and Vinnerljung conclude by arguing that although their results do not support the claim that FGCs are more effective, they do not argue against their use. This study is one of the most rigorous quasi-experimental studies in the field, and it can be seen that process issues emerge more positively than outcomes.

In a fourth study, the California Title IV-E Waiver Evaluation (Center for Social Services Research, 2004) provided an opportunity to carry out a randomised control study of FGDM in relation to child welfare outcomes (see Berzin et al., 2008). Families were randomly assigned to a 'treatment group' who were served by the FGDM model and a 'control group' who were served by the usual Child Welfare Service. The project was carried out in two areas, Fresno and Riverside, and were aimed at differing population groups. The Fresno project targeted children at risk of further maltreatment, whereas the Riverside project targeted those who were in foster or relative care and were at risk of placement moves. Their sample consisted of 60 children in Fresno (39 in the treatment group and 21 in the comparison group) and 50 children in Riverside (31 in the treatment group and 19 in the comparison group). The Riverside staff utilised a version of FGDM that did not include the private family time, thus raising the issue of programme fidelity: all parties remained present during the meeting and they drew up with the plan together, in contrast to the chapter case study. Information related to placement and child safety was extracted from the California Children's Services Archive, most of the data in the archive came from the Child Welfare Services (CWS). The study compared both treatment and control groups for reports of substantiated maltreatment during the study period and found that there were no significant differences between treatment and control groups. The study also examined the number of cases closed and the exit routes: they found no significant difference in the number of cases closed or the reasons why they closed between treatment and control groups. Berzin et al. (2008) summarise these findings to suggest that children who received FGDM were 'no worse off' than traditional services in the areas of safety, permanence and placement stability. Berzin et al. (2008) also make some important observations: they suggest that due to the relatively small sample size, the study may have been unable to detect subtle differences between the groups. They also argue that workers who were exposed to FGDM philosophies may have altered their approach with families in the comparison group who subsequently may have received some benefits of the FGDM value base. Another important finding is that follow up studies reported that family members had difficulty completing tasks and 'maintaining momentum' (Berzin et al., 2008: 50). Berzin et al. suggest that FGDM projects may focus too heavily on the preparation stage and conference itself and neglect the important post-conference stage. The chapter case study illustrates the role of the follow-up review.

In the fifth, and largest, study explored here Wang et al. (2012) explored the impact of FGDM on in-care placements. They had a large sample of 7,986 young people who were subject to FGDMs, assessing placement outcomes over time: they focus on outcome rather than process issues. The researchers conclude that, overall, 'Family Group Conferences after removal increased the odds of reunification with family by 28% and placement with relatives by 7.3%... FGDM increases the likelihood of desirable permanent placements' (Wang et al., 2012: 845).

These studies have uncovered a wide range of research findings – with findings that are mainly positive in relation to the process of FGCs but mixed (with positive, negative and neutral findings) in relation to outcomes. This raises a number of complex issues regarding context, methods and sampling which are discussed fully elsewhere (see Frost, Abbott and Race, 2015, Chapter Nine). The mixed results may be connected with different service provision, different models of FGC/FGDM, different research methods and greatly varying social and political conditions. The chapter case study suggests a positive outcome where the system is properly resourced and the model is followed fully. Crampton (2007), a leading commentator in the field, argues that the apparent failure of FGC/FGDM projects in producing measurable and consistent outcomes could be accounted for by failure to support families after the conference. This argument may be supported by data from Weigensberg, Barth and Guo, who point to early gains in service connection, which do not seem to be sustained:

> The meaning of…strong early connections to services is not clear, because when evaluating service receipt after 36 months, there were no significant differences in received services among those who did and did not experience FGDM meetings. These findings together suggest that although FGDM meetings may facilitate initial connections to counselling, mental health, and parenting services, over time children and families who do not experience FGDM meetings may be just as likely as those experiencing FGDM meetings to receive these services. (Weigensberg, Barth and Guo, 2009: 389)

This again points to the need for longitudinal studies of the outcomes of FGCs.

Given the complex challenge of assessing the process 'empowerment' and 'engagement', and measuring 'outcomes' and 'change' as well as the many differing factors already discussed it may be the case that in assessing the effectiveness of FGC a pluralistic, mixed-method research methodology is required.

Policy and practice implications

This paper has explored outcome and process evidence from data relating to FGCs and FGDMs. Studying outcomes proves to be problematic: the relatively small number of studies that have tried to assess the outcomes of FGC have faced difficulties in finding comparison groups and in recruiting participants which has led to small samples in specific localised settings. There are also further difficulties in applying methods of research such as randomised control studies to a socially complex situation, a common issue in social work research. Even the most rigorous of studies, such as that by Sundell and Vinnerljung, conclude in a nuanced manner by stating that although their results do not support the claim that FGCs are more effective, they do not disqualify their use.

The studies analysed in this paper thus suggest mixed results for FGCs: some studies have reported positive outcomes (Pennell and Burford, 2000; Crampton and Jackson, 2007; Wang et al., 2012) while others have reported neutral outcomes (Sundell and Vinnerljung, 2004; Berzin et al., 2008). However the process evidence is overwhelmingly positive, suggesting a clear role for FGCs. The evidence gathered here suggests that service users' evaluation of the process of FGCs is overwhelmingly positive. The participants feel listened to and valued which, it could be argued, demonstrates the value of FGCs, even in the absence of powerful outcome evidence. This helps to create the strong practitioner value-based support for FGCs/FGDMs.

There is across the world positive, value-based professional and non-governmental organisation support for FGCs (see, for example, Hoover, 2005). Furthermore, this support can be underpinned by theoretical frameworks that support the idea that empowering, restorative, strengths-based approaches can help effect change (see Frost, Abbott and Race, 2015).

There is a need for more longitudinal studies to examine whether, as theory suggests, FGCs can effect change and subsequently produce positive outcomes for children. Whatever these results it is important to note that FGCs can provide an environment in which empowerment can occur: 'it is not an end in itself but an on-going process of collaboration and empowerment' (Pennell and Burford, 2000). In other words, process experiences as well as outcomes matter.

Underpinning our discussion are the challenges in implementing and mainstreaming FGCs. The difficulties faced by a bottom-up approach to mainstreaming FGC is that it can lead to a variation of models and the dilution of the original New Zealand model. It also relies on the support of social workers who may be reluctant to use the model because they operate in a risk-averse context.

FGC implementation requires extensive and codified support if it is to become universal – as is the situation in New Zealand. The use of a referral 'trigger' such as imminent legal or child protection proceedings as suggested by the Family Rights Group (2011b) may be necessary for a more consistent approach.

Following our exploration of a range of studies into the effectiveness of FGC, evidence suggests that with regards to outcomes, FGCs are certainly no less effective than the traditional child protection services. Studies of the experience of children and families using the FGC model suggest that it is a family-centred and strengths-based approach that promotes partnership between family and State and can consequently act as an empowering process. The Case study below illustrates and 'brings to life' many of the evidence-based points made throughout this chapter.

Family Group Conference: a case study

Sarah is mother to Anna, aged ten, Sam, eight, Alfie, three, and Evie, aged nine months. Richard is father to Alfie and Evie. Anna and Sam's father is Paul. The children were made subject to child protection plans under the categories of physical, emotional harm and neglect due to the following concerns.

There have been six domestic violence incidents where the police have been called – Richard has been verbally abusive towards Sarah and on one occasion has physically assaulted her when she had Evie in her arms. Sam tried to intervene to protect his mum and sister. Sarah had a black eye and a cut to her lip. The police were called but Sarah refused to make a statement. Richard is a heroin user who is not currently engaged with drug services, although he has been on a methadone script in the past. He also drinks to excess. Sarah uses alcohol on a daily basis and sometimes uses cannabis as well. The couple want to remain in a relationship.

Anna and Sam have good school attendance but are late most days, sometimes not arriving until 9.30am. Alfie misses nursery at least once every week. Evie is behind with her immunisations and there are concerns about both her and Alfie's development. A number of health appointments have been missed and no one has been at home when the health visitor has visited. The children have not been to the dentist for a number of years.

Sarah is struggling to set routines and boundaries for the children and is feeling overwhelmed and anxious. She and Richard don't always agree about what the children need and Richard often criticises her.

Paul has Anna and Sam to stay every other weekend and they go to his house for tea every other Saturday. He also speaks to them on the phone at least once a week. He is really worried about them but works away during the week. He and Richard don't get on well and Paul tries to avoid any contact with him.

The family agreed to have Family Group Conference and the allocated coordinator met with the referring Social Worker to discuss the social workers 'bottom line' and the questions for the family meeting.

The social work service 'bottom line': Richard has to live away from the family home while an assessment is undertaken. His contact with Alfie and Evie has to be supervised.

Questions for the FGC:
- What needs to happen to ensure that the children are kept safe from the physical and emotional harm resulting from domestic violence?
- What support do Sarah and Richard need to address their drug and alcohol issues?
- What needs to happen to ensure the children arrive at school on time and that health appointments are attended?

Preparation for the FGC:
The coordinator worked with Sarah and Richard to identify their network of family and friends and decide who they wanted to invite to their family meeting. Sarah agreed that Paul and his family needed to be part of the meeting as well. Sarah identified her parents, two sisters and brother, an aunt and cousin, a close friend who lives on the same street, plus her great grandma. She has a good relationship with Paul's mum so was keen for her to be there.

Richard's relationship with his family has been difficult and he was unsure if anyone would want to get involved. He identified his brother and parents but did not want his brother to know about the domestic violence incidents. He did not want any other family members to be involved. Paul identified his mum, sister and brother, as well as his granddad.

With Paul working away during the week and other family members' availability, it was agreed that the family meeting would take place on a Saturday afternoon at a local church hall. The coordinator met with Anna and Sam to prepare them for the meeting and they discussed what they wanted to share with their family at the FGC. Anna and Sam made a welcome poster and invitations for the meeting and drew pictures sharing how they were feeling. Alfie was also seen by the coordinator and drew a picture for the conference.

During the preparation for the family meeting Sarah shared her worries about her family knowing the extent of her alcohol use and the coordinator agreed to support her in telling them about this prior to the meeting. Safety at the meeting was also discussed and a safety assessment completed.

Richard initially minimised the extent of the domestic violence but during the course of the preparation moved to acknowledge the harm being caused. The coordinator supported him to talk to his brother about the domestic violence incidents. Richard shared his anxieties about how Sarah and Paul's family members would behave towards him in the conference.

Paul shared with the coordinator his worries about being in the meeting with Richard, as he was feeling angry that Sam had been exposed to the violent incident. The coordinator and Paul discussed strategies to help him to manage his feelings in the meeting.

The Family Group Conference was held, and was attended by eight members of Sarah's network – her cousin was unable to attend. Richard's brother and parents attended, as did Paul and the family he had identified.

FGC:
During the first stage of the meeting – information sharing – the referring social worker outlined the concerns and the bottom line and the family were given an opportunity to ask questions. Anna and Sam, supported by the coordinator and Sarah's friend Tracey, told the family how upsetting it was for them when Richard got angry. They said that they didn't want their Mum or Richard to use drugs or to drink so much.

After an hour the family had the information they needed to enable them to move into private family time to put their plan together. Private Family Time lasted for nearly two hours and at times the discussion became heated, as family members expressed their anger and upset at Richard's behaviour towards Sarah and the children. Anna, Sam and Alfie came to play with the social worker and coordinator during this part of the meeting as it was 'boring' when everyone was talking.

The family plan:
The family agreed that they would support Sarah and Richard in continuing their relationship but only on condition that they accessed support with their drug and alcohol use and that Richard took part in the social work assessments. The family were clear that the children's safety was their priority and that they would contact the social worker if they had any concerns.

- Richard acknowledged that he needed to change his behaviour and agreed to attend Caring Dads (a domestic violence programme), or equivalent, and to contact the drugs agency to start his methadone script again.
- Sarah said that she would put the children first and while she hoped that Richard could change his behaviour, she would consider ending the relationship if he didn't do what he had agreed.
- Sarah and Richard both agreed to attend appointments to address their drug and alcohol use.
- Sarah agreed to make a GP appointment to discuss her anxiety and to meet with a worker from a domestic violence support agency.
- Sarah's parents and sister agreed to care for the children at the family home so Sarah could meet up with Richard twice a week. Richard agreed not to come to the family home.
- Sarah's aunt and Richard's parents agreed to supervise contact for Richard with the children three times a week at their respective homes.
- Sarah's friend agreed to call every morning to help her get the children ready so that they weren't late for school.
- Anna and Sam's paternal grandma agreed to make dental appointments for them and also for Alfie.
- Sarah agreed to let her aunt know about any health appointments so that she could support her in attending them.
- All family and friends agreed that they would contact the Social Worker if they saw Richard at the family home or became aware that he was seeing the children without being supervised.
- Paul agreed to continue to have Anna and Sam to stay every other weekend and for them to come for the day every other Saturday, instead of just for tea.

The family discussed a contingency plan that if the situation did not improve and the children were still being put at risk, then Paul would make an application for a Child Arrangement Order so that Anna and Sam could live with him. Sarah's parents said that they would consider caring for Alfie and Evie if that became necessary.

The Social Worker felt that the plan safeguarded the children. The Social Worker agreed to complete the child and family assessment prior to the FGC review.

The family decided that they wanted to meet again in eight weeks to see how their plan was working and if it needed to be amended.

Review FGC: eight weeks later

The review was attended by everyone with the exception of Richard's brother and Paul's granddad due to work commitments.

The family discussed progress with their plan and it was acknowledged that there had been no further police callouts. Richard had not been to the family home and had attended all contacts arranged with the children, apart from one. No concerns had been raised by family members about the contact and the children were happy to go.

Richard had been accepted onto 'Caring Dads' (a domestic violence programme) but was waiting to begin attending a group.

Both Sarah and Richard had been attending appointments to address their drug and alcohol use. Sarah had provided clean samples but Richard had given two samples which were negative, very soon after the FGC. Samples had been clean since.

The children had arrived at school on time every day and Alfie had not missed any sessions at nursery.

The Social Worker had completed the child and family assessment and acknowledged that the risks identified around the domestic violence and the drug and alcohol use were being addressed by Sarah and Richard.

Anna and Sam attended the review and were much happier about the situation.

The Social Worker informed the family that if progress continued it would be recommended at the next child protection review conference that the child protection plan was ended, as the family plan was working well to safeguard the children.

Emergent themes

The following themes emerge from our discussion and draw on a study undertaken by Frost and Elmer (2008):

- FGCs require expert independent preparation and facilitation if they are to work well. This is central to enabling an atmosphere of trust and openness between family members and professionals. Adherence to the New Zealand model seems to improve both process and outcomes.
- FGCs seem to operating effectively in differing cultural and political settings. Maximising family network attendance seems to be an essential element of a successful FGC.
- The family plan is the essential outcome of the FGC process. The FGC process itself gives a voice to parties and may well have a positive, empowering impact, regardless of the actual plan.
- Participation levels from family network members at the FGCs seem universally to be high. It is important that all parties are able to make active contributions during the meeting. This seems to be dependent on:
  - effective preparation;
  - an enabling and supportive atmosphere at the Conferences;
  - a facilitative chairing style.
- More research work is required on the participation of children and young people and the role of child advocates in facilitating full participation by children and young people.
- A clear strength of FGC is mobilising wider family networks. Grandparents in particular seem to have a particularly key role. Even where the parent(s) are struggling with substance abuse, domestic violence and/or mental health issues, in Conferences strong and capable relatives often emerge.
- Review meetings can be utilised to review the plans and check implementation and progress, as in our case study. These can work well, with feedback being similar to that for the initial conferences, but further research is required.
- The referring social workers are pivotal to the FGCs in sharing their assessments to the families. Guidance and training is required for social workers, and related professionals, as FGCs are developed and become more extensive.
- It is important to note that FGCs exist at an interface with other processes – most notably care proceedings, child protection processes and private law processes. Agency policy needs to address these

interfaces – there is no reason why FGCs cannot actively contribute to all these processes.

This chapter has focused on the role of evidence in implementing FGCs, while recognising there are also value-based reasons for implementing FGCs. The evidence is mixed – and more powerful in relation to process (how things are done) rather than outcomes (what changes as a result of an intervention). There is no doubt that more research is required – in particular long-term follow-up studies and the participation of children and young people. Meanwhile, as many researchers argue, there is enough evidence and professional and family-based experience to make a powerful argument for the embedding of FGCs in child welfare policy and practice.

Conclusion

We would argue that there are powerful value-based reasons for engaging with FGCs. In addition, as we have demonstrated, the evidence base around the process of FGCs is strong – families find the process, in the main, empowering and engaging. The evidence base in relation to the outcomes of FGCs is mixed in relation to both safeguarding and care placements, as studies have found positive, negative and neutral outcomes following FGCs. To supplement our existing knowledge there is a requirement for more outcome-focused studies of FGCs. There is a particular need for long term follow-up studies.

Further reading

Frost, N., Abram, F., and Burgess, H. (2014a) 'Family group conferences: context, process and ways forward', *Child and Family Social Work*, 19 (4): 480–90.

Frost, N., Abram, F., and Burgess, H. (2014b) 'Family group conferences: evidence, outcomes and future research', *Child and Family Social Work*, 19 (4): 501–7.

These articles provide a comprehensive overview and analysis of the research relating to FGC/FGDM.

SIX

Family members' experiences

*Deanna Edwards and family members
who have been part of an FGC*

"Brilliant – inclusive – no scary solicitors,
just butties and flapjacks."

*Comments from a service user on her experience of an FGC,
with thanks to Stockport FGC service*

This chapter explores the views of family members who have been involved in child welfare FGCs. The case studies presented have been written by family members involved in FGCs. These are their own stories written in their own words. In order to safeguard the identity of other family members, names and identifying details have been changed or not included. Authors of case studies have been acknowledged at the end of the chapter (with their agreement) but not associated with individual case studies presented.

Why service user involvement?

As stated in the introductory chapter, FGCs originate in New Zealand from roots that are firmly embedded within service user rights and empowerment (Connolly, 1994). Some of the key principles of FGC practice are those of empowerment and being a family-led process. Therefore it is not surprising that FGC projects have developed strategies for involving families in developing services (Ashley (ed.), 2006). While this has been somewhat sporadic and piecemeal there have been a number of services and events that have stood out during this history. Torbay FGC service, for example has had a young people's group for many years. This group have been heavily involved in service and policy development and indeed have influenced national FGC developments with invites to several FGC conferences. Alongside Stockport FGC young people's group they met with MPs on several occasions to lobby for FGCs. In 2004 Family Rights Group hosted a family members conference in Birmingham called 'Families Voices' in which people who had experienced an FGC came together to share experiences and discuss how they might shape future provision (Axford, 2007).

At present there are pockets of good practice in terms of service-user involvement. This includes the aforementioned work in Torbay and work on family member inclusion in Camden (Camden Family Advisory board). However, it must be acknowledged that service user involvement in all areas of social care remains a pipe dream for many reasons which include scarce resources in terms of staff and financial commitments (Branfield and Beresford, 2006).

Satisfaction rates for FGCs

It is widely acknowledged that FGCs provide good direct involvement of family members in FGC meetings. For example, Coventry FGC service in 2013 reported that children over four attended in 56% of FGC cases and that fathers attended in 44% of cases. Robertson (1996) reported that children attended 79% of FGCs and when Frost and Elmer (2008) reviewed the Leeds FGC service he found that participation levels were 'high'. We also know that satisfaction rates are often high. Early research reaching this conclusion includes Titcomb and Lecroy (2003) who found that 94% of families reported a high level of satisfaction and 96% of respondents said that they 'felt respected'. Similarly, Walker (2005) found that family members who participated in FGCs were more satisfied with the child protection process than those who didn't. More recent research substantiates these findings (Asscher et al., 2014, Oosterkamp-Swajcer and De Swart (2012), Schuurman (2011) and Frost and Elmer (2008)). Frost and Elmer (2008) reported that this positive response remained even when the family were not able to produce a plan. However, studies such as these are often criticised for being small scale, having selection bias and no comparison groups (de Jong, Schout and Abma, 2014). Moyle (2014) also points out that much of the research is short term and while satisfaction rates are high, outcomes are more difficult to assess.

Quotes from family members involved in FGCs abound and are generally positive and complimentary about services. One example from Coventry FGC services' annual report (Coventry Council, 2013) stated

> "It was a far better process than I would have imagined. We felt listened to and the process was explained well. We were able to reach our own decisions, which was refreshing."

Frost and Elmer's (2008) evaluation of the Leeds FGC service recorded the following comments:

> "I would recommend it to anyone."
> "It was alright."
> "I wish I had known about this before. If I had known about it, it would have helped sort things out. I would have used it."

Frost also cited an example of a 10 year-old boy who led the feedback in the meeting.

Frost and Elmer's (2008) findings that families still report satisfaction with FGCs, even when a plan is not agreed by the local authority, contradicts earlier research by Lupton and Nixon (1999) which had found that in order to feel empowered families must experience beneficial outcomes. Again, it is clear to see that research is mixed and often contradictory in terms of understanding families' attitudes to FGCs. However, what is clear from the research is that overall families are more positive about FGCs than other statutory processes (Holland et al., 2005). It is important for those providing FGC services to listen to the views of service users and engage service users in the delivery of FGC services. This will enable an understanding to develop in terms of what helps and what hinders the FGC process. FGC services need to look at how we can support family members to have their voices heard and how we can make the process better for families.

Article 12 of the UN Convention on the Rights of the Child (UN General Assembly, 1989) states that when adults are making decisions that affect children that those children should have their opinions taken into account. In terms of social care services this means that we should be listening to children and young people when we make decisions about them. However, there remains persistent doubts about whether the voices are heard in decision making processes (Dalrymple, 2002). Even in FGCs (where children are directly involved) according to Heino (2003) they are often overlooked as a source of knowledge, leadership and power, which means that adults are still the decision makers and children and young people hold little power in the meeting and rarely lead it. Indeed Moyle (2014) argues that much of the FGC research rarely includes children and young people as participants. A notable exception to this is Sundell and Vinnerljung (2004) study which followed 97 children for three years and compared these with a control sample of 142 children who were dealt with using traditional child protection approaches. While satisfaction rates were high, this study did not seek the views of children, and did not support the effectiveness of the FGC model. Instead it found that re-referrals to child protection were higher for those families who had experienced FGCs which led the authors to question the efficacy of FGCs. However, Tinworth and Merkel-Holguin (2006) have suggested that this may indeed be an indication of the success of the FGC, in that families continued to seek help and be supported, feeling empowered to do so.

Moyle (2013) further argues that children are not always seen as capable of the responsibilities of decision making. Indeed, Barnsdale and Walker (2007) found that in some FGCs, while children and young people were positive about the process, some young people found that they exercised little influence. Young people's involvement in services, then, will help us to determine how best we can support young people in FGC practice.

The Children's Commissioner for England's 2010 report on family perspectives on safeguarding and on relationships with service users made it clear that there is potential for a 'stand-off' between service users and those working with them. One service user likened social workers to a 'social police force' (Children's Commissioner, 2010: 11). People reported feeling 'judged' and 'violated' (p. 11) and complained that in child protection conferences "there can be people who don't even know the family members of children" (p. 15). While FGCs fared better and families suggested that they wanted FGCs and advocates available, we need to learn lessons from these voices. Families said they wanted workers to:

- respect them;
- understand the barriers they faced;
- work in partnership with them;
- communicate well with them;
- develop relationships with them.

From the Children's Commissioner's report, it is clear that it essential to keep listening to family members. FGC services can achieve this through:

- project evaluation;
- service user involvement in FGC projects and practice including service development and delivery;
- FGC research which listens to the voices of services.

This chapter has captured some of these voices and provided some family narratives of their FGC experiences below.

> "I did not know you could invite your granny to meetings, that would have helped me but I just didn't know." (Children's Commissioner, 2010: 33)

FGC stories

A mother's story

> "I'm a mother of two children, a boy aged nine and a girl aged three. My FGC was about the best possible outcome for myself and my children. My son at the time before our meeting was struggling with a lot of different things at home and at school. What I liked about my FGC was that all my family turned up to the meeting to support and help me and my children. We all came together as a family to work out the best plan to help with my children and myself. The FGC coordinator and social worker were really understanding and helpful. My coordinator explained beforehand how the meeting would be set up and that we would have our own family time to discuss in which ways we could help each other. Since I've had my FGC meeting my son has been diagnosed with ADHD so as a family we have all learned more about his condition and ways we can help him out which is best for him."

A father's story

> "Soon after giving birth my wife started suffering from post-natal depression. She started using alcohol as a coping mechanism and our family started to suffer. All three children (my son and my wife's two children) were deemed to be at risk. My job involved frequently working away from home; trying to put bread on the table, I'd forgotten what was most important in life. My pride closed my eyes to any help.
>
> When social services appeared in our life we hoped that this nightmare would end soon. We found instead that the situation deteriorated and the threat of losing our children became a reality. Almost two years followed implementing

restrictions on us, forcing us to comply with social services policies, procedures and requests. This culminated in frustration and my anger exploded. An unannounced social work visit ended with a massive argument. I was observed to have handled my son in [a way that] the social worker felt was heavy handed and I was challenged about this. This made me very upset and angry; I love my little boy so much, I would never do anything to hurt him. I have to admit that I became intimidating towards the social worker; I demanded she left our house. That same evening someone knocked at the door. There were five social workers and three police officers. A police officer came inside holding a taser, ready to use. Outside our home were six vans waiting as a support. They perceived me as a monster, maybe one they had created. Our son was taken away. Fortunately his mum could go with him. I had to seriously start thinking what to do next not to lose my family. After a few days I rang the social worker and tried to apologise. I had to swallow my pride and apologise, sincerely apologise and truly start to try and cooperate with services.

A court application for a care order was granted to place the children in care until both myself and my wife were judged to have improved or parenting skills. Fortunately my wife's parents were considered suitable. My wife went to stay with them too but the relationship between myself and my in-laws became more and more strained. Shortly after this my wife died. My whole world collapsed; my wife was dead and I was about to lose my son.

Step by step, slowly and with tremendous pain I started to try and prove my innocence and suitability to be a father. I had fantastic support from my solicitor. Even though my 'rehabilitation' process in the eyes of social services was going pretty well I still had some remaining issues with my son's grandparents. We were not communicating and when we met the atmosphere was very tense. We blamed each other for what had happened and saw ourselves as almost enemies not members of the same family. This was the moment when Family Group Conferences appeared on my horizon. My first reaction to the offer of an FGC was sceptical as so far very little I had been offered helped. It felt like a battle to win my son back. I didn't trust anyone but on the other hand my stubborn nature whispered 'prove them wrong'. I decided to take every possible step to win my son back and take part in an FGC. Grandparents weren't as keen and it took the coordinator a while to convince them to take part. The meeting was attended by myself, the social worker, coordinator and grandparents. The meeting took place in a little cosy room and the coordinator managed everything. She went over what we could expect from an FGC and set some ground rules which we all agreed would help the meeting run smoothly. Food and drink was provided to help us feel more relaxed and comfortable.

After an uneasy start we started to relax. Grandparents took a very practical approach. They wanted their lives to go back to normal with no intrusion from social services. They were willing to help me to look after my son, especially when I'm at work. They wanted to maintain contact between him and his siblings. They wanted to help build a routine and a safe life for him. I wanted to show my willingness to cooperate and be more flexible. I opened up and started to feel lighter. It was the first time in a good few months when it felt we had started to look in the same direction. My son's well-being was our common aim.

We came up with a plan and my son came back to live with me with support from his grandparents. My relationship with my in-laws began to improve. We started talking, not just speaking, and started respecting each other again.

I feel that the way I was originally treated by social services absolutely didn't respect my cultural background, traditions and attitude. With the FGC I felt I was able to make choices and decisions. I felt enabled and respected. The family 'own' the meeting and are respected as experts when making the family plan.

My Family Group Conference took place in June 2013. In August the same year the court allowed my son to come back to me. He was initially to be supervised for six months, a period which passed with absolutely no problems whatsoever. He is still with me and is a happy bubbly little boy. At the time of writing he is six years old. My relationship with his grandparents is just what we all wished, back to normal. I recently got married again. According to my son he now has two mums. One lives in heaven and one here on earth.

Meeting my FGC coordinator was an unforgettable experience. Today, a few years after very traumatic events in my life I have moved on. I help out with training new social workers and others about FGCs and want to act as an FGC ambassador. My life would have been possibly very different – and difficult – without access to the project. Thank you for allowing me to share my story."

A young person's story

"I had an FGC because of parent and family problems. I was living with foster carers but wanted to spend more time with my mum and other family members and we had the meeting to discuss how this would work. At the meeting I said that if I could move back in with my mum I would stop running away. The social worker agreed that we could try living back with my mum and now I'm much happier and I've stopped running away like I said I would."

An uncle's story

"My sister-in-law was experiencing difficulties in her life and she had two young boys who were being affected. She came to live with us. While they lived with us we supported her as best we could. Support from us and social care resulted in her hugely reducing her alcohol and prescription drug intake. She was also successful in obtaining a two-bedroom house and after a short while her youngest son declared he wanted to live with her, but after a while he started to show erratic and disruptive behaviours. We had a Family Group Conference and as a result he came to live with us and we set out our expectations. He was treated like we treated our own children, we discussed schooling, our expectations, his expectations i.e. times to be in at for food and times to be in at night, which he engaged with fully. After two years he moved back with his mother, which soon deteriorated into not attending school, staying out all night etc. so he came back to live with us. However, we were now expecting our third child so we couldn't keep him living with us long term; so he went to live with his elder brother who by now had a flat."

A mother's story

"I self-referred for an FGC, after getting the contact number from my GP. I was having problems with A, my 12-year-old daughter. Problems began after I had a breakdown. She started high school and began to not attend, arguing with me and just totally disrespecting me. No matter what I did it became harder to cope and communicate with her. After contacting the local FGC Service, I met our coordinator. She was a lovely kind lady who visited me, listened to me and most importantly heard me. I wasn't judged as a mother, I felt I could confide in her totally.

The coordinator visited my family, the ones that were directly involved in what was happening between A and me and our crumbling relationship. She spoke to everyone individually and listed to their thoughts. She met A and gave her chance to say how she felt. I thought this was very important – she needed an outlet as much as me. After weeks of one-to-one meetings a date was set for our FGC. I must admit I was scared to death; it worried me that our coordinator would not be in the same room but we were prepared. We all expressed our thoughts, feelings and concerns. It made me really upset that I was going to be so honest and relive some of my own childhood experiences that may have been underlying issues regarding how I'd handled mine and A's problems. I was terrified of upsetting my own mum who had been a constant in my life, but things needed to be said. Now or never. We all spoke and listened to each other, some things were hard and upsetting to hear. It was an emotional experience but we did listen to each other, no-one walked out, no-one ranted, everyone did get upset. We now as a family often have 'family meetings'. No, it doesn't always solve everything, but it gave us the grounding to be open, honest, to listen and to accept one another's opinions. I will always be truly grateful to FGCs for what they did for my family. I wish self-referrals still existed. I would recommend it to any family in crisis and feel like they have nowhere to turn before things spiral out of control. Our outcome could have been so different. We weren't on the verge of court proceedings but I was desperate and FGCs saved me."

What I liked about FGCs

Family members were asked to state what they liked about the FGC process. The words will speak for themselves:

"These meetings were better than any other reviews I've ever had. In other meetings there was always too many people and I was never listened to. Everybody ignored the things I wanted. When I had the FGC I did feel I was being listened to and afterwards my social worker was trying hard to get me what I wanted. I also really liked having the food – it really matters and makes it feel less serious. I was also happy that I could choose who I wanted to come because I said I'd only come if my partner could come along and I was told this would be ok." (Skye, young person)

"Open, honest communication, delivered in a clear non-jargonistic manner, wholly restorative in their nature, encouraging participation. This is a process which empowers the individuals who take part, gives all a voice and encourages active listening skills leading to greater understanding of their own and other people's thoughts, feelings, actions, reactions and the impact all these things have on each individual." (Brian, uncle)

"Reinforces family members to bring the child to the forefront of their minds, to put a plan in place to keep the children from harm's way. Also puts a plan in place to safeguard the children. FGCs are a really important tool for making a family come together in a controlled environment. I found this extremely useful to be able to plan and to get my voice heard via a children's advocate. Now I'm an adult, understanding the process has made me more equipped for helping relatives' kids through a child protection plan. It was important to me to bring all the necessary people to the conference to allow everyone to be involved in creating a plan for the children." (Zoe, young person)

"Less stressful and people feel free to speak and open up. In my FGC I was taking on the children and mother was crying, she needed to be there and for people to listen to her too. I like the space that is given to the family to express their views, explore the situation and give an opinion on how much support can be provided without a professional intervening. Because of the FGC I didn't have to go round and round the whole family and tell each one of them what was going on. I didn't have to go to them and ask each one of them for help individually, they came to me, we all had the FGC." (Kevin, father)

"I was alone and isolated; to overcome that fear was the most important thing for me. There was a unity of coming together. It gave me control when decision making. It gave you back up, not one person facing this. It makes you more brave to tell your issues and get help." (Karman, mother)

"When you get your friends and family in a group they get it all at the same time and they can confer with each other. In my experience a lot of people want to show their faces. It showed me who can help and who can't. The FGC was good for me in the sense that the support (as the kinship carer) that I am looking for comes from the mother as well. The relationship with her was improved by an FGC. It gives everyone genuine first hand story of what needs to happen and how it could be fixed. It helped me get my head round the support the kids need after everything they have been through including witnessing domestic violence." (Gary, kinship carer)

How can we improve FGCs?

Like all services, FGC services and practitioners can benefit from hearing what service users say about how it can be improved. For the purposes of this chapter service users were asked to comment on two areas in relation to this:

- What improvements I would like to see in FGCs?
- What advice I would give to FGC coordinators about preparing for an FGC?

Zoe, a young person who had attended an FGC, commented that she would like to see reviews on an annual basis and that she thinks plans drawn up should be written by the primary carer in order to improve 'ownership' of the plan. While the first point may be difficult to implement given the heavy caseloads and financial constraints that local authorities are increasingly facing (Moriarty, Baginsky and Manthorpe, 2015), the latter may be a simple and effective way of engaging primary carers. This would, however, depend upon a number of factors such as levels of literacy of the main carer, feeling confident enough to write up the plan and the wishes of other family members including young people.

Karman pointed out that the social worker initially approached her about an FGC and that she wasn't interested and didn't know what it was about. She wondered whether coordinators could approach the family themselves rather than the initial consent coming from the social worker. Some services (for example Stockport, Gateshead, Cwlwm [Anglesey and Gwynedd] do already take self-referrals. Many services would agree, however, that the social worker would need to get informed consent from the family for a referral to be made to FGCs (Ashley (ed.), 2006). Once this is done the coordinator can help the family to decide whether an FGC is suitable for them.

Kevin was very grateful for the flexibility of the FGC stating that it was important that it was on a Saturday, outside of traditional office hours. Most services would agree that this flexibility is essential and FGC services need to be proactive in ensuring that these unique and family-friendly features of FGC practice are not eroded by the mainstreaming of services. In 2002 and 2011 Family Rights Group produced practice standards for FGCs. These remain as guidance for good practice and are available from FRG. Alongside the FGC toolkit (Ashley (ed.), 2006) they provide a guide for services using FGCs and include recommendations for flexibility and that family decision making should include family-led decisions on the timing of the meeting.

Kevin also adds that the FGC meeting "should feel like the coordinator is in charge", which is something that can be promoted in our training of coordinators. He thinks coordinators should have "good pointer questions that are universal to all families, promoting positive stuff" which fits well with the strengths-based ethos of the model. He goes on to offer advice for coordinators that they "need to be prepared on what is going to be discussed" and provide "lots of copies of any information". He adds, "be ready to repeat yourself, people starting talking a lot about other things. (You) need to be ready to call people back and make sure people (are) talking about the subjects".

Skye would like coordinators to ensure that "comfier chairs" are provided in an FGC in a "nice place that doesn't feel like it belongs to the council". She makes an important point that meetings tend to go on for a long time and so it's important to be comfortable in the venue. While she felt she greatly benefitted from her FGC she found the venue, particularly the chairs to be uncomfortable so she advises coordinators to check the venue ahead of time and not to underestimate the importance of these factors.

Brian, a service user who became an FGC coordinator gives sage advice:

> "Once you know you have good listening skills, are understanding, have great organisational skills, are genuine to the core, able to give full ownership and empowerment then…prepare, prepare, prepare, then prepare for the unexpected. *Prepare* yourself for the people you are working with, give yourself time to understand each person's viewpoint, *prepare* each individual for the process making it inclusive, clear with expectations and non-confrontational. *Prepare* the setting for the meeting ensuring all who have a vested interested are involved and the meeting place is neutral and welcoming for families. Then *prepare* the best you can for the unexpected – ask experienced FGC facilitators what they have experienced."

Gary thinks that meetings should be as early as possible ("earlier the better") and warns us against just inviting people for the sake of it, arguing that it is not just about numbers of people that come but "quality not quantity." He goes on to tell us that it "took me a couple of meetings to work out that (the FGC coordinator) is not a social worker and writing things down against you." This perhaps points to an important aspect of both coordinator and social worker training in FGCs which should encourage workers to be clear about role distinctions. One way to aid this distinction is for FGC service users to see a visual representation of an FGC before preparation starts and Gary suggests that an FGC film would have been useful during his preparation. He thinks this might help prepare people and was concerned that during his meeting he "couldn't put (his) hand on (his) heart and say that everyone knew what it was even by the end".

Involving service users in FGC services

As illustrated at the beginning of this chapter, family members have always played a pivotal role in the development of FGC services. Many of the family members who contributed to this chapter have gone on to become involved in service development and it is not uncommon for family members to become FGC coordinators, as Brian shared: "I got a job with the FGC service and have also worked promoting restorative justice." He was one of a number of FGC family members who went on to secure jobs as FGC coordinators with the Stockport service.

Zoe tells us that she initially trained to be an FGC advocate:

> "I went on to become a children's advocate and actually miss it. An advocate is a great way to start to become a coordinator as you can gain experience while looking after one person."

Andrzej, a service user from Bury, has been involved in training social workers to use FGCS and has recently chaired a national conference on FGCs at the University of Salford (2016). He believes that the role of the coordinator is pivotal to the progress and healing which takes place in an FGC and feels that his life would have been "very different – and difficult – without access to the project." For this reason he wishes to remain involved with FGC development and stated his wish to become a "FGC ambassador".

Jaine, who self-referred for an FGC, proudly states that she was asked to take part in an FGC video which re-enacted a conference and that she "loved every minute of participating in a very useful and informative video." She went on to support a Family Rights Group initiative funded through the then Department of Children Schools and Families. Along with a number of other service users Jaine chaired and spoke at a number of regional 'roadshow' events across England to promote FGCs to the judiciary and other interested parties. The aim of this, as Jaine tells us, was, "so they could gain knowledge on what an FGC was about and how it could help prevent maybe court proceedings". This had the dual effect of supporting and the promotion of FGCs in pre-proceedings and proceedings cases but at the same time helping Jaine to improve her confidence. She enthuses about this: "I absolutely loved this experience, one I will embrace for the rest of my life. Not only did I feel I was helping to pass on valuable information but it empowered me and built confidence in me that I had lost".

This statement illustrates the mutual benefits that can be derived from service-user involvement in FGC development. On the one hand service user stories can make a powerful impact on those delivering the service and those referring to the service. It is also a useful contribution to the service users' experience, as hearing from others who have used the service can be enlightening and reassuring. Service users can talk about the service from a perspective that a social care professional can never experience unless they have also been a service user too, like Brian and Zoe. On the other hand, sharing their experiences of FGCs can be an empowering experience for service users, enabling them to develop confidence, like Jaine's experience. Furthermore, presenting information about FGCs is often a useful addition to job CVs.

That said it should also be recognised that many people give up free time to become FGC consultants, trainers and ambassadors. Therefore reward and remuneration are worthy of consideration. Services could offer certificates that can be used for CVs or give vouchers, gifts and financial rewards. It would also be helpful to pay travel and other essential expenses to allow service users to attend events. A number of FGC services including Torbay, Camden and Bury all have active service user groups and include family members in training, staff development, interviewing and project development. Projects can benefit from involving service users in their steering groups, leaflet and other publicity design, promotional events and DVDs. Projects may also wish to facilitate FGC service user groups too. These groups give FGC family members the opportunity to come together and can provide a useful starting point in terms of service user consultation. As stated earlier in this section, Zoe used her experiences as a family member to become an advocate for other young people involved in meetings. She trained as part of an initiative to develop 'peer advocates'. This was a project inspired by a young family member who wanted a young advocate to support her at her FGC. Zoe and a number of other young people were able to provide this service with the added bonus of being able to speak from experience which can act to reassure other young people about the process.

It is clear that the family members who contributed to this chapter have valued their FGC and their participation in service user groups and their contributions to service development. It is important to acknowledge, though, that the editors have, of course, been guilty of selection bias to some extent in that people who have shared their experiences for this chapter have all had positive experiences of FGCs, many of whom have gone on to join service user groups and involve themselves in service development. It is therefore recognised that the experiences of those who have less positive stories about their FGC need to be acknowledged and understood in order to develop service delivery. Indeed one of the principle philosophies underlying the FGC model is that family members are the experts on their own situation. Therefore in order to develop true grass roots services that build on the expertise of families, service user consultation needs to be developed and expanded.

The final word is left to family members Billy and Carly. Billy felt his FGC felt "safe and comfortable, it wasn't too much either physically or emotionally. It was sensitive to my immediate needs and I could stop at any time". Carly said: "I don't think there needs to be any improvements in an FGC meeting as I found mine really helpful and I would recommend an FGC to anyone in need of support of help from family members or friends".

Billy and Carly's comments illustrate the power of the FGC to be family-led and to harness the support of the family.

Conclusion

This chapter has given us an insight into service user experiences of FGCs and has told us stories of people's FGC process and outcomes. The message from this chapter is that we need to listen to these experiences in order to maintain and enhance our FGC services. Therefore the recommendations from this for new and established projects are:

- to involve service users in service developments;
- to continue to evaluate service user experiences of FGCs and to use these evaluations to enhance provision;
- to give FGC service users the opportunity to contribute to FGC training;
- the contributions that service users make can enhance both their CVs and confidence. These contributions should be recognised by the service.

Thanks and acknowledgements
Thanks to chapter contributors Andrzej Ledochowski, Zoe Pearson, Jaine Higginbotham, Brian Pendlebury, Billy, Skye, Kevin, Karman and Gary. Thank you to Cath Connor and Michelle Phipps, Stockport FGC service, Donna Havill, Bury FGDM service and Tim Fisher, Camden FGC service.

Further reading

Ashley, C., (ed) (2006) *The Family Group Conference toolkit: a practical guide for setting up and running an FGC service*, Department for Education and Skills, the Welsh Assembly Government and Family Rights Group.

Axford, C. (2007) 'Families' experiences', in C. Ashley and P. Nixon (eds) *Family Group Conferences – where next? Policies and practices for the future*, London: Family Rights Group, pp 97–112.

Frost, N., and Elmer, S. (2008) 'An Evaluation of South Leeds family group conferences', Leeds: Leeds Metropolitan University (unpublished).

SEVEN

An international perspective

Kate Parkinson

Introduction

This chapter explores FGCs as an international model of decision making. First it will examine the global context for FGCs, providing a picture of the spread of FGCs across the world. It will move on to examine the differing levels of service implementation, referring to Huntsman's (2006) typology for understanding the implementation of FGCs. The chapter will then focus on some of the outcome studies from seven countries: New Zealand, US, Canada, the Republic of Ireland, England and Wales; and key themes emerging from the literature will be identified. The chapter will end with a focus on China, as a case study for a country attempting to introduce FGCs as a culturally appropriate method of child protection practice.

The context

FGCs are used in at least 20 countries across the globe (Family Rights Group webpage), including the US, Canada, South Africa, Thailand, Sri Lanka, Russia and Slovakia. They are internationally recognised as an effective way of engaging families in decision-making processes (Barnsdale and Walker, 2007). As the model has been applied in other countries, it has been adapted to reflect the cultures, historical and policy context of individual countries and jurisdictions. Some of the processes are very similar to the original New Zealand model while others are very different and are hybrids of the original model, having been adapted to reflect the context of a particular country or region (Browne Olson, 2009). Often the name of FGCs has been changed. Alternative names for FGCs or hybrid approaches include Family Group Meetings, Family Unity Meetings, Family Care Meetings, Care Circles, Family Welfare Conferences and Family Group Decision Making (Barnsdale and Walker, 2007; Crampton, 2007; Harris, 2008). There has been some criticism of the adaptation of the FGC and it has been referred to by some as 'model drift' (Pennell, 2003). Other suggest that adaptation is necessary to ensure that FGCs meet the needs of their population (Browne Olson, 2009).

Historically FGCs have been largely focused on the fields of child welfare (including education) or restorative justice (Fox, 2008). More recently, FGCs have been applied in the fields of social care and health, where decisions need to be made about vulnerable adults (Wallcraft and Sweeney 2011; Wilson et al., 2011).

As a result, much of the literature on FGCs has focused on child welfare or restorative justice (Barnsdale and Walker, 2007: Crampton, 2007; Fox, 2008; Frost, Abram and Burgess, 2014a,b; Merkel-Holguin, Nixon and Burford, 2003; Mirsky, 2003; Morris and Connolly, 2012). There have been some difficulties, however, in developing an international evidence base for FGCs (Morris and Connolly, 2012). Evaluation studies of FGC services and their outcomes have tended to be quite small in scale and localised in their approach (Crampton, 2007; Fox, 2008). This is further compounded by the difficulties in comparing a model that has been adapted to meet the needs of individual countries and regions (Connolly and Morris, 2004). Despite these difficulties, a clear evidence base is starting to emerge and some key outcome themes are emerging from the literature (Connolly and Morris, 2011). These themes will be addressed later in the chapter.

Understanding the Implementation of FGCs

Perhaps the most significant difference in the implementation of FGCs across the globe is the status afforded to FGCs within the legislative and policy structures of individual countries and regions within countries (Doolan, 2007; Huntsman, 2006). FGCs are a legislative requirement in both child protection and youth justice contexts in New Zealand, under the Children, Young Persons, and their Families Act (1989). The Children, Young Persons, and their Families Act provides for an innovative system of youth justice, introducing a hybrid justice/welfare system where young people, their families, victims, the community and the State are involved in taking responsibility for offending and its consequences (O'Driscoll, 2006). Furthermore, within the child welfare context, the act states that:

> Wherever possible, a child's or young person's family, whanau, hapu, iwi and family group should participate in the making of decisions affecting that child or young person, and accordingly that, wherever possible, regard

should be had to the views of that family, whanau, hapu, iwi and family group. (Children, Young Persons and Their Families Act, 1989 (NZ), Section Five)

FGCs also have a legislative mandate in South Australia, New South Wales and Queensland (Australia), the Republic of Ireland and the Netherlands (Ashley and Nixon (eds.) 2007; O'Brien and Alohen, 2015; Wachtel, 2011). In South Australia, legislation requires that a conference be convened if a child is at 'risk' and prior to seeking care or protection orders that affect custody or guardianship (Harris, 2008). In New South Wales, the Children (Care & Protection) Act 2000 includes FGCs in a list of alternate dispute resolutions that should be offered to families prior to seeking care or protection orders that affect custody or guardianship (Morgan et al., 2012). Morgan et al. (2012) state that in practice, however, FGCs had not widely been offered to families in New South Wales prior to 2011, when a pilot FGC service was established to measure outcomes for children. FGCs are now being widely promoted within New South Wales, as the pilot service highlighted the potential of FGCs to enhance the safety of children, within their families (Morgan et al., 2012).

In Queensland, legislation mandates that an FGC is convened when a child is considered in need of care and protection (Harris, 2008).

In the Republic of Ireland, the Children Act 2001 makes provision for Family Welfare Conferences (FWCs) to be held where child welfare issues are identified in juvenile justice cases (The Children Act 2001, Part Two). Under Part Two of the Act, which commenced in September 2004, the Health Service Executive (HSE) is obliged to convene a FWC before applying for a special care order for a child, with the aim of diverting children away from the residential care system and enabling them to remain within the care of their families. Furthermore, the legislation enables a judge to request the HSE, to hold a FWC if a young person is in court for criminal behaviour and the judge considers that there is a care and protection issue to be addressed (Section 77). The Act also provides for the holding of a FWC if the child welfare agency decides that an application to the court is warranted to provide a secure placement for a young person that may be at risk of harm and needs such security for their own protection (Section 23).

Finally, in the Netherlands, the Dutch parliament approved an amendment to the country's Law on Child Welfare in 2014 that gives every citizen of the Netherlands, as of January 1, 2015, the right to make their own plan first (via an FGC) when social services has been called upon to intervene in the care of a child or young person (Wachtel, 2011).

Other regions have legislation in place that refers to FGCs but does not directly mandate for their use. For example in Hawai'i, a law has been passed making it mandatory to explain why an FGC has not been convened in voluntary cases, that is, where there is no court order in place (Adams and Chandler, 2004). In the UK, the Public Law Outline (2008, most recently updated in 2014) recommends the use of FGCs prior to initiating care proceedings (Family Rights Group, 2009). Furthermore, in Tasmania, the Children, Young Persons and Their Families Act 1997 states that an FGC may be convened if a child is at risk or in need of protection and that an FGC must be convened if a court orders one (Huntsman, 2006).

Most countries and regions operating FGCs, however, do not have a legislative mandate for doing so. Some countries, despite not having a legislative mandate, have embedded FGCs into their policies and procedures, such as the US, some territories in Australia and some states in Canada (Barnsdale and Walker; Harris, 2008; Huntsman, 2006). Others, such as the UK, offer FGCs as an 'add on' to existing statutory services, as FGCs are recommended as being good practice in child protection or justice settings (Edwards, 2007; Haresnape, 2007).

Doolan (2002) developed a typology of FGC implementation as a framework for understanding the global implementation of FGCs. He argues that three mandates exist to understand the implementation of FGCs:

- a legal mandate, where a requirement to use FGC is enshrined in law;
- a procedural mandate, where authorities adopt the use of FGC as policy;
- a best practice mandate, where professionals who are convinced of the value of the model are able to set up conferences within their local system.

There are differing perspectives on whether having a legislative mandate for FGCs is necessary or indeed desirable for the successful implementation of FGCs (Adams and Chandler, 2004; Brown, 2003; Doolan, 2007). Doolan argues that there are problems with all three approaches, outlined by Huntsman (2006) above. He argues that under a legislative mandate, the philosophical underpinnings of the FGC approach can be undermined by the legislation, as lawyers seek an adversarial approach and often involve clients to refuse to engage.

Indeed, evidence from New Zealand suggests that nearly 30 years after their implementation, FGCs have become a part of an adversarial legal process and that the model has been 'watered down'. Indeed, there are many cases, for example when families are not offered private family time, which is a core part of the process and where FGCs are being viewed as a 'tick box' exercise, rather than a way of meaningfully engaging families (Child, Youth and Family, 2012). Connolly (2006) in her study on the attitudes of 46 FGC coordinators, 'Care and Protection Coordinators', 15 years after The Children, Young People and their Families Act 1989, found that coordinators highlighted a tension between finding solutions that preserved the integrity of the family and meeting the legal requirements of the child protection process. Concerns raised focused on: questions about how much power families really have in the FGC process when professionals ultimately have to agree to a family's plan; how the philosophy of FGCs fit into an increasingly risk-averse chid protection system; the professionalisation of the coordinator role and the lack of resources and services sometimes available to meet a family's plan.

Adams and Chandler (2004) on the other hand argue that legally mandating service provision leads to a sharper focus and better decision making. They cite the case of the state-wide FGC (O'hana) service in Hawai'i, where between the implementation of the model in 1996 and 2012, there were 13,500 O'hana conferences across the state. Since 2006, there have been more than 1,000 conferences each year (Department of Human Services, Hawai'i, 2012).

Doolan (2007) goes on to offer a critical perspective on a procedural mandate for FGCs. He argues that a procedural approach runs the risk of instability with regards to what is considered to be best practice at the time and when faced with critical incidents, such as child deaths, the practice agenda could change. One could argue that the current climate of austerity and public sector cuts could further threaten a procedural approach, with non-statutory services potentially being the first to go.

Examples of where a procedural approach is in place is in many states of the US, such as North Carolina, Oregon and Washington State (Chandler and Giovannucci, 2004). Most FGC services in the US were established following the implementation of the Adoption and Safe Families Act 1997 (ASFA) whereby FGCs were recognised as being an ideal method of meeting the key principles of the Act; protecting children and preserving family integrity (Barnsdale and Walker, 2007). Outcome studies from these areas demonstrate the potential of FGCs to lead to positive outcomes for children and young people involved in child protection processes (for example, Pakura, 2003; Walker, 2005; Brady, 2006; Kemp, 2007; Marsh and Walsh, 2007), which will be discussed in more detail later in the chapter. The studies show that merely having a procedural rather than a legislative approach, however, means that FGC services face many barriers to their effective implementation. Barriers highlighted were the lack of resources to support a family plan and the instability in funding of services (Connolly, 2006; Skaale Havnen and Christiansen, 2014).

Doolan (2007) argues that the 'best practice' mandate has even more potential to be unstable than the procedural mandate. It relies on enthusiasts of FGCs to maintain the drive for FGCs, in a practice context, where FGCs are not included in statutory processes. The context for FGCs in England and Wales very much emulates the 'best practice' mandate, where despite the fact that FGCs do not have a legislative mandate, 76% of local authorities have an FGC service (Family Rights Group, 2015). One could argue that to some extent there is a legislative and policy framework that could embrace FGCs. Indeed, FGCs meet fundamental principles of the Children Act 1989, namely partnership with parents and that children are best cared for within their families (Brayne, Carr and Goosey, 2013). The model is recommended as good practice (Department for Education, 2015c) and in the Munro Report (Munro, 2011). Furthermore, the Public Law Outline (Ministry of Justice, 2008) states that an FGC or another form of family resolution process should have been undertaken before care proceedings are initiated (Evans, 2011). FGCs have not become an embedded part of practice culture in England and Wales and they are still regarded as an 'add on' service, used at the discretion of individual social workers in individual cases (Ashley and Nixon, (eds.) 2007). Despite this, there are several areas within the UK where FGCs have become an embedded part of policy and practice, such as in Hull, Stockport, Leeds, Kent and some London boroughs (Leibmann, 2015; Morris, 2007; Marsh and Walsh, 2007). In some areas, FGCs have become part of a wider culture of restorative practice, which is changing the landscape of child protection (Liebmann, 2015). Indeed several cities in the UK have now become 'restorative cities', such as Hull, Stockport, Leeds and Bristol, where restorative practices underpin the delivery of education and social care services (Liebmann, 2015).

Doolan (2007) argues, however, that for FGCs to be implemented effectively, there needs to be an existing legislative mandate in countries and jurisdictions using this model. Writing specifically about child protection, he argues that this is the only way that the dominant child protection context and discourse can be challenged and the current professional-led culture transformed. On the other hand, Brown (2003) states that there are risks to incorporating FGCs into existing professionally dominated systems and suggests that FGCs should comprise one of the tools that social workers can use, at their discretion. Indeed, when considering the New Zealand experience, the assertion that having a legislative mandate for the implementation of FGCs is the best approach is somewhat misleading, as it is clear where FGCs have been implemented under a policy or practice mandate that FGCs have been effective in affecting positive outcomes for children and their families. Some of the outcomes from research will be discussed below.

Examining the research from seven countries

The following seven countries have been chosen, as between them they represent each model in Doolan's (2002) typology. In addition to this, a number of evaluation studies have emerged from these countries, enabling some key themes to be identified.

Table 7.1 identifies where each country sits in Doolan's typology. Due to the federal nature of governance in the US and Canada, there are differing levels of the implementation of FGCs across the two countries, which are referred to in the discussion below.

Each model will be taken in turn and some of the research from the countries identified will be discussed. The authors advise that this chapter is read in conjunction with Chapters 4 for a discussion on the legislative and policy context of FGCs in the UK and Chapter Five for a more comprehensive analysis of the research in the use of FGCs and child welfare.

Table 7.1: Countries according to Doolan's typology

Model	Area Used
Legal Mandate	New Zealand, Republic of Ireland
Policy Mandate	USA, Canada
Practice Mandate	Sweden, England, Wales

The legal mandate

New Zealand

Data available in 2004 showed that since the implementation of FGCs, over 50,000 FGCs had been undertaken in New Zealand (Connolly, 2004). Despite the numbers involved, there has not actually been much vigorous evaluation of the outcomes of FGCs, and New Zealand has been slow to develop an evaluative process (Connolly, 2006). Furthermore, much of the research is quite dated and there appears to be little research from the past decade.

What research has been undertaken, however, has demonstrated positive outcomes for children and young people.

In the field of child protection, early studies on the impact of FGCs found that FGCs have significantly reduced the number of children subject to judicial decision making: in 1990 only 17% of conferences held in New Zealand needed court action to determine the final outcome (Maxwell and Robertson, 1991). Furthermore evidence has shown that the number of children being cared for within their families has increased since the implementation of FGCs (Thornton, 1993; Connolly, 1994). Maxwell and Robertson (1991) found that in almost two thirds of all care and protection cases, the children remained in the care of their families; 42% with their original care givers and 23% with extended family and only 34% were placed outside of the family.

Research by Pakura (2003) has substantiated these initial research findings and found that most families develop safe plans, fewer children and young people enter state care, and care and protection arrangements are seen by professionals as being improved for children and young people. This is despite the initial fears expressed by some that families developing their own plans would result in failings to protect children and lead to worse outcomes (Pakura, 2003). More recent research by Connolly and Smith (2010) highlights the benefits of a partnership approach in child protection for both families and professionals alike. Since 2006 the number of children in out-of-home care has fallen by 13%, and front-line staff retention in child protection teams has risen from an average of 5.6 to 6.7 years since 2005, suggesting that professionals are happier in their work when a partnership approach is adopted.

Republic of Ireland (ROI)

Studies into the outcomes of FGCs in ROI have found that FGCs have led to positive outcomes for children and young people involved in child protection processes. FGCs are referred to as Family Welfare Conferences (FWCs) in ROI.

Kemp (2007), in his three-year study on the implementation and outcomes of FWCs in the county of Wexford, found a consensus among professionals that immediate outcomes for children following an FGC were positive. These included improving the chances of a family-based placement being secured, creating a climate for improved relationships and contact arrangements between a child or young person and their family during a local authority care placement, improved stability and assisting in the process of returning a child to his or her family.

Evidence of long-term outcomes can be found in the evaluation of the FWCs in the HSE western area (Brady, 2006). This research found that when families were interviewed a year or more after their initial conferences, 69% reported positive outcomes from their FWCs. The factors that contributed to the success of FWCs appeared to relate to: family motivation and engagement in the process; intervention by professionals where needs are high but before the risk is particularly acute; and having a good family network with 'quality rather than quantity' support. Furthermore, it was found that successful outcomes also required realistic expectations on the parts of all parties involved, a belief in the values of the model and an undertaking of commitments made in the plan from family members, professionals and agencies.

A further study undertaken by Brady and Miller (2009) of the South Tipperary FWC service found that FGCs led to families having better engagement with services, improved communication between family members, increased contact with their family members for children in the care of the local authority, an increase in children returning to the care of their family and young people engaging in less risky behaviours.

More recent research by O'Brien and Alohen (2015) into 335 referrals made to the Dublin Family Welfare Service between 2011 and 2013, found that FGCs had addressed the issues identified by the referral in most cases, more children were found kinship placements, relationships between family members improved, as did the relationships between family members and professionals.

The policy mandate

The US

FGCs in child protection are widely used in several states in the US to varying degrees. Many states have FGCs firmly embedded in policy and practice (Chandler and Giovannucci, 2004) including Hawai'i, where the model referred to as the O'hana Conferencing (OC) model is used state wide (Walker, 2005).

The OC model has demonstrated positive outcomes for children and young people. Walker (2005) in her study of the use of OC in child abuse and neglect cases compared outcomes for children who had been referred to OC with those who were not referred for a conference. The study found that acceptable plans to keep children safe were agreed at OC in 97% of cases, children were significantly less likely to be placed in state care and were more likely to have stable and long lasting placements.

A more in-depth evaluation study was initiated between 2001 and 2003 to consider the state-wide effectiveness of the OC model (Litchfield, Gatowski and Dobbin, 2003). Child protection outcomes for children evidenced in this study are extremely positive with approximately 99% of families not being reported for harm (or threatened harm) within one year of the conference and not requiring subsequent court intervention after the conference had been held to address the original allegations. Furthermore in nearly two thirds of cases children remained within the care of their families, with professionals interviewed acknowledging that one of the benefits of OCs has been the identification of extended family members as permanent placement options for children. Another positive outcome evidenced by the evaluation was the fact that 82% of participants felt that the OC model helped the family, DHS workers, and service providers to work together to meet the best interests of the child(ren) involved.

Outcome studies from other states in the US where FGCs are embedded in state wide policy and procedure demonstrate similarly positive results (Veneski and Kemp, 2000; Pennell, 2003; Titcomb and Lecroy, 2003).

Canada

FGCS are not embedded in legislation at a national level in Canada. Decisions about the use of FGCs are made at a provincial level. The use of FGCs in Canada is widespread, however, with different provinces using FGCs to varying degrees in child protection, welfare and youth justice (Barnsdale and Walker, 2007). FGCs were first introduced into Canada in 1994 in Newfoundland and Labrador (Pennell and Burford, 2000) to address family violence and domestic abuse, although funding for FGCs has recently ceased (The George Hull Centre, 2011) and are currently implemented in Manitoba, British Columbia and Ontario (Barnsdale and Walker, 2007; The George Hull Centre, 2011).

Evaluations of FGC services have demonstrated positive outcomes for children and young people in child protection contexts.

For example, the evaluation of the first FGC service in Newfoundland and Labrador found that; the majority of respondents reported that families were 'better protected' as a result of the conference, there was improved care of children and decreased family violence as a result, the well- being of children improved and family members engaged with positive family support networks (Pennell and Burford, 2000).

Further comparative research into outcomes of child protection FGCs in Toronto was undertaken in 2006. Cases where children were referred to an FGC were compared with other child protection cases that were not referred to an FGC. The research found that in cases where children were the subject of an FGC, they were more likely to return to or remain in the care of their extended families than children who were the subject of alternative decision making approaches, 85% and 72% respectively. The authors concluded that like the Pennell and Burford's study in Newfoundland and Labrador, the research highlights the potential of FGCs to lead to positive shifts in child welfare indicators, such as a reduction in the number of children being looked after (Cunning and Bartlett, 2006).

More recently, a 2013 evaluation of FGCs in British Columbia found that outcomes for children were positive; in 50% of cases, no further child protection work was needed following a conference and 86% of respondents including family members and professionals felt that the family plan was adequately protecting children three months later. The authors conclude that the evidence suggests that an FGC approach has the potential to reduce the number of children in care and increase the number of children placed with extended family members.

The practice model

England and Wales

A detailed examination of the legislative and policy context of FGCs in the UK can be found in Chapter Four. Some of the research evidence from the UK will be examined below.

Despite the 'optional' nature of FGCs in England and Wales there is quite a significant body of research into the efficacy of FGCs in child protection contexts, however some of it is quite dated, and most of it is small scale and localised to individual services or small geographical areas (Fox, 2008). It is significant to note that there is very little research on outcomes from FGCs over the last decade and the most recent research tends to proceed 2010.

Research findings appear to echo those from studies in jurisdictions where FGCs have been implemented at a legal and policy level but, perhaps unsurprisingly, findings are not as robust and links between FGCs and positive outcomes for children are much more tentative.

Some of the research into outcomes for FGCs in England and Wales is summarised below.

Marsh and Crow (1998) examined the outcomes of FGCs from the six initial FGC pilot areas and their findings were that: the majority of families developed safe plans for children; FGCs reduced the demand for expensive services such as state care, court proceedings and the child protection process and that the model can increase professional understanding of complex situations and enhance the partnership relationship between professionals and service users. Furthermore Crow and Marsh (1997) state that children referred with child protection concerns are thought by practitioners to be as well protected or better protected in the great majority of cases through FGCs; the number of children being removed from the child protection register subsequent to the FGC is higher than would be expected in other circumstances and re-referral rates are comparatively low.

More recently, an evaluation of the Camden FGC service (Morris, 2007) found that the data suggested that FGCs were successful in diverting families away from legal proceedings and enabling children to remain in the care of their extended families. Furthermore there was a significant reduction in the number of families requiring social work services following the FGC process.

A key focus of research on outcomes of FGCs in England and Wales has been in the potential of FGCs to engage with families more effectively in child protection processes (Dalrymple, 2002; Holland et al., 2005 and Horan and Dalrymple, 2004). Findings from research suggest that families feel increasingly empowered in the FGC process, are positive about FGCs and that more fathers are engaged than in traditional processes. Furthermore, children and young people report feeling listened to at their FGC and felt that they had more say over decision making about their lives.

Holland et al. (2005) in their study of the use of FGCs in Wales found that FGCs have the potential to create a more democratised relationship between the state and the family in child protection services. Furthermore, an evaluation of the Kent FGC service (Marsh and Walsh, 2007) found that families were positive about the FGC process and viewed it as very much a collaborative approach with professionals. The research found that families tended to view the FGC process as somewhat separate from child protection procedures as a whole, having a negative perception of child protection services generally but being positive overall about the FGC process.

Sweden

FGCs were introduced into Sweden in 1996 as a pilot service and national funding of FGCs was provided until 2000. Between five and ten out of the total of 290 municipalities in Sweden use Family Group Conferences on an optional basis. In at least one of these municipalities, Hoor, FGCs are a part of mainstream practice (Naslund, 2013).

It has been argued that the Swedish child protection system does not lend itself to the FGC approach, as it reflects a 'strong paternalistic welfare state and shared popular values of social control that sanction interventions in families' (Sundell and Vinnerljung, 2004). Hence the FGC model represents an opposing approach. Naslund (2013) argues, however, that the values underpinning the FGC approach are consistent with current child protection legislation, just as in England and Wales.

Sweden is the only country arguably to have undertaken a methodologically robust long term study on the outcomes of FGCs in child protection (Sundell and Vinnerljung, 2004).

In order to evaluate the initial pilot, a three year comparative study of outcomes for those children involved in FGCs and those involved in traditional child protection processes was undertaken. Findings from the research (Sundell and Vinnerljung, 2004) suggested that children involved in FGCs had no better outcomes than those involved in existing processes and indeed in some cases were worse. For example, more children from the FGC group were re-referred to child protection services during the three years, suggesting less stability in their lives during this period; FGCs were no more successful in preventing further child maltreatment than other processes and more FGC children were re-reported for abuse. This research has been influential in the sense that it is the only long term, national comparative study of its size on FGCs and the fact it contradicts all other research in the efficacy of FGCs in child protection (Fox, 2008). The research has been used as a rationale by some to suggest that FGCs are not an effective way of protecting children and that further comparative research is needed to demonstrate their efficacy (Fox, 2008).

Sundell and Vinnerljung (2004) do acknowledge, however, that the child protection system in Sweden does not lend itself to the FGC process due to its paternalistic nature. They describe the child protection system as one which privileges professionals as experts and locates the family as passive recipients of services and intervention. Hence, a model that privileges the family as experts does not sit easily within this context. This can go some way to explaining why FGCs have not been successful in Sweden. After all, a question is raised about how successful FGCs can really be in child protection cultures that contradict the FGC approach. This relates back to Doolan's (2007) assertion that for FGCs to be successful in a child protection context, they need to be embedded in child protection cultures and processes, not merely an 'add on' to existing service provision. Examples from practice in the US, Canada, England and Wales highlights that cultures and processes can change without a legislative mandate.

Emerging research themes

It is important to note that the above is not a comprehensive review of the research into FGC outcomes. Furthermore, most of the studies referred to are small in scale and focused on small geographical areas. Despite these research limitations, however, it appears that a number of key themes have started to emerge from the literature, which suggests that as a result of FGCs: significantly fewer children enter state care and remain in the care of their families; contact arrangements between children in care and their families are improved; families develop safe plans for children; children and families feel more engaged in the process; and more fathers are engaged than in traditional child protection processes (Edwards and Parkinson, 2016).

While there is acknowledgement that further more robust, comparative research is needed to create a solid evidence for FGCs across the globe (Morris and Connolly, 2012; Fox. 2008; Morris, 2007), one could suggest that the FGC model offers a credible alternative to existing child protection systems and in particular could address some of the concerns raised about the increasing bureaucratisation of child protection services in the developed world (Connolly, 2004; Freymond and Cameron, 2006; Higgins and Katz, 2008; Gilbert, Parton and Skivenes (eds), 2011; Munro, 2011). Connolly (2006) suggests that, internationally, child protection systems have become procedurally driven with a focus on administrative tasks and this has been at the expense of more family centred practice. Hence an increasing number of countries are attempting to redress this balance by introducing child protection processes that are focused on supporting families to address child protection concerns (Parton, 2012).

FGCs also neatly fit with the International Federation of Social Work's (IFSW) global definition of social work, which states that,

> Social work is a practice-based profession and an academic discipline that promotes social change and development, social cohesion, and the empowerment and liberation of people. Principles of social justice, human rights, collective responsibility and respect for diversities are central to social work. Underpinned by theories of social work, social sciences, humanities and indigenous knowledge, social work engages people and structures to address life challenges and enhance wellbeing.
>
> The above definition may be amplified at national and/ or regional levels. (International Federation of Social Work, 2014)

The fundamental principles of FGCs are about empowering families to make decisions for themselves and to take collective responsibility for individuals within their family. The model embraces the diversity of families and the research has demonstrated that it can be applied cross-culturally, which is evidenced by the number of countries across the globe that have adopted FGCs into social work practice (Barn and Das, 2016; Barnsdale and Walker, 2007). With regards to the issue of culture, one of the weaknesses of the research is that it has tended to focus on children as a homogenous group. Outcome data has not tended to take into account the race, ethnicity and culture of children involved in FGCs, although there are a couple of studies that focus on aboriginal children (Arney, McGuinness and Westby, 2012; Harder, 2013). This is surprising considering the fact that FGCs were introduced in response to the needs of a first nation population.

Indeed, what is interesting about those countries where FGCs have been successfully embedded in legislation, policy and procedure is that these tend to be countries with a significant first nation population. This raises a question about whether the traditions and cultures of certain groups of people lend themselves more readily to the FGC approach or whether policy makers assume this to be the case, due to the origins of FGCs. Comparative research into outcomes for children from different cultural groups is necessary to address this question of cultural relevance. It could be argued, however, that the notion of families meeting together to discuss their issues and difficulties is relevant across cultures, as evidenced above with the number of countries using FGCs. Relatively recently, a discourse about the importance of culturally competent social work practice has developed (Harrison and Turner, 2010). The FGC model should be at the centre of the discourse. The research has evidenced the potential of FGCs to be applied cross culturally and to meet the needs of minority ethnic groups (Barn and Das, 2016).

The example of China is given below to exemplify the cross-cultural relevance of the FGC model. In the absence of legislation and policy relating to child welfare, FGCs have been implemented under a best practice mandate (Huntsman, 2006).

Implementing FGCs in China: a case study

Dr Louise Brown (author) with contributions from Dr Jie Lei

The Chinese government has in recent years been facing mounting pressure to tackle the growing concerns regarding child maltreatment. Recent national media coverage in China has drawn extensive attention towards child maltreatment which has resulted in a growing pressure from the general public for action to be taken. The exact prevalence and rates of child maltreatment remain unclear as there is no official reporting system in China, yet studies have indicated that the rates are comparable with Western countries (Chen, Dunne and Han, 2004). China continues to lack a comprehensive system for managing child protection, with an absence of statutory agencies, a reporting system or alternative institutional care arrangements for children at risk of harm (Shang, 2012). An enormous gap in the institutional framework exists for meeting the needs of children, yet conditions are changing and opportunities opening up for the development of interventions for working with children at risk of maltreatment. With formal, professionally dominated systems in their infancy it was considered that the FGC model might lend itself to a Chinese context, where Confucius principles dominate family life and where great weight is placed upon informal, family and community networks.

Small-scale funding was secured through a University start-up and Alumni Fund. This was matched locally with funding from two Chinese NGOs and a project team formed. The 'FGC Project Team' consisted of a mainland Chinese academic, a UK academic (with a social work practice background) and two Chinese NGOs with established neighbourhood family centres. Local political support was gathered and permission granted to go ahead with the pilot, and ethical approval to evaluate the trial was secured through the UK university. The conditions (and size of the trial) led to an action-based approach to evaluation which allowed for adaptation of the model to occur during implementation. A social work consultant was employed from Hong Kong to supervise the ongoing 'casework' of social workers using the model and an experienced trainer from the UK Family Rights Group trained social workers in the model. The two social work NGOs took responsibility for the quality of the social work service offered. The pilot project was set in the context of responding to child maltreatment and aimed to test a culturally adapted, Chinese version of family group conferencing.

The first stage of the implementation process concerned preparing the ground. Local public events were held and over seventy practitioners, managers, policy makers and potential volunteers were introduced to the core components of the FGC model. To secure local political support a closed seminar was held to which a further thirty professionals and representatives from key organisations attended. The participants raised the following potential barriers with the model:

- Would Chinese families be reluctant to get involved and not be prepared to discuss their problems with a wider network of family and friends?
- Would the absence of a legal mandate for social workers to intervene in family life result in the failure of the model?
- Would social workers have the skills and capacity required to deliver the model?
- Was it too soon for China?

Alongside the concerns raised, participants were also positive about its potential, suggesting that, with the right support, social workers could be empowered to support families using this model. The pilot project received 'permission' to go ahead. A series of meetings were subsequently held with social workers and managers at the two NGOs to present how the FGC model worked in practice elsewhere, present its key components and process and consider how they might wish or need to adapt it locally. Encouraging adaptation and thinking through how the model might need to be changed proved quite difficult as participants had little social work experience upon which to draw or reflect upon different approaches to working with families. Unlike other countries where the FGC model has been tested, in China, in the absence of existing formal systems, the model was not competing or being used as an alternative to an existing system. Without previous experience of having first used the model it was difficult for participants to know whether the model needed adapting or in what ways. The NGOs chose to test the model in its original form and if necessary look to adapt it over time. The only change suggested by the group at this stage was to change the name from Family Group Conference to 'Family Group Decision Making' (FGDM). The word 'conference' (*huiyi*) was considered too formal which might deter family involvement. Information leaflets for families were produced in Chinese.

Much time was spent on the 'referral criteria' that would be adopted by the two teams. Following much debate it was eventually agreed that families would be identified and offered the service where there was a presence of 'parental mental health illness or parental addiction (drugs, alcohol, gambling) which was impacting on parenting capacity'. An experienced trainer from Family Rights Group presented the FGC model (as used in the UK) and trained two managers and eight social workers as coordinators. The participants then educated colleagues in their organisations in the model (and referral criteria) encouraging them to refer the families that they were working with. The project was launched with social workers confident that there were large numbers of families who would meet the referral criteria.

The second stage of the project involved operationalising and adapting the model. Initial progress was slow and referrals did not arrive at the anticipated rate. Despite a slow start, within the first six months two FGDMs were successfully held with families. During the initial period of implementation a third NGO (another community-based social work organisation) joined the project and additional social workers were trained in the FGC model. A further two FGDM meetings with families were convened. During the initial implementation period, the referral criteria were amended to include cases of lower risk in order to increase referrals and enable social workers to at least practice the model. The third NGO entering the project broadened the referral criteria to include the definitions provided by the Ministry of Civil Affairs (2014). They added 'children with special needs' (*kunjing er'tong*) and 'children from families with special needs' (*kunjing jiating er'tong*) but within families where there were also identified issues of 'child neglect'. The criteria included children who were 'disabled', 'sick' or 'street children'. 'Children from families with special needs' referred to: parents with a severe disability or illness; long-term imprisonment or in compulsory rehabilitation; where a parent had died and the other failed to fulfil the parental responsibility or they were living in poverty. In addition to extending the referral criteria the age range of children who could be referred was extended to include children aged from 0 to 18.

Other adaptations included changing the coordinator's role in the FGDM process. Instead of the social workers referring families from their caseload to other social workers who acted as coordinators, the social workers themselves would convene the FGDM and fulfil the role of coordinator. In other countries the independence of the coordinator from the ongoing, 'powerful', statutory social worker/caseworker had been seen as important. Yet in a Chinese context this tension did not exist and the worker with the most trust within the family was the social worker. One of the major barriers to initiating the family meeting was that there were often insufficient numbers of people in the Chinese families' network to invite. A unique adaptation that was adopted in China concerned the role of volunteers in family meetings. Family members gave consent for volunteers to be matched with the family and they attended the meetings and remained present during private family time. Furthermore, 'sponsors' were identified to help provide resources for families. In China in the absence of any statutory services to resource the plan, social workers identified other families who were in a position to 'sponsor' the family plan. The experience of the social workers in the pilot was that the potential to offer resources, particularly material resources was crucial for the motivation of calling the family meeting. Without this the family would have little confidence in the benefits of discussing their problems in public. A sponsor attended one of the FGDMs and provided indispensable funding to support the family.

The four FGDMs that were held covered a range of different needs relating to the children or young people. For example, case one involved a 14-year-old boy with learning difficulties. His mother left the family home when he was very young and did not return, and he lived with his father and grandparents. His father had learning difficulties, his grandfather had dementia and his grandmother was losing her mobility due to rheumatism. The school social worker referred the family to the FGDM project following concerns that the boy could not care for himself and the adults in the family were increasingly unable to meet his needs. Five family members and the boy attended the FGDM and a family plan was drafted in which each family member agreed to teach the boy specific tasks around the house such as bathing, laundry and cleaning. When the coordinator revisited the family six months later, the aunt reported a significant improvement in the capacity of the boy to care for himself.

The use of an action-based approach to the pilot meant that adaptations to the intervention could occur and be tracked. This design and the small number of cases in the first 12 months do not allow for any meaningful outcome data to be collected. The findings of this initial attempt to develop a culturally sensitive FGC model in China suggested that it was in part successful. The process evaluation highlighted a range of barriers and opportunities to implementing an FGDM model in China, which are similar to findings seen in other FGC pilots in other countries. They included:

- low referral rates;
- small or absent family networks;
- social workers not believing they had the skills or knowledge to identify children 'at risk';
- lack of knowledge by professionals about the model, how it works, its potential benefits, how to sell it to families and what types of cases to refer;
- lack of a 'champion' on the ground to keep promoting the model;
- NGOs unable to prioritise FGDM work within overall workloads and targets;
- lack of resources.

In relation to what was deemed to be working well participants identified three key factors:

- strong, trusting relationships between families and the social workers meant they were more inclined to agree to try using a FGDM approach;
- resources: appointing additional social workers with time dedicated just to the FGDM Project helped;
- using successful cases to demonstrate that the model worked led to a more positive response among teams.

A key finding from the pilot was that the process in China encountered many of the same barriers and opportunities that have been found in other countries. Adaptation was essential to implementing the model. A key difference between China and other FGC pilot sites was the absence of formal services and resources to draw upon in China. The FGC model was therefore not being adopted in order to counter an existing system in which it was felt families had lost their power or ability to participate. It was also not being driven by concern over excessive removal of children from home. In the absence of a legal mandate to intervene in family life, when families in China were reluctant to engage in a FGDM this meant that there was less incentive or leverage with which they could be persuaded to give it a go. Despite those issues great creativity shown by social workers in introducing volunteers and sponsors to expand the resources available to resource family plans. Despite the difficulties encountered FGCs or FGDMs are now being trialled in a further site in China in relation to education-based issues.

Conclusion

This chapter has explored the use and implementation of FGCs across the globe. It has used Huntsman's (2006) typology as a framework to understand the application of FGCs in different countries and regions. It has explored some of the body of global research and identified some key themes emerging from the research in the field of child protection. It has introduced FGCs as a model of cultural competent practice which can be globally applied to address some of the shortfalls in current child protection systems. In presenting China as a case study, it has demonstrated some of the challenges that can arise when implementing FGCs into a different cultural context.

Acknowledgements

The research was supported by the Youth Funds of Research for Humanities and Social Sciences by the Ministry of Education (13YJC840017); the Research Foundation Funds for Returned Overseas Staff and the University of Bath Alumni Fund. The Project Team would like to acknowledge the support that they have received from Family Rights Group, the brave social workers and the children and families who went first.

Further reading

Barn, R. and Das, C. (2015) 'Family Group Conferences and cultural competence in social work', *British Journal of Social Work*, 46(4): 942–59.

Barnsdale, L. and Walker, M. (2007) *Examining the use and impact of Family Group Conferencing*, Social Research Centre, University of Stirling.

Frost, N., Abram, F. and Burgess, H. (2014b) 'Family Group Conferences: evidence, outcomes and future research', *Child and Family Social Work*, 19(4): 501–7.

Huntsman, L. (2006) *Family Group Conferencing in a child welfare context: literature review*, NSW Department of Community Services, Australia.

Part Two
Family Group Conferences in Practice

Part Two
Family Mediation: Perspectives in Practice

EIGHT

Addressing domestic abuse through FGCs

Kate Parkinson and Michaela Rogers

Introduction

This chapter will focus on the use of Family Group Conferences (FGCs) in cases of domestic violence and abuse (DVA). It begins with an explication of DVA, both as a global phenomenon and within a UK context, focusing upon the impact and issues for children and young people. Then discourse and practice surrounding intervention and service responses will be analysed in relation to current multi-agency approaches and the Coordinated Community Response model which incorporates child protection practices. The chapter will then move to discuss the use of FGCs in cases of DVA across the globe in order to provide a broader context for their usage, recognising that within the UK this is fairly limited. The chapter will draw on existing research and evidence to demonstrate the potential of FGCs to address DVA. It will take a critical perspective and address the challenges for using FGCs in this complex area of practice. In the final section of the chapter, a case study is presented which exemplifies how FGCs are currently being used with success to address DVA in the UK. The chapter will conclude by providing some recommendations for practice.

A global problem: domestic violence and abuse

The World Health Organisation (WHO) (2013: online) has described domestic violence and abuse as a 'global health problem of epidemic proportions' and WHO defines violence against women as:

> any act of gender-based violence that results in, or is likely to result in, physical, sexual or mental harm or suffering to women, including threats of such acts, coercion, or arbitrary

deprivation of liberty, whether occurring in public or in private life. (WHO, 2016: online)

While WHO acknowledges the gender-based nature of domestic abuse in that the definition it provides is focused on violence against women, the Home Office (a UK government department, responsible for immigration, security and law and order) uses a gender-neutral definition of DVA as a way to depict it as an umbrella category. The Home Office describes DVA as:

> any incident or pattern of incidents of controlling, coercive, threatening behaviour, violence or abuse between those aged 16 or over who are, or have been, intimate partners or family members regardless of gender or sexuality. The abuse can encompass, but is not limited to: psychological; physical; sexual; financial; emotional. (Home Office, 2013: online)

Within this chapter, we use the definition offered by WHO as in most literature, research and within the evidence base, DVA is depicted as a gender-based phenomenon (see, for example, Stark, 2007), while we acknowledge that DVA can occur in a relationship regardless of gender or sexuality, and women can be perpetrators in heterosexual and homosexual relationships. Moreover, throughout our discussion, we are focusing on the scenario when women are victims/survivors and men are perpetrators as this is the most prevalent and injurious form of DVA (Office for National Statistics, 2016).

There are various sources of prevalence data, however, a WHO (2013) project, *Global and regional estimates of violence against women*, was the first systematic study of global data on the prevalence of DVA. The study found that 35% of all women will experience either intimate partner violence (DVA perpetrated between two adults living as spouses or partners) or family violence. The study found that intimate partner violence is the most common type of violence against women, affecting 30% worldwide. UK statistics also suggest that a high number of women will experience abuse with one in four women experiencing DVA at some point during their life time (Guy, Feinstein and Griffiths, 2014). More concerning is the statistic that on average two women per week are killed by a current or former male partner in the UK (Walby and Allen, 2004).

The impact of DVA on families and children

The above statistics have implications for women living in families and it has been suggested that for women who are parents, the chance of experiencing DVA is double that of women who are not (Walby and Allen, 2004). Moreover, when victims are parents there can be considerable consequences in terms of their parenting capacity (Stanley, Cleaver and Hart, 2010). For instance, research studies have depicted the ways in which DVA erodes a person's mental health, can lead to conditions such as depression and post-traumatic stress disorder (PTSD) and can result in problematic behaviours such as substance and alcohol misuse (Humphreys and Thiara, 2003; Jordan, Campbell and Follingstad, 2010; Minieri et al., 2014). As such, the impacts of DVA can result in mothers becoming emotionally unavailable, being unable to cope and struggling to ensure the safety and wellbeing of their children, and being physically unable to care for their children due to the extent of their injuries. Thus, a key task in work to safeguarding children is to gain insight into these multiple and overlapping issues for parenting capacity as they often co-occur in the families seen by children's services (Blythe, Heffernan and Walters, 2010).

Indeed, within the setting of the family, it is suggested that one in four children will experience DVA by the time they reach 18 and that six per cent of all children will be exposed to more severe levels of DVA when perpetrated between the adults in their homes (Radford et al., 2011). Moreover, in the UK it is thought that around 130,000 children live in households where DVA is at its most severe and perceived to present a high risk (defined as having a significant risk of harm or even death) (CAADA, 2012). While DVA can present at a range of severities, and children can be direct or indirect witnesses (in the latter, hearing abuse taking place in other parts of the house), experiencing DVA as a child will *always* have a harmful effect (Clarke and Wydall, 2015).

In terms of outcomes for children, these are extensive and vary according to a child's age, developmental stage of childhood, personality and social characteristics (ethnicity, ability, gender and so on). Impacts include, but are not limited to: emotional and psychological distress; physical and health-related conditions; disrupted relationships; education (in terms of attendance, concentration and achievements); limitations in terms of play; poor identity development; social and behavioural changes, including anti-social behaviour (Stanley et al., 2010; CAADA, 2014; Houghton, 2015). Living with DVA can also influence children at a cognitive and attitudinal level, with some children adopting distorted views about relationships, gender, power and control, and even normalising the violence that they observe (Murphy and Rogers, in press). Children can also feel a sense of responsibility for the abused parent and with that the feelings of shame, self-blame and guilt. While to some extent these effects are mediated by a child's age, developmental stage, personality and resilience, the impacts to a child are also affected by the frequency, severity and nature of the abuse. Additionally, Stanley and Flood (2011) state that a number of key studies have affirmed that the significant majority of children exposed to DVA are affected by their experiences in both the short and long term.

It is not just witnessing violence and abuse that affects a high number of children as the co-occurrence of DVA and child abuse is clearly shown in a growing body of literature (CAADA, 2014). For example, a prevalence study found a high percentage of those reporting physical or sexual abuse as children had also lived with DVA (Cawson, 2002). In a recent study by Safe Lives (formerly CAADA) of 877 children's case records from frontline child protection services and data collected directly from 331 children, it was found that 62% of children living with DVA had also experienced some form of child abuse (CAADA, 2014). In 91% of the cases of child abuse, the perpetrator of harm to the child was the same person perpetrating the domestic abuse: principally the child's father or mother's male partner. The report suggested that those children who were exposed to the more severe levels of DVA were more likely to directly experience physical harm or be physically and emotionally neglected. The study also found that many of the families had additional vulnerabilities as children were often exposed to parental mental ill health and substance misuse (CAADA, 2014).

Finally, there is ample evidence which emphasises that children and women are at greater risk following separation than they were before it and this is the time that women and children are more likely to be killed or seriously injured by an abusive male (Richards, 2003: Brandon et al., 2008; Brandon et al., 2011). Indeed, child contact arrangements provide the greatest opportunity for the continuation of post-separation violence, and in many cases these arrangements are used as a vehicle for the perpetrator to continue to exercise power and control of children and the ex-partner (Laing and Humphreys, 2013).

Young people and DVA

It must also be recognised that DVA does not occur just within the context of adult relationships. An influential study in 2009, commissioned by the NSPCC, found concerning levels of psychological and emotional abuse along with physical and sexual violence within the relationships of young people aged 13 to 16 (Barter et al., 2009). Since the publication of the NSPCC report, more research has been conducted on teenage domestic abuse and while differences between research methodologies makes it difficult to establish prevalence rates, there are indications that this is a significant growing issue.

In terms of the ways in which DVA is perpetrated within teenage relationships, there are similarities with adult forms (in terms of emotional, physical and sexual abuses). Additionally, there is an emergence of newer forms of abuse, which exploit power and control through social media and digital technologies (Zweig and Dank, 2013). The STIR research study (Safeguarding Teenage Intimate Relationships) used a multi-method approach to investigate the face-to-face and online/digital experiences of young people aged 13 to 18 conducted in five countries across Europe (UK, Norway, Italy, Bulgaria and Cyprus) (Hellevik et al., 2015). Findings from the STIR survey found that 58% of young people (of 4,564 survey respondents) had experienced at least one form of DVA, although there was variation between countries. Twenty-six percent of these young people chose not to disclose their experiences to anyone, illustrating the problem of recognition of abuse behaviours as well as stigma and other barriers to seeking help.

DVA, social work and safeguarding children

As noted earlier, there is considerable evidence highlighting the concerns about post-separation violence and the risks for women and children (Richards, 2003: Brandon et al., 2008; Brandon et al., 2011). The argument that children could be at greater risk if fathers are not engaged with appropriately is significant when considering that post-separation violence is common and that, rather than being better protected, some children may be at greater risk if child protection services demand that mothers leave their partners (Bagshaw et al., 2011). Despite this, service responses still tend to take the view that if abusive men are out of the lives of women and children, then women and children will be better protected (Featherstone and Peckover,

2007; Laing and Humphreys, 2013; Blacklock and Phillips, 2015). This approach, focusing on separating the perpetrator of DVA from the family, creates a culture of allowing men to fail to take responsibility for caring for their children and does not encourage them to address their abusive behaviour, in order to create a safe family environment (Featherstone and Peckover, 2007; Laing and Humphreys, 2013; Blacklock and Phillips, 2015). This is exacerbated by the current preoccupation with a 'mother blaming' approach and a 'deficit model of mothering' that is often taken by social work services in cases of DVA (Lapierre, 2008; Moulding, Buchanan and Wendt, 2015).

Whatever the family scenario, in cases of DVA a singular social work intervention is rarely adequate (Cleaver et al., 2007) and a multi-agency response is more effective at safeguarding children in the longer term. At the very least, children's social care and adult services should seek to collaborate to ensure a holistic assessment and plan for the child (Stanley, Cleaver and Hart, 2010). This collaboration may include a range of services such as child protection social workers, mental health teams, drug and alcohol services, and voluntary sector agencies such as Women's Aid or Refuge who provide support for families affected by DVA. This approach may involve other agencies under the Coordinated Community Response (CCR) model to DVA which has been around in some form since the 1990s (Pence and McMahon, 1999). The model describes the ways in which a range of agencies and structures have the potential to ensure a holistic approach to managing and combating DVA.

Within the CCR model, if a family is deemed to be at high risk of DVA (where there is a possibility for serious harm or death) then the family's case should be managed within a Multi-Agency Risk Assessment Conference (MARAC). MARACs are constituted by a wide range of statutory and voluntary sector services and are tasked with agreeing plans and monitoring safety in families. While MARACS have benefits in terms of promoting inter-agency working, there are also limitations, particularly during times when resources are stretched (Robbins et al., 2014). One benefit is that all relevant agencies should be represented at the MARAC in order to take a holistic approach to working with the family. This includes child protection services, and this reflects the philosophy of *Working Together to Safeguard Children* (2015). MARACs are attended by professionals only, however, and families are excluded from decision making and safety planning in this context.

Despite a more integrated approach to safeguarding children, numerous studies have illuminated the challenges and gaps in multi-agency work to safeguard children (Machura, 2016). An example of this is the way in which need and risk are conceptualised in different and contrasting ways by agencies who respond to DVA and who have distinct remits, cultures and perspectives (Hester, 2011). This results in deep-rooted, systemic barriers to collaboration (Humphreys and Stanley, 2006; Hester, 2011) and it has been highlighted that services appear to be overwhelmed by the considerable extent of DVA in terms of its prevalence, impacts and in the way in which it is rooted to entrenched gendered inequalities (Stark, 2007; Peckover, 2014). Long-standing deficiencies in multi-agency work have been identified in terms of poor communication between agencies, and DVA is a regular feature of serious case reviews (SCIE, 2016). Different codes of practice around confidentiality and consent can obstruct communication resulting in poor communication and information-sharing to the detriment of a child's safety and wellbeing. So, while a multi-agency setting may present benefits to families affected by DVA in terms of a more holistic and comprehensive assessment, current processes are not sufficient (Humphreys and Stanley, 2006; Hester, 2011). Therefore, we propose the widespread adoption of a different structure for safeguarding children living with DVA through multi-agency work using Family Group Conferences.

DVA and FGCs

FGCs have been used to address cases of DVA since the early 1990s, when FGCs were developed in New Zealand (Kohn, 2010). Many other countries now implement FGCs to this end including Australia, UK, Canada, the US and parts of Europe. From the outset, two types of FGCs have been used to address DVA: restorative conferences and child welfare conferences (Kohn, 2010). Restorative conferences are used to ensure that the perpetrator takes responsibility for the abuse and that the victim/survivor feels that sufficient reparation has been achieved. Child welfare FGCs are used to plan for the safety of children, where DVA is a feature of family life (Salcido Carter, 2003; Pennell and Francis, 2005; Inglis, 2007). Much of the current research evidence tends to focus on the use of FGCs in a restorative context because until relatively recently, this is the area where FGCs were most readily used to address DVA (Pennell, 2006; Liebmann and Wootton, 2010). As services in this area have developed, however, a growing body of research which focuses on the use of child welfare FGCs in DVA cases has emerged (Pennell and Burford, 2000; Social Services and Research Information Unit, 2003; Inglis, 2007).

Historically, the use of FGCs in this regard has been challenged by feminist commentators, with expressed concerns about the use of FGCs to address DVA questioning the appropriateness of bringing a family together in a conference where there has been a significant level of violence (Grauwiler and Mills, 2004; Cheon and Regehr, 2007; Kohn, 2010). Critics have tended to express concern for the safety of survivors of DVA in meetings where the survivor and the perpetrator are both present. Furthermore, questions have been raised about how empowering a FGC can be for survivors particularly as the FGC process could 're-victimise' those who have been subjected to male violence (Mills, Grauwiler and Pezold, 2006).

Despite these reservations, FGCs to address DVA are being used more frequently across the globe (Rogers and Parkinson, 2018). For example, in the UK, several services provide FGCs to address DVA, particularly within the area of child welfare (Family Rights Group website). One service in particular, The Dove Project in Hampshire, has been established since 2000 and it is the forerunner for more recent FGCs specialising in DVA. An evaluation of the service in 2000 found that in all cases, a safe plan for children was developed, with the majority of plans being successful three months later (Social Services and Research Information Unit, 2003). Other services specialising in offering FGCs to address DVA include the FGC services in Camden, Swindon and Leeds (Family Rights Group website). Across the globe, research examining the use of FGCs in DVA cases has highlighted the potential benefits in this area of practice (Coker, 2006; Kohn, 2010). Pennell and Francis (2005) emphasise the potential, highlighted by evaluation studies, including respecting the cultures of families and communities and promoting the wellbeing of children and women. Furthermore, Strang and Braithwaite (2002) argue that restorative justice approaches (including FGCs) serve victims, perpetrators and communities better than traditional justice practices. Significant benefits of FGCs evidenced by research are listed below:

- engaging with male perpetrators;
- enhanced safety for children and women;
- enabling families to stay together;
- addressing the disconnect between families and relevant services;
- survivors feeling that 'justice' has been served. (Coker, 2006; Kohn, 2010)

Engaging with perpetrators

One of the clear messages in the research is the potential to better engage with perpetrators to enable them to take responsibility for their behaviour, to encourage them to address their abusive behaviour and when abusers are also parents, to take responsibility for contributing to family safety (Holland et al., 2005; Pennell and Francis, 2005; Kohn, 2010). These are significant outcomes, particularly when considering research that suggests that if abusive partners are better engaged in child protection processes, then children and victims/survivors would be safer (Featherstone and Peckover, 2007; Alderson, Westmarland and Kelly, 2012; Baynes and Holland, 2012).

Salcido Carter (2003) argues that FGCs can be used to engage perpetrators to address their abusive behaviours and receive appropriate support. She argues that the FGC process can enable violent abusers to access offender intervention programmes and other services that can support them to end their violence. This claim is substantiated by Kingi, Pulim and Porima (2008) who, in their research into the use of restorative justice processes (including FGCs) to address DVA, found that the majority of offenders involved in the study stated that the process helped them to take responsibility for their violence, with two thirds taking steps to address and change their behaviour. Despite this being a small-scale piece of research (19 victims/survivors and 19 perpetrators), it highlights the potential of FGCs to engage with perpetrators to address their offending behaviour. In addition to this, Grauwiler and Mills (2004) state there is some evidence to suggest that FGCs in DVA cases actually reduce reoffending and as intimate partner violence lessens within the family, the intergenerational transmission of violence is also reduced.

From a child-welfare perspective, FGCs, when used to plan for the safety of children in DVA cases, can more readily involve fathers than traditional child protection planning processes. The lack of involvement of fathers in child protection decision-making is well documented (Featherstone, 2003; Scourfield, 2006; Brown et al., 2009). Moreover, research evidence also suggests that fathers are excluded from planning processes when they have been perpetrators of DVA, the underlying assumption appearing to be that they do not have a right to be engaged in this way (Peled, 2000; Scott and Crooks, 2004; Featherstone and Peckover, 2007) or that they would be a threat to their partners or professionals involved in planning meetings if they attended (Hopkins, Koss and Bachar 2004; Stanley and Humphreys, 2015). The FGC model supports an alternative paradigm for practice where all parents should be involved in decision making about their children as they have a responsibility to ensure their wellbeing (Rogers and Parkinson, 2018).

Research illuminates the positive contributions that perpetrators of DVA can make to planning for the safety of their children through the FGC process (Holland et al., 2005; Inglis, 2007). In a study conducted in South Wales, Holland et al. (2005) found that there was a much higher involvement from men at FGCs than in traditional child protection processes. They also found that those men who it was feared would be difficult, or potentially abusive, at the conference conducted themselves appropriately and made constructive contributions to decision making about their children. In addition, Inglis (2007) states that research evidence from the UK and Canada emphasises the positive contributions that fathers make at FGCs. She cites early findings from the Daybreak Dove project in Hampshire, which found that all FGCs were violence-free, family members reported that they preferred a FGC to a child protection conference and women reported feeling empowered in the process (Ashley and Nixon, 2007). The concept of women feeling empowered in the process of a FGC was introduced by Pennell and Burford (2002). Using evidence from the Newfoundland and Labrador FGC service (known locally as family group decision-making or FGDMs), they claimed that the FGC process can enable women to take a leadership role and take back control over their lives and those of their children (Strang and Braithwaite, 2002).

Enhanced safety for children and women

A further message that is evident from research is the potential for FGCs to enhance the safety of women and children in families affected by DVA. This is only the case, however, if services engage with women, children and perpetrators (Ashley, 2011). Moreover, there is an increasing recognition that child protection practices that focus only on the mother are not only 'unfair' but are also unsustainable in the sense that abusive parents may join other families and if their abusive behaviour is not addressed, then the cycle will continue (Featherstone and Peckover, 2007). It appears that this change in discourse has been influenced by a developing understanding of the pervasive impact of domestic abuse on children. Research by Lamb (1997) emphasised the importance of a healthy relationship between parents in order for children to flourish and that hostility between parents is generally associated with poor outcomes for children (Featherstone and Peckover, 2007).

The fundamental philosophy of FGCs, of involving the whole family in planning for safety, and their proven ability to engage with men more effectively than traditional social care practices ensures that they are ideally placed to address safety concerns within a family, with the emphasis on keeping families together, where safe to do so. This is borne out in the research evidence (Ashley (ed.), 2011; Inglis, 2007; Pennell and Burford, 2000). Comparative research emanating from Newfoundland and Labrador in Canada (Pennell and Burford, 2000) focusing on outcomes from FGDMs and traditional case planning approaches found: a marked reduction in indicators of both child abuse or neglect and abuse of partners following the Family Group Conference process; positive outcomes relating to children's development; and an extension of social support for families. One year after the conference, there were 50% fewer incidents of abuse or neglect compared to the year before, while incidents increased significantly for 31 families in the control group who did not participate in a Family Group Conference.

Further, an evaluation of the initial pilot of the Daybreak Dove Project in Hampshire by the Social Services and Research Information Unit (2002) found that following conferences addressing issues of DVA:

- families were able to make safe plans for themselves and their children;
- in most families, children were taken off child protection plans;
- women showed a decline in signs of depression immediately after the meeting and in the subsequent follow up period of three months;
- families reported that their situations changed for the better following a FGC;
- for the majority of families, the three-month period following the FGC was free of violent incidents;
- women were empowered to take control of the situation. (Inglis, 2007)

Subsequent evaluations of the service have substantiated these initial findings (Ashley, 2011). Evaluations in 2007 and 2010 showed reductions in DVA incidents in the six months following an FGC. After attendance at a Dove Project Conference there was a 50% reduction in the number of crime reports received by Hampshire Constabulary. In the six months following the project phase (April 2006 to March 2007) 11 of the 15 families that took part did not come to police attention again, a 73% success rate (Hampshire Constabulary,

2007). Despite being small in scale, these research studies emphasise the potential of FGCs to improve outcomes for children and women in DVA cases.

Given that one of the major criticisms of applying the FGC model in DVA cases has been the potential for women and children to be 're-victimised' by the process, putting them at risk of further violence and abuse (Mills, Grauwiler and Pezold, 2006) it is important to examine the approaches that FGC services use to ensure that women and children remain safe at a FGC.

Primarily, it is important to note that it is the choice of the women and children involved whether to have a FGC, as is consistent with FGC practice. Furthermore, the support of an advocate at their FGC is offered, if they feel that they need it, in order to support them in contributing to the meeting (Pennell, 2004; Inglis, 2007). Therefore, from the outset women and children are 'in control' of the process.

In some cases, it may be appropriate for the perpetrator not to attend the meeting, if the potential risk to others at the meeting is significant (Pennell, 2004; Mills, Grauwiler and Pezold, 2006; Inglis, 2007). In these situations, the perpetrator may represent their views through an advocate or a written report for the meeting (Pennell, 2004; Ashley and Nixon, 2007; Inglis, 2007). Many advocates for the use of FGCs in the area of DVA consider that perpetrators being present at a FGC is significant, however, and enables them to take responsibility for their behaviour and the care of their children (Holland et al., 2005; Pennell and Francis, 2005; Kohn, 2010). Furthermore, research has highlighted that careful planning and preparation, for the FGC, with a clear focus on safety, ensures that the FGC is a safe and empowering environment for the vulnerable parent and children involved (Pennell and Burford, 2002; Strang and Braithwaite, 2002; Inglis, 2007; Rogers and Parkinson, 2018).

Enabling families to stay together

Earlier in this chapter, the potential risks to parent and children following separation from an abusive partner were discussed. In addition to the risks posed, the current emphasis on encouraging women to separate from their partners to protect their children, does little to address the perpetrator's abusive behaviour and enables them to potentially move on to the next relationship and repeat the cycle of violence (Walker, 1979). Indeed, many commentators consider that children and women are better protected if families remain together (Featherstone and Peckover, 2007; Laing and Humphreys, 2013;

Blacklock and Phillips, 2015). Research focusing on outcomes of FGCs highlights the potential of FGCs to enable families to remain together, re-build fragmented family relationships and encourage parents to take responsibility for meeting the needs of their children (Burford and Pennell, 2000; Strang and Braithwaite, 2002; Litchfield, Gatowski and Dobbin, 2003; Hayden et al., 2014).

Evidence from New Zealand has shown that the number of children being cared for within their families has increased since the implementation of FGCs (Thornton, 1993; Connolly, 1994) with 'Fewer children...living separate from their families...for many years' (Thornton, 1993: 29). Maxwell and Robertson (1991) found that in almost two thirds of all care and protection cases, children remained in the care of their families following a FGC; 42% with their original care givers and 23% with extended family. Only 34% were placed outside of the family. More recent research by Pakura (2003) has substantiated these initial research findings and demonstrated that most families develop safe plans, fewer children and young people enter state care, as care and protection arrangements are seen by professionals as being improved for children and young people.

Research outcomes from outside of New Zealand add further weight to this view. For example, research undertaken by Litchfield, Gatowski and Dobbin (2003) of the state-wide implementation of FGCs in Hawai'i found that approximately 99% of families had not been reported for harm (or threatened harm) within one year of the conference and not requiring subsequent court intervention after the conference had been held to address the original allegations. Furthermore, in nearly two thirds of cases children remained within the care of their families.

Survivors feeling that justice has been served

As noted earlier critics of FGCs have not only highlighted the potential of the FGC process to reinforce the abuse that children and women have experienced but they have also presented the argument that the FGC, as an alternative to court processes is potentially a 'soft' option for perpetrators of DVA and potentially 'lets them off the hook' (Cameron, 2006; Kohn, 2010). In this chapter we have shown how not only are women and children potentially better protected as a result of FGCs, or at least not placed at further risk as a result of the FGC process, but they are also empowered by the FGC and feel that they have regained some control over their lives (Inglis, 2007). Furthermore, there is some evidence to suggest that women feel that the FGC process enables them to feel that justice has been served (Hopkins, Koss and Bachar, 2004; Stubbs, 2007; Kohn, 2010).

Hopkins, Koss and Bachar (2004) state that what victims/survivors of DVA want in addition to the violence stopping, is not necessarily a punitive approach taken for the offender such as a fine or a prison sentence, rather they wish for the opportunity to have their say, be heard and for an acknowledgement of the harm done to them and/ or their children. This is what a FGC can provide: the opportunity for a woman to have her say with a focus on the perpetrator taking responsibility for the harm they have caused. This is reinforced by Stubbs (2007) who, citing empirical research, argues that women primarily want safety for themselves and their children and a right to love without violence, rather than punishment for the offender. Stubbs expresses caution for the use of restorative processes in cases of DVA, however, if the expectation is that a victim/survivor 'forgive' a perpetrator and feels compelled to accept an apology. She warns against such expectations contributing to the continued coercive control of victims of abuse.

Kohn (2010) argues that potential concerns about using restorative justice approaches in DVA can be addressed and that the potential benefits to women of engaging in these processes are significant. She highlights the potential of restorative FGCs to more readily meet the justice needs of women and provide them with a sense that the perpetrator is taking responsibility for their actions, in a way that court-orientated approaches cannot, stating that 'The restorative justice setting may well empower the victim and enhance her agency in a way that is impossible in current justice system programs' (Kohn 2010: 566).

The above section has discussed the potential of FGCs to address the needs of children and women in DVA cases, responding to concerns raised about the use of FGCs in this area. A case study exemplifying the application of the FGC approach in a case of DVA is detailed below.

The following is a case study from Camden FGC service, which has been using FGCs in DVA cases since 2014. All names and personal details have been anonymised to protect the identity of the family.

Aruna: a parent tells the story of her Family Group Conference

"Our Family Group Conference was suggested by a social worker who was worried about Rubi, my three year old daughter. I was in an abusive relationship with her dad Abhik for four years before we split up. The relationship with him and his family is still difficult despite the fact there has been no violence since the split.

The coordinator who organised the Family Group Conference spoke Bengali so that she could communicate with my whole family as she came to visit us in turn. At first I was uncertain and embarrassed about discussing things in front of my family but it was reassuring that I was in control of how it would happen. The social worker said it was needed for the wider family to make a plan to keep Rubi safe. To me it felt like I had to grab the moment and change things for the better.

My parents were willing to take part and the coordinator met with them as well as my aunt who is supportive of me and had been aware of the relationship difficulties between me and Rubi's father. Several other family members were visited to explain and have them involved at the Family Group Conference meeting.

Abhik and his family meanwhile were worried about taking part and said at first 'definitely not', concerned with the 'exposure' of him as perpetrator of violence. They didn't want to come to a meeting with social services and there was a general feeling that relations with our side of the family were strained. The coordinator discussed these concerns with Abhik and his family; his fears were eased and he got on board.

On the day of the Family Group Conference we came together in a community hall, we had brought some food which added to the different feel of the meeting from ones we had attended regularly in the professional offices. The domestic abuse was on the table for discussion from the start of the meeting – that it was bad for the child and for our family; the social worker was clear about that, but Rubi's father also genuinely acknowledged this too. My family raised their concerns with what had happened and also were able to make it clear that they were not going to accept any type of abuse. It was important for me that both sides of the family accepted what had happened and also that it was wrong.

One thing we all agreed on was that Rubi should be given an opportunity to have a relationship with her father. He expressed his sadness that he had not had contact with her for more than four months.

We moved into private time and wrote down our plan, without the social worker. We had listened to their viewpoint earlier and we were then trusted to make our plan. Agreements were made where Abhik was able to have weekly contact with Rubi at my parents' home where they could supervise his time with her.

The plan also had my family stepping in to give me support, including regular respite offered and transport to appointments. I was able to see that my family were supportive of me in a practical sense as well as backing me up when it came to the abuse I had experienced. Thinking back this gave me a certain amount of confidence where before I was really quite low. Abhik also agreed that he will take up counselling support for himself to identify his own issues and difficulties in managing his anger.

We did also discuss back up potential short-term and long-term carers for the children if something unforeseen happened and I wouldn't be able to continue caring for the children. This gave me peace of mind.

Since the Family Group Conference we find it easier to cope, to talk and plan for Rubi's best interests – the most important thing. She looks forward to seeing her father on a weekly basis. We have decided to remain separated until Abhik can show to me and the family he has benefited from the therapeutic help he is getting. Through the Family Group Conference we got to understand each other more and that includes the social worker. We got stuff done and it also improved relationships and our confidence for the future."

Families come from many communities in the borough of Camden; this case study is from one of several with Bengali families. There have been some forty FGCs in Camden which all addressed domestic violence and abuse. In half of them the fathers attended and acknowledged the abuse (in personal communication with Tim Fisher, Manager of Camden FGC Service, 2016).

Conclusion

Earlier we introduced Hester's (2011) persuasive argument that in the case of DVA there is a disconnection between the family, domestic abuse services, child protection services and child contact. In this chapter, we have argued that there is ample evidence to suggest that FGCs have the potential to bridge this gap (Rogers and Parkinson, 2018). Evidence highlights the potential of FGCs to galvanise relationships between families and professionals, and among professionals themselves. For example, research into the state-wide implementation of FGCs in Hawai'i (referred to as O'hana Conferences) found that the conference approach enabled professionals to understand each other's professional responsibilities, enhancing communication and leading to an improved service response to meeting the needs of families. Furthermore, both social workers and families reported an improved relationship among each other and a shared understanding of concerns developed (Litchfield et al., 2003). While this research evidence has a focus on the use of FGCs in general child protection practice, rather than having a specific focus on DVA cases, the messages can be applied to DVA cases, as the FGC process remains largely the same irrespective of the issues being discussed. Indeed, more specific research into the use of FGCs in DVA cases (referred to as safety conferences) undertaken in North Carolina found the potential of FGCs to offer an inclusive and coordinated response to families, bringing together families, domestic abuse support professionals and child welfare professionals to plan for the safety of children (Pennell and Francis, 2005).

To conclude, this chapter has introduced the reader to the use of FGCs in DVA cases. It has provided a discussion about the nature of DVA in families in the UK and service responses to address the issue drawing on evidence from across the globe. Using this evidence, we have emphasised that the current disconnect between the family and services which address DVA and safeguarding in families, can be addressed by an existing structure: the Family Group Conference. As such, we have highlighted the potential of FGCs to address the shortfalls in service provision. While discussing how FGCs can be appropriately utilised in DVA cases, the chapter also provides a critical perspective and addresses concerns expressed by some commentators on the use of FGCs to address DVA. Finally, while this is a niche area of practice, we hope that the reader will be better equipped to imagine a holistic and democratic way of involving families affected by DVA to become better involved in safeguarding the children within those families and to more effectively move forward without falling into the pitfall of existing practices which currently rely on separating family units.

Further reading

Family Rights Group (n.d.a) www.frg.org.uk/involving-families/family-group-conferences

Pennell, J. and Burford, G. (2000) 'Family group decision making: protecting children and women', *Child Welfare*, 79(2): 131–58.

Pennell, J. and Francis, S. (2005) 'Safety conferencing: towards a coordinated and inclusive response to safeguard women and children', *Violence Against Women*, 11(5): 666–92.

Salcido Carter, L. (2003) *Family team conferences in domestic violence cases: guidelines for practice*, San Francisco: Family Violence Prevention Fund.

Strang, H. and Braithwaite, J. (2002) (eds.) *Restorative justice and family violence*, Cambridge: Cambridge University Press.

NINE

FGCs with marginalised communities

Iyabo Ayodele Fatimilehin

Introduction and context

Marginalisation or social exclusion encompasses social disadvantage and pertains to the practice of treating people as if they are not important (Cambridge Dictionary) or relegating them to the fringes of society (Collins Dictionary). It is an active process that is the opposite of social inclusion and results in the alienation or disenfranchisement of certain groups of people in a society. This marginalisation can be based on socioeconomic status, social class, educational status, ethnicity, race, gender, sexuality, legal status or a combination of a range of factors.

> Social exclusion is a complex and multidimensional process. It involves the lack or denial of resources, rights, goods and services, and the inability to participate in the normal relationships and activities, available to the majority of people in a society, whether in economic, social, cultural or political arenas. It affects both the quality of life of individuals and the equity and cohesion of society as a whole. (Levitas et al., 2007: 9)

Discrimination and being treated differently and less advantageously in society can be related to a number of social characteristics such as gender, race/ethnicity, social class, disability, sexuality, age, and others. These groups are not homogenous in composition and experience, and there may be areas of social life in which some sections of a group are doing relatively well, while for others there is stark disparity.

It is beyond the scope of a single chapter to address all the groups that are marginalised in Britain today (for example on the basis of sexuality, religion, disability, age, gender) and therefore this chapter will mainly focus on communities that are marginalised due to socioeconomic status (poverty) and ethnicity.

Socioeconomic status and marginalisation

Low socioeconomic status (SES) is related to profound levels of social exclusion. Bramley and Fitzpatrick (2015) reported on research funded by Lankelly Chase Foundation on severe and multiple disadvantage (SMD). This was defined as involvement in homelessness, substance misuse and the criminal justice system. Poverty was a universal experience for the group in their study and mental ill health was an additional complicating factor. They found that people affected by SMD are predominantly white men, aged 25–44 with long term histories of economic and social marginalisation and in most cases, childhood trauma of various kinds. Black and mixed race people, however, are over-represented in the homelessness category and in the offender-only category but not in substance misuse. In the overall population of people with SMD, 85% had experienced traumatic experiences in childhood. Forty-two percent had run away as children, 45% had no qualifications, 55% had a mental health condition that has been diagnosed by a professional, 75% reported problems with loneliness. The cause of persistent offending was overwhelmingly about poverty, and the attendant social and economic disadvantage.

It has been estimated that 39% of families in England live below the poverty line (Marmot, 2010) and that nearly four million children are living in poverty in the UK (Department for Work and Pensions, 2017). The majority of poor children live in a household where at least one adult works (Department for Work and Pensions, 2015). The effects of poverty on children are wide ranging. Poverty shapes children's development such that before reaching his or her second birthday, a child from a poorer family is already more likely to show a lower level of attainment than a child from a wealthier family. By the age of six, a less able child from a rich family is likely to have overtaken an able child from a poor family (Field, 2010). Furthermore, children growing up in poverty are more likely to leave school at 16 with fewer qualifications (Department for Education, 2015a). Ultimately, poverty shortens lives: a boy in Manchester can expect to live nine years fewer than a boy in Barnet; a girl in Manchester can expect to live six years fewer than a girl in Kensington, Chelsea and Westminster (Office for National Statistics, 2014).

Involvement with and entering the social care system is strongly associated with poverty and deprivation (for example low income, parental unemployment). While there is no official data for the UK countries of the number of children who were on child protection plans and also living in poverty (Bywaters et al., 2016), it is clear that children from lower socioeconomic backgrounds are more likely to be subject to family care proceedings than those from higher socioeconomic backgrounds.

Ethnicity and marginalisation

There is a wealth of information indicating that social exclusion and marginalisation is a significant and comprehensive part of the lives of many black and minority ethnic people in Britain. Data from the UK censuses has consistently evidenced the inequalities and social disadvantage experienced by people from some minority ethnic groups. This is demonstrated clearly in areas of academic achievement and employment. Results from the 2011 census showed that men from all minority ethnic groups were less likely to be employed than white men, and full-time employment of white men in the 2011 census was 72% compared to 35% for Bangladeshi men. The closest was Indian men at 69%. This is in spite of the fact that people from some minority ethnic groups were more likely than white British people to have degree level qualifications or equivalent, for example Chinese, Indian, black-African. The most disadvantaged group in terms of educational attainment was the white Gypsy or Irish Traveller group. In 2011, 60% of white Gypsy or Irish Traveller people had no qualifications. This was the highest proportion for any ethnic group and was 2.5 times higher than for white British people. Similarly, only around one in ten (9%) white Gypsy or Irish Traveller people had degree level qualifications or equivalent. Academic achievement did not necessarily confer better outcomes in the labour market, however: young men of black African, black Caribbean and other black ethnic groups had unemployment rates ranging from 16% to 20.3% compared with 5.85% for white British men (Nazroo and Kapadia, 2013a). Arab (19.2%), Bangladeshi (19%) and black African (17.2%) women of working age were over four times as likely to be unemployed as white British women (5%) (Nazroo and Kapadia, 2013b).

Other areas in which people experience marginalisation and social exclusion on the basis of ethnicity include criminal justice, mental health and social care. The Ministry of Justice (2015) reported that black and minority ethnic groups were twice as likely to be stopped and searched as white people, and that black (or black British) people were four times more likely to be stopped and searched. People who identified themselves as black (or black British) were almost three times as likely to be arrested as white people (Ministry of Justice, 2015) and while the most common outcome for white and mixed ethnic group offenders was a community sentence, the most common sentence for black, Asian and Chinese offenders was immediate custody (Ministry of Justice, 2013).

The relationship between social exclusion and ethnicity is also evident in the mental health system. People of African-Caribbean ethnicity living in the UK are 9–12 times more likely to be diagnosed with schizophrenia than white people. Second generation immigrants have a higher risk than first generation (Fearon and Morgan, 2006) suggesting that there are social or environmental reasons for the high rates of schizophrenia within this ethnic group, as does the fact that this rate is not found in people of African Caribbean heritage living in other parts of the world. People from black and minority ethnic groups are under-represented in primary care systems and over-represented in referrals using more coercive routes into services. Thus, over 60% of inpatients from mixed white and black African, Caribbean, and any other black backgrounds were subject to detention under the Mental Health Act compared to fewer than 40% of white British inpatients (Thompson, 2013). Furthermore, South Asians of all ethnic groups are least likely to be referred to specialist services (Bhui et al., 2003).

The processes and outcomes of social exclusion are also evident in the social care system. Children from black, black British and mixed ethnic groups are over-represented in the looked-after population and make up 16% compared to approximately 9% of the population of England (Zayed and Harker, 2015). This disproportionality has remained relatively stable over time. Research in the US has highlighted similar findings with African American, Latino and American Indian children being more likely than white children of European descent to be placed in care and stay there longer (Pennell, Edwards and Burford, 2010). Asian or Asian British children and young people, meanwhile, are under-represented in the looked-after population in England at 4–5% compared with 10% of the population (Office for National Statistics et al., 2017).

Thus the research and statistical data describes the effects of social exclusion and marginalisation on communities. The link between ethnicity and poverty is complex with some ethnic groups being more likely to experience marginalisation than others. For example, while approximately two-fifths of people from minority ethnic groups live in low-income households (twice the rate for white people), the highest rates were for Pakistanis (60%) and Bangladeshis (70%) (Department for Work and Pensions, 2015). Bangladeshi and Pakistani people are more likely to live in income-deprived neighbourhoods than people from other ethnic groups. In addition almost half of all children from minority ethnic groups live in low–income households compared to a quarter of white British children, demonstrating the compounding effect that ethnicity can have on the experiences of marginalisation and social exclusion.

FGCs as a response to marginalisation

Empowerment and participation

Empowerment and the promotion of social inclusion and participation are consistent approaches that have been used to address the marginalisation of families and communities. There are many fields of inquiry and practice in which these terms are used, and at many levels of analysis from the individual to the societal. Within mental health settings, models of empowerment have included psychological, social and political components and have identified domains such as self–esteem, power and powerlessness, community activism and autonomy, optimism and control over the future, and righteous anger (Rogers, Ralph and Salzer, 2010). Models of participation have been elaborated within services for children and young people where hierarchies of participation have been described that range from manipulating children to follow instructions provided by adults, to equal partnerships in which children and young people initiate and direct the interaction and involve adults as equal partners (Treseder, 1997).

Unfortunately, families who find themselves in the children's social care system are subject to systematic processes of disempowerment and manipulation. They are required to focus on their shortcomings (rather than their strengths and competencies) and to address them by following the instructions of professionals (Featherstone, White and Morris, 2014). The systems are powerfully coercive and aim to seize control of the decision-making processes within the family system. The outcomes for children and families can often lead to increased marginalisation and social exclusion as they become part of the social care system with the associated poor outcomes in terms of health, education, employment and involvement in the criminal justice system (Department for Education, 2011b; Zayed and Harker, 2015).

FGCs and empowerment

Family group conferences (FGCs) offer an alternative and more sustainable approach to working with families who are marginalised or socially excluded. It has already been stated in the Introduction that the origins of the family group conference model lie in the empowerment of the indigenous people of New Zealand to reduce the numbers of children who were being removed from their communities into the social care system. It promotes the sharing of power and decision making between families, professionals and communities (Merkel-Holguin, 2004) thus promoting active citizenship. Studies of FGCs have shown that there are positive outcomes on a number of levels including the higher numbers of children who are returned to the care of their extended families, the involvement of wider family systems, a higher involvement of fathers, higher satisfaction levels for parents and relatives, a greater sense of empowerment expressed by parents and relatives (Sheets et al., 2009; Pennell, Edwards and Burford, 2010). In addition, children who had taken part in FGCs were less anxious than those who had not (Sheets et al., 2009), and were likely to have benefited from witnessing important adults in their lives participating positively in difficult decisions about their lives (Merkel-Holguin, 2004).

FGCs and cultural competence

The family group conference model is widely agreed to be culturally competent because it takes account of the values, cultures and beliefs of families (Pennell, Edwards and Burford, 2010, Sheets et al., 2010, Barn and Das, 2016). There are many definitions of cultural competence and wide-ranging debate about the nature of cultural competence.

For example, Papadopolous defined cultural competence as 'the capacity to provide effective health and social care, taking into consideration people's cultural beliefs behaviours and needs' (2006: 10) A more in-depth definition is that it is

> a set of problem-solving skills that include a) the ability to recognise and understand the dynamic interplay between the heritage and adaptation dimensions of culture in shaping human behaviour, b) the ability to use the knowledge acquired about an individual's heritage and adaptational challenges to maximise the effectiveness of assessment, diagnosis and treatment, and c) internalisation of this process of recognition, acquisition and use of cultural dynamics so that it can routinely be applied across diverse groups. (Whaley and Davis, 2007: 564–5)

The question for the FGC model is whether it is essentially culturally competent, and whether or not the way in which it is practiced can undermine or enhance its cultural competence. Definitions and models of cultural competence assume that the skills that are needed reside in the practitioner and are not an integral part of the intervention.

The FGC is unusual in that it has cultural and political roots in a non-western country. It was the result of protests by Maori people in Aotearoa New Zealand about the Eurocentric professional approaches that undermined children and young people's connections to their extended families and cultural heritage (Pennell, Edwards and Burford, 2010). It is based on a collectivist cultural system as opposed to an individualist one that is more prevalent in western countries. Involving and inviting the wider family and community to the FGC is consistent with collectivist cultural systems (Fatimilehin and Hassan, 2010), and sharing power for decision making between professionals and families is consistent with values of democracy (Merkel-Holguin, 2004). Furthermore, FGCs are able to incorporate and support the cultural values, beliefs, practices and strengths of families (Sheets et al., 2009).

Although there are only a handful of studies on the outcomes of FGCs with children and families from a range of non-western cultures (Sheets et al., 2009, O'Shaughnessy, Fatimilehin and Collins, 2010), it appears that the model is accessible and acceptable to families who are from minority ethnic groups in western countries as well as to the indigenous white ethnic groups who have historically had more collectivist approaches to family and community. For example, Sheets et al. (2009) conducted a comparative study and found that positive outcomes were especially pronounced for African American and Hispanic children and led to faster exits from care. O'Shaughnessy, Fatimilehin and Collins (2010) reported on the implementation and evaluation of a FGC project aimed primarily at black and minority ethnic children and families.

Ironically, there is also evidence in the literature that families from black and minority ethnic cultures in the UK and US are under-utilising the model. They are under-represented in referrals and take up of support services including FGCs (Barn and Das, 2016; Haresnape, 2009, Barn et al., 2009; Merkel-Holguin, 2004). The reasons for this are unclear but one suggestion is that the long-standing tensions between child welfare services and minority ethnic communities have contributed to a lack of engagement (Pennell et al., 2010). This would also be true, however, for many white working class communities in the UK and more research is needed to explore this issue. Several studies have explored and identified key components of culturally competent FGC services (Waites et al., 2004; Flynn and Ashley, 2007; Barn et al., 2009; Haresnape 2009). For example, engagement with local BME communities is essential (Flynn and Ashley, 2007; Barn and Das, 2016) as is the availability of coordinators or facilitators from diverse cultural and linguistic backgrounds that reflect those of the families that are using the service (Waites et al., 2004; Haresnape, 2009; Barn et al., 2009; Barn and Das, 2016). Other key considerations are the culture of the organisation running the FGC as well as that of the social care services (Haresnape, 2009), the location of the service, recognition and use of cultural traditions and involvement of community elders or leaders (Waites et al., 2004; Barn, Das and Sawyer, 2009; Haresnape, 2009; Sheets et al., 2009).

FGCs, ethnicity and poverty

The ability of the FGC model to respect the family's culture and prioritise the voices of family members were identified by O'Shaughnessy, Fatimilehin and Collins (2010) as the key dimensions that make it effective with BME families. Both dimensions are particularly important when considering the context of marginalisation on the basis of poverty and ethnicity. The model is premised on mobilising community and family resources, however there are instances where these have already been utilised to a large extent and there are significant issues with access to services. In their work in Liverpool, O'Shaughnessy, Fatimilehin and Collins (2010) described BME communities with high levels of unemployment, socioeconomic deprivation and racial discrimination over several generations as well as entrenched problems with drug and alcohol use and involvement in the criminal justice system. It is important for the coordinator to address the barriers to accessing services (for example language and cultural barriers) and to advocate for the family. This is consistent with the empowering nature of FGCs, and is important when working with all communities that are experiencing socioeconomic deprivation. Practice experience has also demonstrated that the model has to be adapted for each community and family and there has to be constant review of the way in which it is delivered. When working with linguistically diverse communities, the practice is often to consider providing the family plan in the first language of the family. It has also been necessary, however, to address literacy needs and offer voice recordings of the family plan to families who cannot read in their own language (including English speakers with literacy needs).

Case study

The cultural competence of the Family Group Conference model can be illustrated through the use of the following case study:

The Nkrumah family was referred for a FGC by children's social workers due to the need to establish long-term living arrangements for the children: Kwame (aged 11), Afuah (aged nine) and Mensah (aged six).

The family is of Ghanaian heritage. The mother, Mercy, was born in Ghana and came to the UK as a young adult to join her parents. She was the main carer for the children, and Kwame had a different father to his younger siblings. The father of Afuah and Mensah was not involved in their lives and currently lived in London, while Kwame's father lived in Ghana with his wife and family and had occasional telephone contact. The family had been known to children's services for three years due to Mercy's ill health and had been placed on an interim care order. At the time of referral, Mercy's health had deteriorated. She had recently been in hospital for some time. The children had been placed in the care of the maternal grandparents on a Section 20 of the Children Act 1989. The children visited their mother regularly in hospital and looked forward to seeing her. The maternal grandparents wanted the children to return to the care of their mother once she was discharged from hospital, and were willing to provide support.

The family was identified as having a number of strengths. These included Mercy's insight into the effect her health had on the care of the children, and her ability to access appropriate support and services. In addition, the children were bright and were doing well at school despite some low level concerns about Kwame's emotional presentation at school. Their mother and maternal grandparents had ensured that their attendance was good. The children were settled with their grandparents and also accessed resources in the community including sports activities and youth activities through their church.

The concerns of children's services included the deterioration in the mother's health that put the children at risk due to neglect. The children had reported feeling hungry and there being no food in the house at times when their mother stayed in bed. The school and grandparents reported that Kwame was still anxious about food and the possibility of it running out. The children's behaviour had been challenging when they moved to live with their grandparents but this was showing signs of improvement.

The FGC coordinator met with the referring social worker to discuss the family. Several home visits were undertaken with maternal and paternal family members (including grandparents, aunts and uncles) during the preparation stage. Telephone contact was made with Kwame's father in Ghana and a visit was also made to his aunt who resided in another city in the UK. All family members engaged fully with the FGC process and welcomed the opportunity to discuss the children's welfare with other family members. Kwame's father did not wish to be involved but his aunt and her husband represented his side of the family. The focus of the visits to the family members in the preparation stage was to explore the family's understanding of the issues, their commitment to supporting the children and what support they could offer. The FGC coordinator was supported by a child advocate who undertook some direct work with the children to ascertain their wishes and feelings. The children were also involved in choosing the food for the FGC and asked for their favourite Ghanaian foods (for example Kelewele, jollof rice) alongside crisps and pizza.

The family came from diverse backgrounds and life experiences. The paternal family of Afuah and Mensah was from an educated, middle class background while Kwame's father was from a poor rural background in Ghana. Mercy had initially trained as a nurse in Ghana but had been unemployed and on benefits for most of the time that she had lived in the UK. The FGC coordinator was from a similar ethnic background to the family and realised that Afuah and Mensah's paternal family were ashamed of the fact that their son had let the family name down by establishing a relationship with a woman who was 'unsuitable'. Ghanaian culture is collectivist and family obligations are seen as more important than individual rights and wishes. Therefore, the coordinator was able to discuss these issues and encourage the family to come to terms with their situation. Ultimately, the family members understood the needs of the children and were able to express their commitment to ensuring that their lives were not unduly disrupted should their mother be unable to care for them in the future. They welcomed the opportunity to speak to other interested and committed members of the family including the aunt of the father of the eldest child, and to maintain a sense of harmony.

Eight family members attended the FGC. They developed a coherent plan to address the issues and a contingency plan should Mercy's health deteriorate again in the future. The FGC plan included provision for the maternal grandparents to provide respite at weekends, increased contact of all three children with the paternal grandparents of the younger children, establishing contact between Kwame and his paternal aunt through visits to Birmingham during school holidays. Afuah and Mensah were also invited to accompany Kwame on these visits.

A review of the FGC plan was held three months later and most family members attended or sent a report of the progress made with regard to the actions agreed at the family group conference. The maternal family had been able to support the return of the children to their mother's care, and the paternal family reflected on how they could have provided more support to the mother in the past. The children attended the meeting and were able to identify how much their situation had improved. They described positive changes in their mother's behaviour and personality since they had returned to her care. Kwame was clear about the purpose of the FGC and when asked about his understanding, he said that the family members had gathered together 'for him'.

This case study shows how the cultural background of the family can be important and also how the process of the FGC was facilitated by taking account of the family's culture from more concrete considerations (such as food) to more systemic dimensions such as social class and family dynamics.

Challenges and opportunities

There are several challenges to be considered in the delivery of FGCs to marginalised communities, and there are also opportunities waiting to be embraced.

The economic climate and austerity programmes can affect the sustainability of FGC services with approaches to funding being driven by attempts to reduce costs. Some local authorities develop their own FGC services using existing staff (such as social workers) with statutory duties being trained to deliver FGCs. The difficulties that arise from this solution include the conflicting roles of statutory social work and the voluntary nature of FGCs making it impossible for the practitioner to hold both positions. Furthermore, practice has shown that the high case-loads carried by social workers means that they cannot protect the time needed to prepare family members for a FGC.

Merkel-Holguin (2004) described how inappropriate or inadequate resources can sabotage family plans. This is particularly relevant for marginalised communities and families that have reduced access to statutory or community resources, and O'Shaughnessy, Fatimilehin and Collins (2010) describe the role of FGCs in empowering BME families to access practical and financial services that they were entitled to. There is the potential for there to be a conflict between the ability of FGCs to empower families to access resources and the desire for local authorities to reduce demands on services.

Other challenges to the delivery of FGCs to marginalised communities include the focus of statutory agencies on their own outcomes of reducing their statutory obligations in the child protection process and less emphasis on the more empowering aspects of the model (for example cultural consultation, additional resources made available, choice of food and venue, use of child and vulnerable adult advocates, access to reviews). Merkel-Holguin (2004) warns of the dangers of child welfare agencies structuring and controlling FGCs in order to achieve benchmarks for system-imposed outcomes, such as the pace of the FGC being dictated by the professionals' need to reach targets rather than the needs of the families. In practice there are times when professionals have sought to limit and control the information that is made available to family members in order to expedite an outcome, and there are times when the FGC has been chaired by someone other than the coordinator who has prepared the family for the FGC. These cost-cutting exercises run the risk of undermining the empowering aspects of the model.

While many FGC services are commissioned as an intervention to prevent children from entering the care system, there are also opportunities for communities to be more involved at an earlier stage and to have ownership of the model (Merkel-Holguin, 2004). The Building Bridges FGC service in Liverpool trained community facilitators and accepted referrals from community leaders. These developments were possible because the FGC project was based in a service that was designed to specifically meet the needs of BME families (O'Shaughnessy, Fatimilehin and Collins, 2010). These developments take years to achieve and cannot be delivered in the short timescales demanded by local authorities. There is nonetheless the potential to develop interventions that increase the capacity of families and communities to address their problems at an earlier stage.

Conclusion

Despite the origins of the FGC model as a culturally competent intervention, there are challenges in maintaining its cultural competence in differing cultural and economic contexts. Used in the right way, and with due regard paid to the culture and context in which families are living, FGCs are a powerful and effective intervention. The danger is that practitioners and services believe that it is automatically culturally competent and need to be aware that it operates as a framework that embraces culture if true partnerships are formed with families and they are empowered to make choices about the way that the model works for them. In order to do this, practitioners must be able to have conversations with families about their cultural beliefs, values and practices and work with them to ensure that the FGC embodies this. Furthermore, FGCs have the potential to strengthen and build communities and social capital (Merkel-Holguin, 2004).

FGCs do not stand alone in this and can be seen as part of a history of community responses to individual and family distress and difficulties. It is consistent with a liberatory orientation approach that is part of a movement for a just society and brings in victims and those affected by difficulties as actors and not just passive recipients of prevention and intervention (Kagan et al., 2011). We need to go beyond interventions that risk locating pathology and blame at the individual level and focus more on interventions with communities that reduce the imbalance of power and privilege people's own experiences and understandings of their lives (Featherstone, White and Morris, 2014). We must recognise the strengths of communities and families and move from an expert to an empowerment model of health and social care practice, hence the importance of participation, involvement and collaboration with both service users and wider communities in the planning and delivery of interventions. These considerations are not just applicable to BME communities but to all communities, especially those who experience social and economic disadvantage. Real change will only occur when there is shared political power and the ability for anyone to 'issue an invitation to dinner'. Meanwhile, it is essential that we, as practitioners, continue to act in ways that make a difference, even if it is just in our own services. FGCs offer us a way to act to reduce the impact of social exclusion and marginalisation in our daily work.

Acknowledgements

The case study was provided by Annette Williams who has been a supportive colleague and ally in the delivery of the Just Psychology Family Group Conference service. I am also indebted to Deanna Edwards for the supervision and support she has provided in the development of the service. Last but not least, I wish to acknowledge the courage of the many families who have engaged with our service in the hope of achieving a better future for their children.

Further reading

Bernard, C. and Harris, P. (2016) *Safeguarding black children: good practice in child protection*, London: Jessica Kingsley Publishers.

Featherstone, B., White, S. and Morris, K. (2014) *Re-imagining child protections: towards humane social work with families*, Bristol: Policy Press.

Jivraj, S. and Simpson, L. (2015) *Ethnic identity and inequalities in Britain: the dynamics of diversity*, Bristol: Policy Press.

TEN

FGCs and harmful sexual behaviour

Monique Anderson

Introduction

The idea of arranging a meeting between a victim and perpetrator[1] of sexual harm might, at first sight, seem undesirable or even unwise. There is mounting evidence, however (Zinsstag and Keenan, 2017), that restorative meetings such as family group conferences (FGCs) can, in certain circumstances, be beneficial for all stakeholders. Drawing upon theory, empirical research and practice examples, this chapter will explore the potential and some of the risks of FGCs (conceptualised as a restorative approach that can address both welfare and justice needs[2]) in cases where young people have displayed harmful sexual behaviour (HSB).

Harmful sexual behaviour

The term harmful sexual behaviour[3] (HSB) refers to behaviour displayed by minors, and encompasses a wide spectrum of contact behaviours, such as sexual assault and rape, and non-contact behaviours, including coercing others to make and share sexualised images. Importantly, HSB is distinct from the curiosity-driven exploration of their own bodies or those of other children, known as 'sex play' (Swisher and Pierce, 2014) in which some young children will spontaneously engage. '[B]enign in its effects on later psychological, social, or sexual development' (O'Brien, 1991: 75), sex play occurs occasionally among children who know each other well and play together regularly (Swisher and Pierce, 2014). It is mutually agreed, absent of aggression, and between children similar in age, developmental level and size (Swisher and Pierce, 2014; Finkelhor, 1980; O'Brien, 1991). These last elements are important factors distinguishing between 'normal' and harmful sexual interactions. Hackett and Masson (2011) conceptualise sexual behaviour as a continuum ranging through 'normal', 'inappropriate', 'problematic', 'aggressive' and 'violent'. This reminds us that there are often 'grey areas', and that HSB can be complex and something into which a child may progress, rather than a binary. This ambiguity can pose challenges with respect to how HSB is assessed and addressed, particularly within the traditional youth justice system.

FGCs' potential

There are no gains in presenting the FGC as a panacea. HSB cases are often complex and sensitive (Ricks and DiClemente, 2015) and an FGC may be inappropriate or detrimental in some instances[4]. Suitability for an FGC should be evaluated on a case-by-case basis. Young perpetrators have important needs, but the priority has to be the victim's safety (Oudshoorn, Jackett and Stutzman Amstutz, 2015). The suitability of an FGC should be questioned if, for example, the perpetrator does not accept the facts of the case. General concerns regarding applying restorative measures to sexual violence cases are often also valid for cases involving young people. Such concerns include participant safety and avoidance of re-traumatisation, the inability to address systemic issues, and fears that censure is not appropriately conveyed (Oudshoorn, Jackett and Stutzman Amstutz, 2015). Additionally, FGCs should certainly not be used to rehabilitate or recondition the perpetrator at the victim's expense (Cossins, 2008).

That being said, at their best, FGCs are flexible, tailored, evidence based and information driven processes in which skilled and reflective practitioners facilitate the group to harness their strengths and empower them to plan for the future. The following sections will outline how FGCs can accommodate and positively respond to some of the important factors in HSB cases, while making reference to some of the risks. Importantly, FGCs can take place within, outside of and in constant cooperation with the legal system (Aertsen, Daems and Robert, 2006), so they do not necessarily exclude the possibility of legal recourse. This means that young perpetrators can be held responsible and young victims can receive a response even in cases where there would have been no legal, and possibly no other, steps towards redress.

FGCs' potential as an addition or alternative to the criminal justice system

A youth criminal justice system (CJS) is often an unsuitable or inappropriate mechanism in HSB cases. A CJS response requires the young perpetrator to be at the age of criminal responsibility, the harm must be legally defined as a 'crime', and the case must meet certain requirements with respect to public interest and the presence of evidence. Many cases that come to the attention of the authorities, therefore, do not result in prosecution action. Where the youth CJS is the main or only option for holding wrongdoers to account, there will be cases where the victim does not receive redress. FGCs and similar 'restorative justice' measures, can respond to harms regardless of the legal status of the incident. CJS processes are often ill equipped to balance the need for individual safety with the best interests of different family members (Keane, Guest and Padbury, 2013).

The youth CJS was not constructed with the aim of prioritising and protecting victims' needs, and this is evident in practice. For example, sexually harmed young people often find participation in court cases stressful and may experience disappointment if, having been subjected to the trial process, the defendant is subsequently found not guilty (Back et al., 2011). There are many challenges to the CJS, which is not yet considered 'child friendly' (FRA, 2017), addressing HSB. Therefore, there are many reasons to look for alternative ways to respond to HSB. FGCs have shown promise in HSB cases, particularly when compared with more traditional criminal justice responses.

Conviction commonly results in young perpetrators acquiring a 'sex offender' label. There is often stigmatisation around sex offenders and negative community responses can be extended beyond the perpetrator and to their family (Hackett et al., 2013). Such labels can be detrimental and lead to negative consequences for the young person's self-image and future outcomes (Hackett et al., 2013; Chaffin, 2008; Beckett, 2006). Daly (2008: 564) suggests that the 'hyper stigmatization and demonization' of sex offences encourages perpetrators to deny their guilt, which can hinder both the victim and the young perpetrator from moving forward (Worling and Långström, 2006). Further, labelling can also exacerbate the often false assumption that young people who display HSB are similar to adult sexual offenders (Letourneau and Miner, 2005). While FGCs do require perpetrators to accept that they caused the harm, they aim to create a positive space, without blame and stigmatising shame (Braithwaite, 1989), which empower young people to 'make amends and shed the offender label' (McCold and Wachtel, 2003: 2).

FGCs are most often used in either youth welfare or youth justice settings, with their primary focus on welfare needs and justice needs respectively. Carefully constructed FGCs can respond to both sets of needs for the victim and also the perpetrator (see Anderson and Parkinson, in press). An important distinction is that social work

FGCs usually focus on planning for a young person or young people from a particular family. This will often involve members of their 'community of care' (CoC) who are often parents, siblings, extended family members and/or friends with whom the young person or young people has or have kinship bonds. In a justice context, the FGC often facilitates direct or indirect communication between the perpetrator and the victim of a harm and/or their respective CoC. In this scenario, therefore, two distinct communities of care may be brought together. Any situation in which a person feels harmed and the individual who brought about that harm can accept the facts of what happened could be suitable for a restorative justice response.

FGCs' potential for HSB perpetrators

Young HSB perpetrators are a heterogeneous group on many factors, including age, ethnicity, type of perpetration and risk (Hackett et al., 2013), making a 'one size fits all' approach inappropriate. A distinction is sometimes made between 'pre-adolescent' or 'adolescent' onset HSB (Hickey et al., 2006). Those with early onset HSB are more likely to have experienced insecure attachment, multiple forms of abuse, inadequate sexual boundaries within the family and poorer parenting (Hickey et al., 2006). They more frequently offend against family members, and within the home (Finkelhor, Ormrod and Chaffin, 2009). Comparatively, those who display adolescent onset HSB are generally more socially competent (Beckett, 2006) and are likely to use verbal coercion, to misuse substances, and to victimise specific groups (Hickey et al., 2006). These differences warrant separate approaches (Yokley, LaCortiglia and Bulanda, 2007), which highlights the necessity for and role of in-depth needs assessments, such as with the AIM2[5] framework, prior to an FGC.

Populations of young people who exhibit HSB often have higher than average prevalence of mental health challenges (Griffin, 2003) and learning disability (Hackett et al., 2013). Generally, young HSB perpetrators have '[s]urprisingly high rates of sexual and non-sexual victimization in their backgrounds' (Hackett et al., 2013: 232). In many cases, they are harmed within their family context (Tidefors et al., 2010). In addition to being perpetrators of harm, many young people have experienced trauma and are themselves victims. Young people who display HSB may present a risk to others, but they may also pose a risk to themselves through the effects that their HSB has on their development and relationships. They may be confused and disturbed by their own behaviour (Erooga and Masson, 2006) and may be shunned by their communities (Hackett et al., 2015).

What certainly unifies these perpetrators is their status as young people with welfare needs and vulnerabilities. FGCs have a strong pedagogic element and can provide the young perpetrators with opportunities to learn and develop (Chapman et al., 2015a). Importantly, Daly et al. (2013) found that participation in restorative justice conferences did not increase the reoffending rate in young people who had offended sexually. The common criticism that restorative approaches to sexual harm are 'easy options' appears to be refuted by the young perpetrators who express that they would rather face prison than their victim (Gxubane, 2016). While many HSB perpetrators can be supported to safely remain at home, others will be removed. FGCs can assist in making family reunification plans. In general FGCs, can satisfy the procedural justice needs for perpetrators (Miller and Hefner, 2015) and also victims (Gal, 2011).

Communication proficiency will form an important part of how young people are perceived and judged, and this will influence the 'success' of the FGC. Generally, young people communicate less competently than adults. Young participants face challenges in negotiating the strong reactions of others while managing their own emotions. The emotional reactions often elicited by restorative meetings (Sherman and Strang, 2007), and layered content may amplify communication difficulties (Snow and Sanger, 2011). In particular, young offenders generally have a 'significant possibility of undetected language impairment' (Snow and Sanger, 2011: 331). Being subjected to maltreatment, as HSB perpetrators disproportionately are, is a risk factor for language deficits (Snow, Powell and Sanger, 2012). Difficulties in expressive or receptive language may hinder a young person's ability to fully grasp what is being communicated and impair their ability to articulate feelings. In addition, feelings of guilt, the social taboo around discussing sex and a lack of vocabulary may also hinder the ability to speak about experiences for both the victim and the perpetrator. This may be compounded by the presence of the CoC. Young people with language deficits often also lack cognition skills, including perspective taking and the ability to understand non-verbal cues (Snow and Sanger, 2011). Although mainly dialogue driven, FGCs are complex social interactions based on multiple level verbal and non-verbal communication (Rossner, 2011). Young people may struggle to understand and portray non-verbal cues such as eye contact, tone of voice and body positioning (Snow and Sanger, 2011) or be shy or inexperienced in talking in groups (Gal and Moyal, 2011) and may be subsequently disadvantaged. These factors should be mediated. This can be true for perpetrators as well as victims.

FGCs' potential for HSB victims

There is much heterogeneity with respect to HSB victim characteristics and again, the flexibility of FGC processes can be beneficial here. Generally, girls are more frequently victimised than boys (Radford et al., 2011) and HSB perpetrators mainly victimise other minors (Hackett et al., 2013). Young people who experience homelessness, disability, state care or domestic violence are at greatest risk (Home Office, 2007). Experiencing sexual abuse as a child is 'a major public health concern' (Dong et al., 2003: 626) and is an 'adverse childhood experience' that can lead to long-term negative health outcomes (Anda et al., 2010).

A victim's response to HSB depends on factors including type of HSB, how it was experienced, the victim's world view and developmental stage, and also factors in the social environment (Finkelhor, 2008). Some young people experience stress and trauma (Gal, 2014) while others do not recognise their victimisation. Those who have an understanding of their victimisation often experience feelings of shame and guilt (Back et al., 2010) and may assume responsibility for the HSB, similarly to adult sexual violence victims. Their confused perception of their own culpability may arise if, for example, the abuse started as a game in which the victim initially willingly engaged (Lamb and Coakley, 1993) or if they experienced arousal (Caffaro, 2014). Self-blaming attitudes are reinforced by the prevalent 'rape-myth' culture (Heath et al., 2013). HSB victimisation will often create further vulnerability and will elicit a number of welfare and justice needs in the victim, the primary being that for safety. HSB cases will have to carefully negotiate the complexities and needs for two vulnerable minors, both with their own sets of welfare and justice needs.

It is easy to understand why practitioners faced with the challenge of managing the risks and not increasing vulnerability in these complicated cases may shy away from FGCs. It is important, however, not to 'feed the risk monster'. While vulnerable, victims often also resilient and have strengths which can be built upon. Practitioners should avoid 'victim rescuing' and, particularly where young people themselves express a desire or need that might be fulfilled by an FGC, seek ways to enable such processes in a safe way. Gal (2011: 3) argues that child victims are too often treated 'as objects of protection rather than…stakeholders' and that restorative processes can counter this by meeting the needs of child victims while upholding their rights under the 1989 United Nation Convention on the Rights of the Child (UN General Assembly, 1989).

The use of FGCs to address welfare needs is discussed further in several other chapters. While not much is known about the justice needs of sexually harmed young people, research suggests some similarities with the needs of adults (Back et al., 2010). Adult sexual assault survivors report justice needs (Clark, 2010; Herman, 2005) including those for outcomes (for example, future safety, official acknowledgement of the harm), information (for example, updates regarding case progress), validation of their position as a victim (for example, the perpetrator being made accountable), control (for example, within the justice process) and voice (for example, the opportunity to recount their story). Many such needs can be accommodated within FGC processes. For example, victims of HSB are often threatened, frightened or otherwise coerced by their perpetrator into not revealing their victimisation and feel 'without a voice'. They may have tried to disclose what was happening to them and felt not listened to or not have been believed. FGCs can provide young victims with the opportunity to tell their story, share their feelings and ask questions. Even when a family lives together, they often avoid discussing the HSB. FGCs help to create the space for dialogue and can be a route to reconciliation and a much desired understanding. This forum for communication is often experienced positively by young people (Mercer et al., 2015).

FGCs' potential for 'families'[6]

Young victims and perpetrators of HSB commonly live in the same neighbourhood (Gxubane, 2016). In the vast majority of cases, victims and perpetrators are known to each other prior to the harm taking place (Gxubane, 2016; Ryan, 2010), and in some cases they will be related (Keane, Guest and Padbury, 2013) or live in the same home. In one study of 700 HSB perpetrators, 25% victimised a relative[7] (Hackett et al., 2013). Some authors hypothesise that sibling abuse is the most common form of intrafamilial sexual abuse (Caffaro and Conn–Caffaro, 1998). Established social bonds prior to the harm taking place are a prominent feature in HSB cases and family relationships are challenged and often damaged by the HSB and its subsequent effects.

The 'fallout and crisis' (McNevin, 2010: 66) that families experience when HSB is discovered or disclosed is often caused because they have to deal with the legal and/or social welfare response while negotiating complex family dynamics. Victims may have bonds with members of the perpetrator's CoC or vice versa. Relationships may exist between members of the two communities of support, and individuals may be members of the CoC for both young people. This pre-existing bond often provides the drive to re-examine, and sometimes attempt to repair, the relationship in the light of the harm (Mercer, 2009). FGCs allow many people who feel they have been affected to be included in the process, directly or indirectly (McNevin, 2010) and to play a positive role in the process of addressing the harm. Given the salience of relationship in HSB cases, this can be an important strength of FGCs.

More than adults, young people are dependent on the social network provided by their families (Finkelhor, 2008). The family serves as an 'environmental buffer', influencing how young victims (Finkelhor, 2008) and perpetrators experience and respond to their victimisation and the associated trauma experience (Caffaro, 2014). For example family members may have strong or complicated feelings, often involving blame and anger, towards the young people involved and/or other family members. Particularly in sibling incest cases, parents may feel conflicted. Family members may not always act in ways that are considered to be in the best interest of the child, for example by pressuring a victim to withdraw an allegation (Children's Commissioner for England, 2015). The way CoC members interact with the young people will be influenced if they have, for example, hostile attitudes towards sexual violence (McNevin, 2010) or victim-blaming attitudes. Such attitudes within the CoC that may have supported or contributed to the sexual harm include intergenerational sexual abuse, denial, or maladaptive attitudes towards sex and sexuality. It is important that such factors do not play out within the FGC process, but these factors do present risks. Thus Cossins (2008) argues that victim vulnerability may be increased where FGC processes are conducted in families. Weijers (2002: 75) warns of the potentially negative impact of the 'heavy moral and emotional medicine' that can arise when families are present in conference and Braithwaite (1989) describes the stigmatising shaming processes that should be avoided during restorative processes. The ecological context has an important role to play but there is an important challenge within FGC processes: to minimise the impact of factors within the family that contributed to and/or sustained the harm while drawing on the strengths of the family and addressing the harm in its ecological context.

A pre-requisite of FGCs should be that the perpetrator admits the facts and takes responsibility for their actions. Properly conducted FGCs can be symbolic, because the victim's CoC (and in some FGC models, also the perpetrator and their CoC) come together to collectively acknowledge the victim's status as the harmed party. FGCs can, therefore, be empowering. Victims should feel fully included and in control, however. Deciding whether to participate (Gxubane, 2016) and contributing to the action plan (Cossins, 2008) are actions that can contribute to this.

Therapeutic practice indicates that engaging with young victims, perpetrators and their CoC in addressing sexual abuse, particularly between siblings, can help to create safe environment from which families can begin their journey towards repairing the harm (Keane, Guest and Padbury, 2013). O'Brien (1991) advocates for an approach involving a balance in attention for systemic issues within the family and individual responsibility. It is beneficial to addressing perpetrating behaviour 'within a developmental and ecological framework, in which…sexual difficulties are located within a wider context of family and community factors' (Morrison and Henniker, 2006: 37). Engaging with the families can be beneficial for both the perpetrator and the victim and FGCs allow for this. Additionally, such conferences provide a space and place for non-abused and non-abusing siblings.

The FGC process

Much depends on how the FGC is conducted. The meeting itself should be set within a wider process that includes detailed pre-conference preparation and post conference follow-up. The preparation stage is extremely important (Chapman et al., 2015b) and should include assessing case suitability, understanding participants' needs, ensuring access and communication, and managing expectations. Preparation for FGCs should be thorough, and can be labour and time intensive. Importantly, FGC effectiveness '…relies as much, if not more, upon the post-conference support as upon the conference itself' (Chapman et al., 2015a: 70).

FGCs may be the only response to an HSB incident or may be part of a package of complimentary interventions that may include therapy or counselling. McNevin (2010) describes a case where a 16-year-old boy was discovered to have been sexually abusing and raping his 13-year-old sister over four years. Systemic family therapy helped family members to come to terms with what had happened, which also prepared them for an FGC process which aimed to allow direct communication between family members about the HSB. Indeed, there are some links between FGCs as they could be used in HSB cases and therapeutic interventions in HSB cases. For example, in their discussion of a counselling approach to working with sibling sexual abuse, the main practice messages suggested by Keane, Guest and Padbury (2013) are: considering the needs of the victim and the offending sibling equally; joint work with all family members to promote safe environments and healing; and safety planning as a partnership between parents and professionals. The first two closely match with restorative values, and future planning, albeit not always or exclusively around safety, is an important feature of conference processes. Meeting individual need is also important in both therapy (Keane, Guest and Padbury, 2013) and FGCs. Given this, it is not surprising to learn that FGCs do sometimes result in therapeutic outcomes such as reconciliation and closure. It would nonetheless be unwise to use FGCs with the aim or expectation of achieving such results and participants should not expect these outcomes (McNevin, 2010). FGCs should definitely not be a substitute for therapy.

Where FGCs take place within institutional contexts, this influences the process. For example, statutory contexts often have strict timeframes. While there can be advantages, such as the swift administration of youth justice, the disadvantages include not providing sufficient time for parties to be thoroughly engaged in FGC processes. FGCs should be tailored to meet participants' needs.

The FGC facilitator

The facilitator is key to the success or failure of FGCs. Facilitator responsibilities include assessing suitability, preparing the parties, managing expectations (McNevin, 2010), risk assessment, and making the FGC accessible for those who want to participate. Facilitators must create an environment in which all participants feel safe, supported, able to discuss the difficult issues (Henniker and Mercer, 2007) and negotiate the feelings or shame, while challenging any denials of perpetration behaviour (Daly, 2012). To do this, they must win the trust of the parties and be seen to be 'multi-partial' or neutral, and should be able to work flexibly to meet participant needs without losing the programme integrity of the restorative approach.

Facilitators should have in-depth knowledge of FGCs, HSB and also of young people, working creatively towards increasing participation and minimise risks. For example, the main questions could be decided in advance so young participants have a chance to prepare responses in advance rather than reacting spontaneously during the meeting. Facilitators can avoid jargon, adapt their own communication and use visual prompts (Chapman, Gellin and Anderson, 2015b). These are often complex and challenging cases for professionals (Hackett, 2006). Facilitators should be appropriately equipped and receive regular support and supervision. Multi-agency working and information-sharing is also considered good practice. Specialist knowledge is essential for avoiding secondary victimisation and re-traumatisation (Chapman, Gellin and Anderson, 2015b).

Co-working can help to balance the process dynamics including the reactions of parents (Hoyle and Noguera, 2008) and can ensure that all necessary competencies are available. Facilitators in family violence cases in New Zealand are joined by a family violence expert who seeks to identify controlling behaviour exhibited by the perpetrator, and helps participants to understand the mechanisms and manifestations of family violence (Hennessy, Hinton, and Taurima, 2014). The adult sexual violence survivors in Wager's 2013 study reported positive experiences of restorative justice processes when they were facilitated by sexual victim experts, indicating that practitioner skill contributes to how the FGC is experienced.

Case study: Lee and Courtney

Lee (17) and Courtney (14) are siblings who live together with their mother Lisa. They generally have a positive relationship. One day while Lisa is shopping, Lee rapes Courtney. Courtney tells her mum the same day and the police are called. A medical examination confirms sexual intercourse has occurred. Courtney receives ongoing counselling from a specialist worker.

Lee is charged with rape and is soon removed from the family home and placed with an aunt. Courtney fears that Lee will go to prison if convicted. She refuses to co-operate with police and consequently the rape charge was altered to 'unlawful sexual activity with a family member'. Lee pleads guilty and is sentenced to a one-year Supervision Order, with a comprehensive programme of offence focused work. He is supervised by an experienced Youth Offending Team (YOT) practitioner who conducts an AIM (Assessment, Intervention and Moving on) assessment. After five interviews Lee is described as having High Strengths–Low Concerns. Identified 'high strengths' include his ability to reflect upon and understand offence consequences, willingness to address offending behaviour, positive plans or goals, good communications, and positive family support. Identified concerns include past family stress, current family stress, and mum's past history of mental health problems. The AIM report describes Lee's behaviour as exploratory in nature, and also suggests that some confusion and mixed messages around nudity and sexual issues exist within the home. Lee progresses well at the YOT. Eventually it is decided that Lee can return home. A restorative meeting is arranged in preparation for this. Lee and Courtney hope the FGC will provide a much needed space for family dialogue. Mum's two sisters have agreed to join the FGC and provide support.

Lee fully accepts that the offence took place and recognises he was wrong. He is ashamed of his behaviour and remorseful about the consequences for all concerned. There is no significant denial about the actuality of the act, but there is some ambiguity about the context of the behaviour: Lee sees Courtney as having given some degree of consent because she joined in with the play-fighting and physical exploration prior to the sexual intercourse. There was no suggestion of force during the event. Lee is anxious about discussing the HSB, and mindful of the embarrassment this will cause Courtney. He wants the opportunity to apologise to Courtney and the family.

Courtney is angry about what Lee did but is clear and assertive that she wants the family to be together. There is no suggestion that she is manipulated or pressurised into this. There has been tension between Courtney and mum, especially after Lee was removed from home. Courtney is aware that mum struggles massively with being the mother of both offender and victim. She is reassured by the support from her aunts. Courtney does not seek an apology from Lee during the meeting, but feels that his acknowledgment of responsibility would help her.

Conclusion

By definition HSB causes hurt and can lead to trauma, particularly for the young victim, who may experience negative consequences into adulthood. Young perpetrators may have transgressed social norms or even broken laws, but they have often themselves experienced victimisation and will have welfare needs (Hackett, 2007). Importantly, FGCs are not zero-sum constructions that require victim needs to be met at the expense of the perpetrator. Rather, FGCs are 'child-sensitive' processes, because they prioritise the safety and value the needs of all young people involved, while promoting their reintegration into the community (Chapman, Gellin and Anderson, 2015b).

There is a strong relationship aspect in HSB cases; both because of the dependence that young people have on their family and CoC and also because of the relationships that are damaged by the HSB. FGCs provide a forum for affected parties, and address individual feelings as well as interactions. The victim's status as the wronged party can be confirmed, the perpetrator takes responsibility, and collectively the participants draw upon their strengths to formulate a plan for the future to address the welfare and justice needs.

The application of restorative approaches to cases involving sexual harm and sexual violence has its critics, and FGCs also have the potential to elevate risk and amplify harm (Cossins, 2008). Certainly, when considering a restorative approach to sexual harm, the priority should be victim safety (Oudshoorn, Jackett and Stutzman Amstutz, 2015) and avoiding revictimisation and re-traumatisation. While the use of FGCs is not risk free, knowledgeable, skilled and reflective facilitators can help to manage these risks.

There is certainly a need for more research and for FGC practices involving HSB cases to be better documented, and for this information to be shared, however the evidence in support of FGCs in HSB cases continues to emerge and continues to demonstrate that FGCs have a great deal of potential.

Notes

[1.] The author acknowledges the problems with the terms 'victim' and 'perpetrator', but they are used here for simplicity.

[2.] For elaboration of the concept of justice needs, see: Bolitho (2015).

[3.] For the purpose of this piece no distinction will be made between HSB and 'problematic sexual behaviour'.

[4.] For further consideration of the potential risks of carrying out FGC in HSB and sexual violence cases see Oudshoorn, Jackett and Stutzman Amstutz (2015).

[5.] The AIM2 is an assessment framework is for children and young people who display HSB (AIM, n.d.). For further information see: www.aimproject.org.uk.

[6.] Here 'family' refers to the social group within which the young person was situated when the HSB was taking place.

[7.] An immediate or extended family member, or a close, non-blood relative.

Further reading

Chapman, T., Maija, G., Aertsen, I., Anderson, M. (2015a) 'Protecting rights, restoring respect and strengthening relationships: a European model for restorative justice with children and young people', Brussels: International Juvenile Justice Observatory.

Chapman, T., Gellin, M., Anderson, M. (2015b) 'Toolkit for professionals: implementing a European model for restorative justice with children and young people', Brussels: International Juvenile Justice Observatory.

McNevin, E. (2010) 'Applied restorative justice as a complement to systemic family therapy: theory and practice implications for families experiencing intra-familial adolescent sibling incest', *The Australian and New Zealand Journal of Family Therapy*, 31(1): 60–72.

Mercer, V., Sten Madsen, K., Keenan, M. and Zinsstag, E (2015). *Doing restorative justice in cases of sexual violence: a practice guide*, Leuven: Leuven Institute of Criminology.

Ricks, J. M., and DiClemente, R. J. (2015) 'Adolescent sex offenders', in T. P. Gullotta, R. W. Plant, and A. A. Evans, (eds), *Handbook of adolescent behavioural problems: evidence-based approaches to prevention and treatment*. New York: Springer, pp 578–530.

ELEVEN

FGCs in the youth justice system

Jonny Cohen and Dave Norton
with Deanna Edwards and Kate Parkinson

Introduction

This chapter focuses upon Family Group Conferencing in the youth justice arena using the ReConnect project, an FGC service based within Leeds Youth Offending service as a case study to exemplify their use in this field. The chapter does not offer a discussion on other types of restorative approaches in the field of youth justice, but there is some suggested further reading at the end for those who wish to explore restorative approaches further.

FGCs in the youth justice field sit under the umbrella of restorative justice. Restorative justice is the process of bringing together the 'victim' of a crime with the 'offender' to enable dialogue between the two parties with a focus on 'repairing the harm' to the victim. The restorative process is aimed at creating an outcome where the victim feels that justice has been served and that the offender is taking responsibility for their crime (Zehr, 2015). The result is a 'personalised' justice process because it is the 'victim' who determines what needs to happen for them to feel that justice has been served.

The House of Commons Home Affairs Select Committee, 2005–06 defines restorative justice as follows:

> Restorative measures offer victims an opportunity to confront offenders with the consequences of the actions, receive apologies and reparation. They potentially open the way for changes of attitudes so that fear may be reduced for victims and offenders may have more understanding of their behaviour, and therefore incentive to discontinue. (paragraph 29)

Restorative Justice was first introduced into the UK in the mid-1980s, when the Home Office funded four victim–offender mediation services (Davy, 2005).

This work was developed further in 1996 with the publication of 'Misspent Youth', an Audit Commission document looking at the way young people were managed with within the justice system; it introduced the idea of cautions and targeted prevention work and emphasised restorative approaches as being best practice (Audit Commission, 1996).

The next significant event was the establishment of Youth Offending Teams (YOTs), following the Crime and Disorder Act 1998. YOTs were set up with the intention of reducing the risk of young people offending and re-offending, and to provide counsel and rehabilitation to those who do offend. Again, the emphasis was on restorative approaches to address the offending behaviour of young people (Williams, 2000).

In 2002 the Referral Order was launched nationally; this was the first youth court *ordered* intervention that was designed to have a restorative element to it. Until this point, while restorative practice was emphasised as best practice, there was no mandate for youth offending services to use this approach. Referral Orders included the convening of a post-court panel comprising of the young person (offender); their parent or carer; the victim, their representatives, or both; and community volunteers recruited and trained by the YOT, with the aim of developing a plan to address the offending behaviour of the offender and to 'repair' the harm to victim (Uglow et al., 2002).

Around this same period, the national provision of Restorative Conference training was introduced. This was a partnership between Oxfordshire YOT, the Youth Justice Board and Thames Valley Police with the intention of upskilling the workforce in the youth justice sector around issues of restorative practice (Stahlkopf, 2009). Since then restorative approaches have been widely used within youth justice, with restorative justice being well embedded in youth offending services (Criminal Justice Joint Inspection, 2012).

There are of course regional variations in the application of restorative practice in the UK. Northern Ireland has had restorative processes at the heart of its approach to youth justice since the establishment of the Youth Justice Board in 1998, and under The Justice (Northern Ireland) Act 2002 a court is required to refer a young person for a 'youth conference' in applicable situations (Edgar and Pickford, 2009). The fact that restorative practice is not mandatory in England and Wales means that there are geographical variations in the application of this approach (House of Commons Justice Committee, 2017). In Scotland, most local authorities implement a restorative justice approach, with Objective Four of the National Standards for Scotland's Youth Justice Services (Scottish Executive, 2002: 7) stating that 'every victim of a young offender referred to the reporter on offence grounds will have the opportunity to engage in a [restorative justice] scheme, where appropriate.' The House of Commons Youth Justice Committee (2016) has, however, recommended that the Northern Ireland Approach to youth justice be adopted across the UK.

The report emphasises the benefits of restorative approaches for both young victims and offenders, using evidence gathered from Youth Offending Services already applying the approach. The evidence suggests that restorative approaches reduce offending and reoffending rates, with data from ten test sites demonstrating reduction rates of between 7% and 77%. Furthermore, evidence demonstrates that overall victims are satisfied with the restorative process, having a sense that justice has been served. Figures from studies cited in the House of Commons Youth Justice Committee report (2016) demonstrated victim satisfaction rates of 77% and 85%.

Research suggests that restorative process helps young people and their families to be future-focused and to work towards positive outcomes. It also places the emphasis on resettlement and desistance, resulting in a reduction of the number of young people entering the criminal justice system and ultimately reducing the number of young people sentenced, or resentenced, to custody (Braithwaite, 2016).

FGCs and restorative justice

Family Group Conferencing (FGC) in the youth justice system originated in New Zealand in 1989, as with FGCs in child welfare, and FGCs have been the cornerstone of youth justice approaches in New Zealand since that time. Under the Children, Young Persons and Their Families Act 1989, young people who offend are referred to a FGC before the court makes a decision about sentencing, with the aim of diverting young people from custody and allowing them to remain within their communities. The model of FGCs used is the same as that applied in child welfare FGCs and 'private family time' remains an essential part of the process (Mutter et al., 2008). The use of FGCs is not prevalent in the youth justice system in the UK, with the exception of Northern Ireland and specialist services such as the AIM project in the North West of England which offers training to local authorities and youth justice services on holding FGCs for young people with Harmful Sexual Behaviour (AIM, n.d.). This way of working is nonetheless very much aligned with the current emphasis on restorative approaches being considered to be best practice. The process is restorative and encourages young people and their families to plan for, and take responsibility for, positive changes to their behaviour and outcomes. It is a child friendly approach that gives the young person a chance to be heard and for those wishes to be recorded as part of a shared family plan in which they are an equal partner with other family members (Rogers and Parkinson, 2018).

As stated previously, youth conferences are routinely used within the youth justice field in Northern Ireland. The Justice (Northern Ireland) Act 2002 mandates that youth conferences should be offered to young people where appropriate to do so (Campbell et al., 2005). The Northern Ireland approach emulates the youth conferencing approach taken in New Zealand (Payne et al., 2009). As with a child welfare FGC, it is the family who play a central role in decision making at a youth conference. The victim and the offender and their families have the responsibility of developing a plan with the aim of repairing the harm to the victim and addressing the offending behaviour of the offender. The families undertake this task in partnership with the police, youth justice professionals and, where appropriate, social workers. Campbell et al. (2005) undertook an evaluation of youth conferences in Northern Ireland and reviewed 362 referrals for a youth conference, 75% of which resulted in a conference. This research found that 97% of young offenders took responsibility for their actions, all victims felt that the process was helpful to them, 95% of conferences resulted in a plan and 74% of offenders and 87% of victims were happy with the plan agreed. Furthermore, 98% of young people attending a youth conferences felt that they were listened to during the meeting. These findings are consistent with research from New Zealand undertaken by Maxwell and Morris (2006) who conducted a six-year study of 14–17 year olds involved in offending behaviour. For those who were not persistent offenders, several factors were found to be significant in supporting young people to address their offending behaviour, including that of being involved in decision making and feeling as though they had repaired the harm that they had created. Further research from the UK by Mutter et al. (2008), who evaluated one of the early UK restorative FGC projects, found that the process was viewed positively by participants and that young people were helped to accept their offending and reduce their strengths and difficulties questionnaire (SDQ) scores (Goodman, 1997). The FGC approach has, however, been described as 'inadequate for recidivist high risk offenders' (Slater, McDowell and Lambie, 2015: 621) and there is debate about whether FGCs are appropriate for domestic abuse and sexual abuse cases (see Chapters Eight and Ten for an exploration of research and discussion on competing perspectives).

There may be occasions when FGCs are held in a youth justice context where the victim and the offender are not both present, as the victim may not want to meet with the offender (Shapland et al, 2007). These FGCs can still be defined as restorative and Haresnape (2007) argues that this may be the case if the following criteria are met:

- the young person willingly engages in the process;
- any victims of the offence are consulted;
- the FGC has a focus on the offence and its impact;
- the FGC considers ways that the offender may make reparation for the offence.

Further Braithwaite and Mugford (1994) argue that the conference must contain three key features

1. an apology for the crime;
2. the victim having opportunity to explain how the crime affected them;
3. the young person and their family plan to develop strategies to address offending.

Indeed the authors would argue that all FGCs which address offending behaviour can be seen as restorative, even without direct and indirect victim involvement since they aim to address the reasons for offending and hence to repair harm.

Another important issue for consideration is the use of FGCs in the Youth Justice arena to address welfare issues so often inherent in offending behaviour (Fox, 2005). Indeed, as stated in Chapter Seven, in the Republic of Ireland, the Children Act 2001 makes provision for Family Welfare Conferences (FWCs) to be held where child welfare issues are identified in juvenile justice cases (The Children Act 2001, Part Two). Under Part Two of the Act, which commenced in September 2004, the Health Service Executive (HSE) is obliged to convene a FWC before applying for a special care order for a child, with the aim of diverting children away from the residential care system and enabling them to remain within the care of their families. Furthermore, the legislation enables a judge to request the HSE, to hold a FWC if a young person is in court for criminal behaviour and the judge considers that there is a care and protection issue to be addressed (Section 77). The Act also provides for the holding of a FWC if the child welfare agency decides that an application to the court is warranted to provide a secure placement for a young person that may be at risk of harm and needs such security for their own protection (Section 23).

The importance of addressing welfare issues in the context of offending should not be underestimated in terms of addressing the origins of offending. The link between child abuse or neglect and offending behaviour is well established (Cashmore, 2012). Therefore, a distinctly welfare FGC service may pick up referrals from Youth Offending Teams to address offending or welfare issues or specialist youth justice services such as ReConnect may use FGCs to address both offending and welfare concerns. Anderson and Parkinson (in press) suggest that in cases for HSB (see Chapter Ten) that one FGC, rather than separate FGCs for both welfare concerns and offending behaviour, can address both offending and welfare issues for the young people involved and propose a practice framework for the delivery of FGCs in this field. The Leeds experience below demonstrates that one FGC addressing both sets of issues can be highly effective in recognising the intrinsic relationship between offending behaviour and welfare concerns.

The Leeds experience

In 2012 the Leeds ReConnect Family Group Conference project was established within the Leeds Youth Offending Service. The project initially focused on young people with a history of custody or burglary with an aim of reducing recidivism rates. It has however since broadened its referral criteria to include all young people involved with youth offending services. The service adheres to the 'pure' FGC model in terms of all referrals being voluntary, neutral venues being used, food and refreshments being provided and the use of 'private family time'. The project has developed strong links with the social care FGC service in Leeds, using a shared recording system and management structure.

Since 2016 ReConnect has expanded to offer restorative conferences – known locally as Resolve meetings. The purpose of a Resolve meeting is to help individuals to repair relationships and improve communication. Resolve meetings can be offered as a stand-alone intervention or as part of a process which will enable a family to move forward to a ReConnect FGC. Like ReConnect, Resolve is family-led and solution-focused. While the family decide what issue is actually discussed, however, it is a more managed process, in preparation and at the actual meeting. In preparation, the coordinator meets each participant to ascertain the nature of the difficulties or incident of harm and then completing preparation with each participant covering the following areas:

- What is the nature of the problem?
- What were your thoughts about the issue at the beginning? How have your thoughts changed over time? What do you feel about it now?
- How has the issue affected you? How has it affected other people? How has it affected relationships?
- What has been the hardest thing for you?
- What needs to happen to repair the harm done and make things okay again? What do you need to do? What do you need other people to do?

This preparation is completed with each person, with full notes being taken regarding their responses. While not a script, these notes will help inform the questioning in the Resolve meeting and ensure that each person gets to say what they need to.

The Resolve meeting has a clear structure to it which states when people can speak and when they must listen, with each person afforded the same opportunity to be heard in turn while others listen without interrupting. After the first person has reached the point where they state what the hardest thing for them has been, the coordinator will then move on to the next person and so on until all have had an opportunity to give their version of events.

At this stage, the coordinator checks that each person is satisfied that they have had an equal opportunity to speak. The coordinator then checks that each person agrees that there is a problem that needs to be resolved in the conference. Finally, the coordinator checks that each person agrees that they are ready to move on and want to be part of finding a resolution to the problem or problems.

Throughout the meeting it is the coordinator's responsibility to keep the conversations focused and not allow participants to follow their own agendas.

This has been a particularly useful tool when dealing with family crises, such as the relationship breakdown between a parent and their child or between siblings, or if the offending has been intra-familial. Cases which used to be dealt with by Victim Liaison Officers (VLOs) are now routinely referred to the ReConnect or Resolve service when incidents appear to be related to family issues, with VLOs focusing on those cases without this familial angle.

It's not just offending...

Clearly, all young people who are in contact with Leeds YOS and, subsequently ReConnect have, by definition, been involved with or identified as being at risk of offending behaviour, it has become very clear over the entire period of the project that a great many of the family plans deal with lots of issues but quite often have no mention of offending. It appears that offending by the young person is the symptom of other issues, rather than the cause. The problems often lie around communication, poor relationships, understanding, boundary setting, vulnerability, education issues, lack of support and substance misuse. This is reflected in research and evidence which emphasises the difficult and chaotic family lives that young people who offend often have experienced (Anderson, Bromley and Given, 2005; Cashmore, 2012). By focusing the work on the issues relevant to the young person and their family, a plan is produced which addresses these pertinent issues often resulting in the reduction or an end to the offending behaviour. Statistics for reoffending within Leeds YOS for the period from April 2016 to April 2017 indicate that the general YOS reoffending rate was 24%, whereas 81% of those engaged with the Reconnect service had no further offending. This reduction should be considered alongside other positive impacts of the Reconnect Service on family relationships and stability at home.

YOS case managers' perspectives

After five years, ReConnect and Resolve has become an integral part of the offer to young people and their families, with a strong buy-in from case manager colleagues.

"As case managers, our only contacts in the family are Mum and Dad – we rarely get the story beyond that. The information that ReConnect provided really helped in understanding how Joe became the young man he is."

"ReConnect gives power back to the family – moves away from the tradition of doing "to" the family and gets families talking about what their expectations of each other are."

"In one case, the young person felt hopeless – nobody seemed to care. Jack had had five previous custodial sentences by age of 17 and YOS had been unable to engage with his carers due to ongoing alcohol issues. ReConnect succeeded in identifying a wider network of family, some people who cared about Jack. This empowered him to become more a member of the wider family and an opportunity to be successful. The process allowed his new carers to compartmentalise expectations: if you live here, this is what you need to do. Previously, there were no expectations and no safety. This helped Jack's emotional health and fostered clarity and a sense of belonging. Four years on, there has been no further offending."

"ReConnect drew on family strengths and gave the young person the clear message that everyone in the family wanted the best for him. As a result, he started attending education and didn't get chucked out for the first time in four or five years – the impetus came from family support which reinforced the need to stick to his [ADHD] medication."

"ReConnect is positively regarded across the YOS – even when the young person doesn't manage to make progress it is still good to see young people in a family situation and from a different perspective. The value is in the process, taking small steps and giving insight which would be otherwise unknown – it helps identify needs."

"Private family time is really empowering – the process facilitates positive communication and families buy into the idea of coming together to support their young person – they understand that they are central to any success."

ReConnect (FGC) – Case Study P

Family background:
Peter, 15 years old, first came to the attention of the Youth Offending Service in December 2015, when he received a Youth Caution for violence against his mum. He has since gone on to receive a Youth Conditional Caution for further offences in the family home, including threatening behaviour.

Around this time Peter was assessed by CAMHS (Child and Adolescent Mental Health Service). Although it was found he had no diagnosable conditions, it was acknowledged that he had some behaviour difficulties and he was subsequently enrolled at a specialist school.

A referral to ReConnect was made around concerns about his behaviour within the home. The referrer held the view that the issues of boundaries, incentives and communication patterns within the home were all areas of which needed to be addressed. In addition, ReConnect was seen as a way of ensuring that Peter's mum had the support she needed in order to look after Peter effectively.

Peter lived at home with his mum (Sheila) and older sister (Helen). His dad (Steven) had been asked to leave the family home several years earlier. He has since remarried and lives with his new partner and her children. When I first met with Peter he was not having any contact with his dad and his relationship with his maternal grandparents was very strained due to his behaviour.

Another issue that came to light during my discussions was that although Grandma (Rita) came across as a very focused and caring person, she had been through some difficult times with regards to relationships when Sheila was young, and that this still had an effect on their relationship now.

As part of my preparation I managed to meet with Steven who was very keen to start rebuilding his relationship with his son; I also talked with him about supporting Sheila with his day to day care and behaviour.

ReConnect family plan:
Reason for the Reconnect Conference:
To help and support the family to work together and set appropriate boundaries, to help them improve communication and reduce the risk of Peter becoming criminalised.

Questions for the Reconnect Conference:
- How can we all support each other to communicate in a positive way, stay calm when we disagree and calm down when we are angry?
- How can we as a family set appropriate boundaries and incentives and support each other to be consistent?
- How can we all support Mum to be Mum?

Family members present:
- Peter
- Sheila (Mum)
- Steven (Dad)
- Helen (Peter's sister)

- Rita (Grandma)
- Fred (Granddad)

Professionals present:
- Case holder and ReConnect conference coordinator

The plan:
1. Peter agreed that Monday to Thursday he would be home no later than 8.30pm and no later than 9.00pm on Friday and Saturday.
2. Peter agreed he will hand his mobile phone over to his mum at 10.30pm each night so that he can sleep with no distractions. It was agreed he can keep his phone on Friday and Saturday nights.
3. If Peter complies with the above he will receive £5 pocket money on a Monday. If he is defiant and difficult he agreed to be grounded the next day.
4. If Peter feels he is becoming distressed or frustrated he has the option of phoning his dad to discuss the issue or to contact his Grandma and Granddad where he can go overnight if he feels it is necessary to remove himself from the situation at home.
5. Peter will go out with his dad on a weekly basis and this will be arranged by telephone. If this is going well over the next month this will move towards Peter staying at his dad's house one weekend per month.
6. Peter, Helen and Sheila all agreed that they would knock on the bedroom and bathroom door before entering the room.
7. Helen and Peter agreed they would stand by their mum's decisions and that they would not get involved in discussions or arguments that were not relevant to them.
8. Mum agreed that she would explain clearly why she was saying 'no', but this would be once.
9. All agreed they would think about how they speak to each other, what they are saying and how they are saying it. They will speak to each other with respect, the way they would like to be spoken to.
10. Sheila, Helen and Peter will go for Sunday lunch as a family to Grandma and Granddad's house once per month.

Family feedback:
MUM: "I found this very helpful and it brought my family back together. We are now communicating.

Peter has tried hard, we have started to act like a normal family with lots of laughter."

PETER: "It was good because it helped me understand better. It has helped us to understand each other and get along with each other. It has helped my behaviour."

HELEN: "ReConnect has brought us closer together as a family, it has worked well for us; we just need to keep it up. It has helped us make rules – I think we are in the best place as a family we have been for a long time."

STEVEN: "It has helped me to rebuild my relationship with my son and he now comes to my house on a regular basis."

GRANDMA: "I found it positive especially in regard to motivating Peter and his mum. ReConnect has allowed us all to look and think about how we treat each other and how we deal with situations without aggression."

GRANDDAD: "ReConnect was a positive chance to engage all parties to contribute to fix all our problems to mend the breaks. It has helped family members to find common ground and stop apportioning blame."

Conclusion

In conclusion, it is clear that Family Group Conferencing can be an effective and useful tool in engaging young people and their families with the idea of positive change (Crea and Berzin, 2009: Mutter, Shemmings and Dugmore, 2008; Pennell, Shapiro and Spigner, 2011).

This is systematically evidenced via the collation of qualitative feedback received from families in every ReConnect case (See Case Study, above). Families respond well to being placed at the centre of a process which works 'with' them rather than does 'to' them. Indeed the recently published Leeds Family Values Evaluation Report found that 100% of families felt involved in decision-making processes and valued this experience (Mason et al., 2017).

The Leeds YOS experience, in the form of ReConnect FGCs and Resolve restorative conferences, has demonstrated that there is a broad need for family-centred responses to youth justice issues. The FGC model is flexible enough to deal with almost any family dynamic, provided that young people and their family members are prepared to engage with the possibility of positive change.

It is also clear that, in order for FGCs to be successful and become an established part of service delivery, management support is crucial. It takes time to embed a service and tweaks to the service may be required over time. It is apparent that many, if not the majority, of young people in contact with the police, Courts or Youth Offending Service have some family difficulties which, if addressed, would reduce the risk of further offending. Therefore, the authors would argue that all youth offending services should include practitioners trained in FGCs and restorative approaches.

Finally, in those areas where FGCs are already used in social work or other settings, a ready-made 'skill-set' and established procedures can already be found, which can provide support to those YOS services that wish to establish a FGC service. Collaboration, liaison, peer support and joint training are all ways to ensure a Youth Offending Team-based project will keep pace with developments in the field and evolve to better respond to the needs of young people and their families restoratively and inclusively.

Further reading

Liebmann, M. (2007) *Restorative justice: how it works*, London: Jessica Kingsley Publishers.

MacRae, A. and Zehr, H. (2004) *The little book of Family Group Conferences New Zealand style: a hopeful approach when youth cause harm*, Brattleboro, VT: Good Books.

Zehr, H. (2015) *The little book of Restorative Justice: revised and updated (justice and peacebuilding)*, Brattleboro, VT: Good Books.

TWELVE

FGCs and adult social care

Tim Fisher, Beth Mooney and Andrew Papworth

Introduction

Using family group conferencing with vulnerable adults has been viewed for a long time as an idea with real potential. Why? Evidence from innovative practice in children's FGCs (documented elsewhere in this book), research from the Netherlands and policy developments in adult social care and mental health (which are dealt with in this chapter) have all been sources for optimism.

In 2010, the Making Safeguarding Personal Toolkit (Ogilvie and Williams, 2010) gave encouragement to those who were considering using FGCs with adults. It urged more local authorities to develop FGC work, throwing down the gauntlet, suggesting that a 'routine offer' for FGC could become part of practice in the future (Local Government Association, 2013). Like a slow train picking up speed there have been practice developments in the UK: a burgeoning practice network, a few established adult FGC services (some longstanding) and the application of the model across an increasing number of service user groups and areas of concern.

This chapter draws upon key research and writing on the use of FGCs with vulnerable adults. Key features of FGCs in adult social care will be addressed by the chapter – including its history, its current practice, and potential points of development. The research and feedback analysed here is encouraging, showing FGCs in adult social care to be both constructive and productive (Marsh with Kent Adult FGC Service, 2007; Camden Family Group Conference Service, 2015).

FGCs for adults: a sketch across Britain

At the time of writing (February 2017), established FGC practices vary widely in their length of operation, however the number of authorities running or considering running a service continues to grow significantly.

- Birmingham has commissioned an Adult FGC service with 'in house' independent coordinators who, at the time of writing, are being trained and preparing to take their first referrals.
- Camden added an adult provision to their FGC service in 2013. An evaluation of this service led to it being confirmed in place by the Adult Services a year later. Referrals have included young people with a disability who are transitioning to the adult services, adults with a disability and older people who require safeguarding. Thirty FGCs have now been held.
- Dumfries and Galloway has commissioned Kalm Solutions to provide FGCs for vulnerable adults (Forsyth et al., 2013). They are currently undertaking a contract for 15 FGCs.
- Edinburgh City Council Family Decision Making Team's focus includes FGCs for children on the edge of care, vulnerable babies and family-finding for children unable to stay at home, which traces kinship links using public registers for young people without known family members. They have begun to take a handful of referrals from the authority's adult services and piloting FGCs in adult social care. Two FGCs – one for a person with alcohol dependency issues and one for an adult with dementia – were held and largely considered successful. It is hoped that the adult care division, possibly with the local health agencies, will continue to grow this service.
- Essex, as part of the NE Essex NHS Partnership Foundation Trust, has a long established FGC service for people with mental health issues: anyone with a Care Programme can ask or be referred for an FGC. Such FGCs often work to avoid the person's readmission to hospital. The service has a close working relationship with health professionals and, in turn, is able to address the needs of numerous mental health problems.
- Hampshire has met demand for FGCs through the voluntary organisation Daybreak, which has been promoting and providing FGCs and FGC standards since the mid-1990s. While Daybreak most often work with children and families, they extended their provisions in 2007 to include vulnerable adults. The Bluebird Project – initially funded by Comic Relief – aimed to use FGCs to meet the needs of adults at risk of abuse. Hampshire County Council began to fund the project from 2010 and have recently extended this contract for another two years, in which time they will provide Hampshire with 20 FGCs annually in relation to elder

abuse, safeguarding adults with disabilities and risk management within the context of personalisation.

- Kent FGC Service ran a successful pilot adult FGC Service in two areas of Kent from 2005–2008. The service accepted referrals of adults with learning disabilities, young adults with physical disabilities and older people. The service found a high referral rate for two years and the pilot received a very position evaluation in 2007 (Marsh with Kent adult FGC service, 2007). This evaluation shared positive responses from service users, families of service users, social workers and other professionals and indicated substantial cost savings. Kent decided to extend the programme across the county but this decision coincided with a major restructuring of the authority. Thus, effective mainstreaming did not happen and the adult FGC service was closed.

- Lincoln City Council FGC Service started a service for adults. Their remit includes those with physical disabilities, learning disabilities, adults with dementia and older people with safeguarding and care planning needs, as well as young people in transition from children services. Early results have been positive with a reduction in complaints to the authority as well as in referrals to the Court of Protection (Adult FGC Network Survey, 2017).

- Midlothian Council commissioned Kalm Solutions to provide FGCs for adults experiencing dementia in 2012 (Forsyth et al., 2013). Kalm Solutions were given resources for ten FGCs which, thus far, have been reviewed three times. The service continues today.

- Swansea FGC Service is currently being piloted with people who have early signs or a recent diagnosis of dementia. The service is in its initial stages but family members have shared positive responses, often grateful for FGCs giving them an opportunity to be involved in care provisions.

Across all of the cities and regions noted above, the Practice Network formed a peer led practice network for organisations and individuals (including academics and educators) involved in the provision of FGCs with adults. Originally set up by Camden, Edinburgh and Coventry, the network now has 25 connected local authorities and organisations, including Daybreak, Family Rights Group and North Essex Mental Health Trust (the longest established adult FGC service).

The application of FGCs with vulnerable adults

Family Group Conferences can be used to safeguard adults in relation to physical abuse, financial abuse and neglect. Adults suffering abuse are more likely than the general population to have been abused by their partner or member of their family (Mowlam et al., 2007) An FGC can help bring relevant stakeholders together to establish a plan that safeguards by working with the people close to the vulnerable adult and the perpetrator of the abuse (Community Care, 2013). The 'no blame' and restorative FGC culture, encourages participants to engage with the process. (Daybreak, 2010; Forsyth et al., 2013).

Professionals can express appropriate worries about perpetrators of abuse being exonerated, victims being blamed and perpetrators using FGCs to manipulate the participants (Camden Family Group Conference Service, 2015). In order to mitigate against these concerns, a thorough risk assessment is carried out in order to determine whether perpetrators and victims acknowledge that the abuse has occurred, whether they have insight into its impact and ensuring the relevant family and friends are in engaged with the process (for example, they are not colluding with an absent abuser) (Camden Family Group Conference Service, 2015; Daybreak, 2010). The overriding aim for this restorative process is that an open approach to discussing the abuse in a Family Group Conference will mitigate risk and make the situation safer. The FGC can 'work against the secrecy of abuse' by widening the circle of support (Tapper, 2010: 29).

Marsh with Kent Adult FGC Service (2007: 3) in his evaluation of the Kent FGC service, highlights that 'changes in service user capacities, changes in carers capacities and changes in service provision' can all be triggers for an FGC and this premise certainly applies to young adults in transition. FGCs should be future-focused – for example, planning education and housing – to maximise the autonomy of the young adult. Advocacy may enable the young person to fully engage and, in turn, work to the principle of group planning in the best interests of the adult (Camden Family Group Conference Service, 2015; Daybreak, 2010; Adult Network Survey, 2017). It has been said by social workers that when one person steps forward to care for someone with vulnerabilities there is a tendency for others to step back (Camden Family Group Conference Service, 2015). As the aim of FGCs is to distribute responsibility and widen the circle of support, support for carers can be a useful focus for an FGC (Marsh with Kent Adult FGC Service, 2007; Forsyth, et al., 2013; SCIE, 2013a). In both the UK and the Netherlands, evaluation and research has shown that

FGCs support the carer network in ways that most existing services struggle to do and in ways carers report they had not experienced before (Marsh with Kent Adult FGC Service, 2007; Camden Family Group Conference Service, 2015; De Jong and Schout, 2013). In 2017 Jamie Spencer, Care Act Implementation Manager for the London Borough of Camden, said:

> Informal care is the hidden foundation of the entire social care system without which the edifice would collapse. The Care Act represented an unprecedented opportunity for carers to receive the recognition and support for what they do. Practice is still inconsistent, however, and many carers report no difference since the Act came into force. Adult FGCs can cut through the bureaucracy of formal assessment processes and can get to the heart of what matters to a carer. Carers are often carrying out their role in isolation, with family members not aware of how much their role might be impacting on them. FGCs allow the carer's voice to be heard and give an opportunity for the wider family network to agree a plan that can support a carer to sustain their caring role while maintaining a life outside caring. (Camden Family Group Conference Service, 2015: 67)

The use of FGCs has recently been extended to issues of hoarding and self-neglect (Adult FGC Network Survey, 2017). The hope is that issues can be resolved by the network through the FGC process and the adult in question would not need to be referred back to the social worker (SCIE, 2013a).

Moreover, FGCs are being used widely for planning care. An advantage of the FGC approach is that it offers a framework for a personalised approach, allowing people to make decisions as far as their capacity allows. Where end of life care is to be discussed or the frailty of the adult is significant, preparation for deterioration in health is often required. The length of the FGC – on the day itself – may need to be considered if the subject of the FGC is too frail to attend a long meeting (Marsh with Kent Adult FGC Service, 2007; Brown and Walter, 2014).

> A plan was made for family members to support the adult to live at home – with myself [social worker] and the independent social worker both in agreement with the family… the process was positive, excellently facilitated

and the families plan to step in with care and support was robust. (Feedback from a social worker; Camden Family Group Conference Service, 2015: 9)

In many of the FGCs which are held to address dementia care, it is important to understand how the Mental Capacity Act 2005 (MCA) and deprivation of liberty safeguards apply in each case. Where a reduction in capacity is assessed, advocacy may be a key element of the process (Ogilvie and Williams, 2010; Forsyth et al., 2013). Daybreak have stressed that FGC can fulfil the requirements of a 'Best Interests' meeting under the Mental Capacity Act by allowing adults to make decisions to the limits of their capacity (Daybreak, 2010).

Areas for consideration

A list of key points that services should consider when implementing FGCs in adult services has been provided below.

Applying the FGC process to adults in need of safeguarding

FGC coordinators working with adults need additional competencies to those working in child welfare – for example understanding of the Health and Social Care legislation and policy (SCIE, 2013a; Marsh with Kent Adult FGC Service, 2007). As there are a number of different barriers to overcome, adult FGCs ought to be regarded as a new development in FGCs (Marsh with Kent Adult FGC Service, 2007) and, as such, coordinators must be familiar with adult-specific practices.

Referrers can tend towards only selecting 'mediation' style cases, where the focus is on difficult relationships, either within the family group or between the adult and the professional network. These types of cases are usually welcome and appropriate for FGC services, however referrers should also feel able to refer with issues and decisions in mind regardless of the state of the relationships in the network. It is possible to have a useful and functioning FGC in which members of the network suggestion solutions and come to an agreement without addressing their specific relationship difficulties. Often joint concern is enough to allow participants to overcome their difficult relationships in order to help. The process of coming together to create a solution can often improve the difficult relationship, despite that not being an original aim for the FGC. (SCIE, 2013b; Camden Family Group Conference Service, 2015).

In other situations an FGC Coordinator will need to negotiate or mediate with members of the network to enable them to come together. De Jong and Schout (2013) emphasis that limited or broken social networks can be a reason for organising FGCs. Such a focus on restoring connections and support networks is part of the Netherland's concept of family group conferencing as a developmental and restorative process (De Jong and Schout, 2013).

It is generally accepted that part of the coordinator's role is to resolve difficulties that prevent key members of the network meeting. It may be that the difficulties are between members of the family network and agencies. Some coordinators will be more confident and better equipped to take this further than others. FGC services may look to bear this in mind as they develop adult FGCs (Camden Family Group Conference Service, 2015).

Adult FGC coordinators have reported that, in some cases, the mediation needed in preparation for the event leads to a dependency on them. (Camden Family Group Conference Service, 2015) Such families may feel that they need the coordinator to support them and, in turn, prevent them from leaving the room during private family time. Despite this, it is important that private family time remains a key part of the process. Without this time, responsibility may be transferred from the family to the coordinator and, in turn, the family may exhibit a weaker commitment to the plan (Camden Family Group Conference Service, 2015). Research has suggested that establishing clear ground rules can mitigate against this problem (SCIE, 2013a).

The Making Safeguarding Personal toolkit (Ogilvie and Williams, 2010) highlights FGC reviews as a necessary part of the process to sustain resilience and maintain momentum. The evaluation in Camden Family Group Conference (2015) found that requests for extra reviews were more common than for child welfare FGCs because of the ongoing nature of the support from Social Care. Multiple reviews are an established part of the practice of the North Essex project. FGC services may want to consider the function of reviews in the FGC process when working with adults and not make the assumption that clients and participating professionals will view the process as a closed-ended one as they often do in child welfare FGC practice (see North Essex review and case study later in this chapter; Camden Family Group Conference Service, 2015).

Relationship dynamics

Forsyth suggests that FGCs may engage support from the adult's informal network and improve the understanding between the 'family' and professionals, which can often be a source of conflict. FGCs see human beings as fundamentally interdependent and contend that sharing vulnerability and accepting help can prioritise the participants' relationships (Metze, Kwekkeboom and Abma, 2015; Tew, 2015). Project evaluations completed thus far suggest that FGCs can build trust between agencies and service users (SCIE, 2013a; Forsyth et al., 2013; De Jong, Schout and Abma, 2014). It would seem it can work both ways: social workers and health professionals can achieve a 'higher level of direct communication with 'hard to reach' family members' while the informal network can ask questions and understand professional worries (Camden Family Group Conference Service, 2015). FGCs prevent the 'ad hoc bombardment' of professionals by providing a platform for family members to be heard and make changes. This in turn improves relationships (Forsyth et al., 2013).

Professionals may feel more positive and motivated because, if they have the support of the family in question, they are more likely to make progress as the FGC becomes a team effort (Ogilvie and Williams, 2010; Camden Family Group Conference Service, 2015). An FGC is an opportunity for co-production: to question diagnoses, change assessments and plan care arrangements (Tew, 2015). FGCs with adults often involve more professionals (Marsh with Kent Adult FGC Service, 2007). While this may be useful for adults with complex needs, a purposeful and organised approach to care provision is required to ensure the need is successfully addressed (Marsh with Kent Adult FGC Service, 2007).

The Making Safeguarding Personal Tool Kit (Ogilvie and Williams, 2010) highlights that the 'widest possible network' is necessary for adult FGCs. In cases where the family are not a part of the adult's life, the community focus is even more important (Ogilvie and Williams, 2010: 12). De Jong, Schout and Abma's (2014) research on the Netherland's 'citizen rights' version of FGC demonstrates this. This research tells the story of 'Arie': a schizophrenic man who was involuntarily referred to a psychiatric hospital after a suicide attempt around his 18th birthday. When he ended up living on the streets in the cold, local residents organised for his shelter and sought advice on how best to help him with an FGC. This FGC allowed them to set up boundaries and make it clear that they wanted 'Arie' to stay in their community long-term. Successfully, nine months after the conference, 'Arie' continues to live in the neighbourhood without coercive measures (De Jong, Schout and Abma, 2014).

Metze, Kwekkeboom and Abma (2015) use the concept of 'relational autonomy' to describe how individuals use their relationships to express their own identity. A meaningful FGC process is one that engages with the subject's sense of self (Metze, Kwekkeboom and Abma, 2015). For older adults 'there is an amount of "compassionate interference" from the informal network which is to be embraced while at the same time paying mind to the autonomy and identity of the adult' (Metze, Kwekkeboom and Abma, 2015). An aspect of the relationship patterns specific to older adults which features heavily in research is the 'separation dynamic' – where an older person and their older carer do not wish to separate, even though the care at home may not be good enough without extra support – which an FGC could be instrumental in planning (Community Care, 2013).

A restorative practice?

FGCs are also discussed as a 'restorative' practice. The term 'restorative' is often used to describe a specific restorative action such as a piece of voluntary work to make amends for a negative act or an apology to those affected by the act. There is a lot of scope for FGCs to be used more in this explicit restorative context (Terry O'Connell 1999; De Jong and Schout, 2013) FGCs can also be restorative, even without a specific act of reparation. As discussed above, an FGC can be a constructive experience of a family coming together and resolving a problem. Giving everyone – children and adults in need of protection alike – a voice can improve relationships between members of the family network and with professional agencies. We believe this can be considered a restorative process.

Offering a forum to discuss clients' shameful feelings with their social network is an important feature of FGCs (De Jong and Schout, 2013). De Jong and Schout (2013) suggest that a process which brings people together to solve problems could also deal with underlying issues of shame. The FGC can be considered to be a 'lubricant' which gives people a formula, a way of overcoming the shame by addressing it with others that are close to them (Metze, Kwekkeboom and Abma, 2015). Researchers in the Netherlands, who point to Braithwaite's work on the importance of shame in restorative practices, second this suggestion. Likewise, in Camden, Brown's work (2007) on shame is part of the FGC training programme (De Jong and Schout, 2013; Brown 2007).

> It was definitely a restorative FGC, making progress on repairing relationships. The fact that I speak Bengali helped. The care agency will be concentrating only on the necessary personal care now, domestic tasks such as cleaning will be managed by a rota of committed family and friends. (Feedback from an FGC coordinator; Camden Family Group Conference Service, 2015: 12)

The question of whether FGCs can repair relationships returns us to our earlier discussion about FGCs and relationship dynamics. There is some divergence of opinion on this from the research and project evaluations, some of which privilege reparative or restorative principles more than others. Is FGC a developmental process, as much of the Netherlands work argues, or is it primarily a practical planning tool? This is a crude characterisation, as most would say it is both, however projects undertaking adult FGC work may want to think about their view on this (De Jong and Schout, 2013; North Essex, Project Study, 2017; Camden Family Group Conference Service, 2015; Tew, 2015).

It has been demonstrated in this chapter that FGCs can be a forum whereby people discuss their shameful feelings and generate support to counter feelings of social isolation (De Jong and Schout, 2013; North Essex, Project Study, 2017; Camden Family Group Conference Service, 2015; Tew, 2015). It has also been acknowledged elsewhere that, for older adults who are planning care at the end of their life, relationship dynamics may be different and more complex due to their long-standing nature. This can make the FGC itself more challenging – especially when anger, shame and other difficult emotions are involved (Marsh with Kent Adult FGC Service, 2007; Camden Family Group Conference Service, 2015). Despite this, adult FGCs can still harness support and base themselves on reciprocity, but may utilise different areas and support structures. For example, if family relationships cannot be rebuilt then the community, friends and faith groups can be used instead (Marsh with Kent Adult FGC Service, 2007; Metze, Kwekkeboom and Abma, 2015; SCIE, 2013a).

Power, democracy and culture change

There is a thread of social care policy and practice that is looking outwards towards the community and the changing relationship between citizen and state (Hobbs and Alonzi, 2013; Doolan, 2012). The phrase 'participation society' has been used to describe this societal change (Doolan, 2012). The term 'co-production' – which features throughout the Care Act 2014 – is a useful concept to describe new ways of working in this changing context: '[c]o-production means delivering public services in an equal and reciprocal relationship between professionals, people using services, their families and their neighbours. Where activities are co-produced in this way, both services and neighbourhoods become far more effective agents of change' (Boyle and Harris, 2009: 9).

This context and its increasingly familiar terminology is helpful to FGCs and to strengths-based approaches more broadly. For professionals working with adults, the co-productive potential of FGC is appealing. At a workshop in Camden social workers set out their aims for the FGC as 'empowering family as decision makers, improving partnership working between family and other partners, harmonising previously fractured relationships and maintaining service users in the community for longer' (Community Care, 2013: 2).

FGCs as vehicles for achieving culture change within professional groups is often discussed in relation to, firstly, working with people and, secondly, understanding risk (Hobbs and Alonzi, 2013; Forsyth et al., 2013). The idea that FGCs can be an emblematic strength-based approach is endorsed by a National Audit Office report (2016), which states

> Although there needs to be some caution as the number of authorities involved is very small, those using family group conferencing have reported a significant cultural shift. Social workers have to think about the person's family network and the resources they can bring from an early stage, i.e. an asset-based or strengths-based approach. (National Audit Office, 2016: 16)

In the detail of FGC practice with adults it is incumbent on the referring professional, the FGC coordinator and the FGC service to consider, case by case, whether the FGC offer is a genuine offer to share power. In plain terms, is it sharing the responsibility for help and solutions? Is the agenda for FGC collaborative? Is it a genuine offer for Adults and their networks to access rights, and co-produce plans? (Ney, Stoltz and Maloney, 2011; Hobbs and Alonzi, 2013).

It has been suggested that social networks can be 'extrinsically motivated' to participate in child welfare-focused FGCs by significant threats such as losing custody of children (Ney, Stoltz and Maloney, 2011); The context and the 'state power' in the adult social care arena is different, but there may be similar 'system' factors at play. The Court of Protection can instruct an FGC offer be made and the necessity of social work intervention and care provision (whether funded by the 'family' or not) may sometimes mean that cooperation is driven more by the state than the citizen. Participants and facilitators of FGCs should be mindful of power dynamics and yet the FGC model was developed as a process which could better rebalance power differentials to include the voice of adults and families (Ney, Stoltz and Maloney, 2011; Hobbs and Alonzi, 2013).

Personalisation, wellbeing and resilience

The corollary of professional culture change is empowerment of the informal network and a change to the perception of the adult and their relationships with professionals acting for the state (De Jong and Schout, 2013; Forsyth et al., 2013). For example the FGC method shows that 'safeguarding situations can be handled in a person centred way' giving social workers, adults and family satisfactory outcomes (SCIE, 2013a: 10).

Firstly the Making Safeguarding Personal toolkit (Ogilvie and Williams, 2010) endorsed the use of FGCs. Then came the Care Act 2014, which privileges the concepts of wellbeing and an 'active citizen' and a measure of successful personalisation (Local Government Association, 2013).

FGC models can adapt to various cultures and languages, ensuring that particular cultural practices are understood and that the identity of the adult is expressed in the process (Camden Family Group Conference Service, 2015; Marsh with Kent Adult FGC Service, 2007). Visible details like venue, food and integrating religious practices can help the informal engagement with the FGC process (Ogilvie and Williams, 2010).

There is evidence to suggest that FGCs can enhance participants' sense of wellbeing, with significant results from Malmberg-Heimonen's (2011) study which found that life satisfaction improved in the intervention group, while mental distress and the measure for anxiety and depression decreased significantly. Positive trends in the research were found for emotional social support and social resources (Malmberg-Heimonen, 2011).

Tew (2015) has highlighted the work in North Essex which also found an improvement in participants' sense of wellbeing. De Jong and Schout (2013) also make similar claims and these examples demonstrate that the impact of FGC can extend beyond the practicalities of the plan made at the FGC itself. Indeed, the therapeutic nature of FGCs has often been discussed (Holland and Rivett, 2008). While some argue that therapy is beyond the scope of an FGC, there is evidence that through the practical focus of FGCs, the relational nature of the process, its symbolism and emotional resonance can make a positive and therapeutic difference to those involved (Tew, 2015; Hobbs and Alonzi, 2013).

In Camden, six-month follow-up with participants found that eight in ten people felt more in control following their FGC and better able to cope with future problems. This research substantiated the view that a timely family group conference process can have a positive impact on both individual wellbeing and family resilience (Malmberg-Heinomen 2011; Camden Family Group Conference Service, 2015; SCIE, 2012a; Hobbs and Alonzi, 2013).

Saving resources

The evaluations highlighted here suggest that FGCs have the potential to save on the costs of care packages (Camden Family Group Conference Service, 2015; Marsh with Kent Adult FGC Service, 2007). This is particularly clear where service users and families feel that FGCs enable them to coproduce a plan themselves that is supported by statutory services (Camden Family Group Conference Service, 2015; Marsh with Kent Adult FGC Service, 2007). Savings in care and support package costs can be calculated in a number of ways. A protection plan that is supported by families and the adult's wider network can avert the need for more expensive interventions such as a move to extra care: sheltered, supported living or residential care. Using an FGC early can help prevent the escalation of issues and the need for multi-agency interview. Moreover, in cases where the FGC is successful in producing sustainable plans, there is likely to be a reduction in demand for professional support over time (Daybreak 2010; Marsh with Kent Adult FGC Service, 2007).

Marsh's evaluation of FGCs in adult services in Kent (Marsh with Kent Adult FGC Service, 2007) found that overall FGCs reduced the budget expenditure of adult services by around £7,000 on average per FGC. Marsh suggested that a £7,000 saving per FGC could be achievable more widely, especially when the FGC is used to support adults and families whose needs are complex. The Greenwich and Central Bedfordshire SCIE studies (2013a and 2013b) each describe ways in which FGCs postponed or averted the need to fund intensive home care or residential care with a range of weekly recurring costs between £100 and over £1,000. Given that supported living or residential care packages for adults with complex needs can exceed £1,000 per week, and in some cases are significantly higher, an FGC which averts or delays the use of intensive intervention has significant saving potential (SCIE 2013a).

Recommendations for setting up an adult FGC service

If you are reading this and are involved in or thinking about using the FGC model with adults then you may find this list of recommendations and points to consider helpful.

- Use local FGC experience, but remember the differences distinguishing adult FGCs as compared with child FGCs.
- Promote the FGC and prioritise creating an identity for the service.
- Connect FGCs to other current schools of thought, for example wellbeing and strength-based approaches.
- Utilise your FGC champions and people in your organisation who are keen.
- Develop interest in FGCs within the service and aim for a whole service commitment to FGCs.
- Emphasise that the service is about decision making and is not a therapy or mediation service (although the process may produce some of these outcomes).
- Conduct all practice with transparency and ensure families understand the 'bottom line'.
- Consider using FGCs for 'best interest' meetings.
- Make good links between the FGC service and local advocacy services.
- Avoid using FGCs only to address entrenched relationship issues (although you can take some of these cases).
- Ensure that coordinators stress that private family time is a fundamental element of the process.
- Emphasise collaborative work between child protection and adults.
- Ensure all coordinators crossing over into adult work from child welfare cases are given specific training and close shadowing opportunities.
- Coordinators should know the history of adults, the policy context and the organisational structures within which they carry out FGCs; for example the differences between Health and Social care.

Focus on four current services: project studies

We will now use case examples of four adult FGC Services to demonstrate adult FGCs in practice. Each service has written their own summary of their service and provided an individual, anonymised case study to exemplify practice.

London borough of Camden

Camden has held 60 adult FGCs in the last three years and is looking to increase the number of FGCs it facilitates as part of its transformation to strengths-based social work. FGC referrals have been made in Camden for young adults with learning disabilities and for older people with physical disabilities or dementia. Some of the issues the FGCs have addressed are: supporting carers, dementia care and safeguarding issues including physical abuse, financial abuse and neglect.

FGCs have enabled individuals and their informal networks to plan care and support adults to live safely in the community, as well as mitigate the impact of self-neglect and prevent abuse. They have been shown to be effective where there may be disputes or relationship difficulties between family members or between family and professionals, preventing the need for (and cost of) Court of Protection and legal involvement. Our pool of independent FGC coordinators, speaking 14 different community languages have been delivering the work in partnership with social workers. The following results have been noted:

- participants saying they felt 'more in control' following their FGC;
- social workers and health professionals achieving a higher level of direct communication with 'hard to reach' family members;
- family members taking on more responsibility in decision making and support for their family member;
- repaired relationships within families;
- adult service users supported to make decisions about their own care using advocacy;
- sustainable care plans with a range of elements that work together to support independence;
- relieving 'bombardment' of professionals by giving family members a process to be heard and make changes.

The Begum family

Mrs Begum was in her 80s and had lived in the United Kingdom for the past 15 years with her two sons. Neither Mrs Begum nor her sons are able to speak English.

There were safeguarding concerns about Mrs Begum's care and her day-to-day finances. Mrs Begum has outside carers for personal care only, however the family were instructing the carer to carry out other tasks. Mrs Begum and her sons have also been threatened with eviction because of disputes with neighbours and the condition of the house.

An FGC coordinator who speaks Bengali agreed to organise the family group conference – it needed sensitive facilitation and an understanding of the cultural dynamics involved.

The FGC took place with useful discussions and some positive outcomes.

A key family member was identified to help Mrs Begum liaise with the social worker and the care agency as well as support with managing finances. The wider family were able, with Mrs Begum, to work out a schedule so that she is less isolated and so that tasks in the home, such as cooking, cleaning and hoovering can be covered by them, with outside carers focusing on personal care. Respite visits to family outside London were agreed.

Family conflict was addressed; the family member who had, by common consent, been using Mrs Begum's money inappropriately apologised. The family felt that the meeting had given them an understanding of the safeguarding concerns and Mrs Begum was pleased they all agreed to work together to try and save their tenancy.

Adult Mental Health Family Group Conferencing, Essex (MHFGC)

Our project was established in 1999 as a result of the number of parents and carers under children's FGCs experiencing mental health disorders or substance misuse (91 out of 155 in March to February 2000).

The need to identify and address the parents' or carers' own needs was recognised and conclusions made that FGCs would benefit all people experiencing mental health difficulties. The project currently employs 2.5 clinicians, 0.5 admin and two independent coordinators.

The service manages around 165 FGC referrals each year and carries out around 80 FGC meetings and 220 review FGCs. Many FGCs will identify and address safeguarding concerns.

Research undertaken by Mutter et al. (2002) found that two key elements were present in mental health FGCs, the alteration of family members' perspectives on the nature of the mental health condition and the generation of family support for the person who is the subject of the FGC.

Further research by Tew (2015) identified key elements of FGCs addressing issues associated with mental ill health found that FGCs:

- bring about true partnership between family, service user and professional systems;
- bring together networks that have been fragmented, overstressed or confused;
- enable recovery on the service user's terms;
- result in decreased dependence on services, and increased social participation in the wider community, alternatively increasing engagement with services;
- result in decreased stress on the family network;
- bring about increased understanding between the whole system of strengths and weaknesses and needs;
- help to truly identify carers' needs and include those in plans and decisions.

B and his family

A young adult male (B) using secondary mental health services for suicidal ideation and extreme anxiety was referred. He chose to address the following issues at his FGC:

- to understand the impact of my mental health difficulties and the effect on myself and family;
- for my family to allow me more freedom of choice;
- to re-engage in hobbies;
- begin to manage my anxieties and social confidence;
- find a way to get into work.

Preparatory meetings with family and professionals were held in which it was clear that the identified family network were concerned regarding suicide risk. They were angry with services, who they perceived as not being 'very helpful'.

Professionals identified difficulty engaging the client or family to work on treatment options.

During the FGC, initially the family found it hard to contain their emotions. They were encouraged to reflect on this and were offered some support from the independent coordinator with distress management. At first, B's dad did not engage with the process and positive discussion around his role and the impact on him was encouraged. The care coordinator shared her understanding of recovery and the family's role in this and they were supported to discuss suicide and management of risk.

Following the FGC, B began to join in family activities, work in the family business, engage with services, and reduce his online gaming. He began fishing with his dad. His mum began to manage stress by gardening and his sister and his mum started spending quality time together. B found that his family were letting him make decisions and giving him space in the home.

The care coordinator found observing the client's role and communication in the family, alongside the plan, helped her work with the client more effectively. She felt the family felt more positive and were effective in their support. The family's focus changed from feeling a lack of help from professionals to developing an awareness of the client's role in engaging with support and how to encourage him with this.

Following the FGC, reported changes are that B is more confident, less anxious, proactive in seeking support and accepting challenges. He is able to go out alone and is more involved in family life.

Overall the process helped bring the family together, become aware of their strengths, skills and resources as a family and enabled them to discuss fears about B's mental health, address these and agree realistic solutions to enhance the recovery process.

Midlothian and Dumfries and Galloway, Kalm Solutions

We currently work with two local authorities, Midlothian and Dumfries and Galloway. We have been working with Midlothian from the outset. Their criterion for consideration is adults with a diagnosis of dementia. We have been working for Dumfries and Galloway since 2014 with the wider criterion of vulnerable adults.

The service in Midlothian was evaluated by Queen Margaret University, Edinburgh and they concluded that FGCs are a valuable way of decision making for care and support for people with dementia, involving service users, family members and key professionals. FGCs ensure that families have time and space to come together with the common objective of considering and planning the care needs of their loved one experiencing dementia. The evaluation also highlighted that as a result of an FGC:

- a person with dementia benefits from support provided by family members rather than paid carers;
- a person with dementia benefits from needs-led input from services focused on quality of life rather than reactive symptoms management;
- professionals have the opportunity to base their intervention on comprehensive information about the individual's needs and circumstances;
- more open and trusting relationships can be developed between service users, their families and the professionals involved;
- changes can be seen in professional beliefs, values and attitudes towards partnership working with families, and in service users' perceptions of and attitudes to health and social care services.

Actual costs savings for local authority services averaged almost £5k per FGC (Forsyth et al., 2013).

Nettie and her family

Nettie is in her 90s and lives in sheltered accommodation. Nettie has a large family and has care workers attending her home four times every day.

The referral was made as Nettie is very frail but is keen to maintain her independence and live in her own home.

When the initial visit was made the family was more concerned about money that was going missing on a regular basis and they felt someone was playing on Nettie's good nature and poor memory.

This concern was passed onto social care services who agreed for the Family Group Meeting to go ahead before they considered Adult Protection Procedures. A social worker, Nettie and nine family members (including the relative who had been stealing to fund a gambling habit), attended the meeting. Due to the 'future focused' and 'no blame' culture of the meeting the family were able to identify a plan that ensured Nettie was protected and her money safe. Nettie's son and daughter-in-law had power of attorney and it was agreed no money would be kept in the house. The family would pay for items and Nettie's son would refund them. Nettie was given money on a Tuesday to pay for a club she attended.

This worked well and as a result Adult Protection Procedures were not required. When the family were contacted to discuss a review, the situation was so settled a review was not required. Furthermore, so much money had been saved for Nettie that she was able to buy a new bed, curtains and new clothes.

Daybreak

When Daybreak was awarded a three-year grant in 2007 to use FGCs to address the abuse of older people, the team exhibited a pioneering spirit in exploring whether this way of working could be equally effective in this context as it has been with children and their extended families. Although we were able to draw on our work with FGCs and domestic violence since 2001, our learning curve in the first few months was almost perpendicular. Among the many lessons learnt, we quickly needed to appreciate the different practicalities of working with referred adults often in their 80s, as well as the importance of ensuring that the adult who was at the centre of the process was empowered to control the pace and context of the FGC. We also learnt that advocacy was almost always required by these participants. In the early days and subsequently, we found that referrals were often at the highest threshold of safeguarding, sometimes in life-threatening situations. The outstanding success of these three years led to Hampshire County Council taking on the funding of the service after 2010, and to expand its focus to include an adult in need of safeguarding of any age. The amount of annual funding has reduced in the current climate, but the commitment of the council to its continuation has been consistent. The programme steering group provides accountability and guides our reflective thinking. Its remit has expanded to include the wide range of FGC work with adults that we are considering and proposing.

We try hard to empower adults who have experienced an FGC not only in their own meeting but in the wider development of the work of Daybreak. We are especially proud of one survivor of domestic violence who became a member of our Board of Trustees, to whom the CEO reports. Since 2007 we have received 239 referrals. This year we have received 15 of the 18 for which we have funding for 2016/17. Our Report of 2014 to 2016 suggests costs savings resulting from FGCs (Daybreak, 2016). It includes a number of case studies to illustrate our learning of working with adults at the centre of FGC referrals.

Domestic violence in an older couple

An early referral involved an older couple whose relationship had involved domestic violence for many years. It was now escalating and becoming much more dangerous with the increasing frailty of the male victim. It was felt that he must leave the home if his safety was to be ensured. The perpetrator was initially reluctant to acknowledge the problem, but eventually agreed to participate in the meeting. The process was a revelatory experience for her, and she finally appreciated what was happening, its seriousness and the necessity for change. This was supported by their children, and the plan for this to happen was agreed and successfully implemented. The couple were able to remain safely together.

Drawing on our experience of work with vulnerable adults, Daybreak has developed a training programme for coordinators to give them the additional knowledge and skills necessary, and we are developing a social franchise which includes a package of training, consultation, and the tools to introduce this work.

Conclusion

What is the future for FGCs with adults in need? We spoke at the beginning of this chapter about the increase in projects in recent years and likened it to a slow train picking up speed. Can that rate of progress continue? We suggest that the challenges facing adult FGC development are less immense than those faced by children and family sector proponents ten and twenty years ago. After all, there is confidence in the children's work model. Moreover, there are examples of good experience, developed learning opportunities and success stories from the pockets of now-established adult work. Especially relevant to this train picking up speed is the evidence that FGCs are economically effective.

The development of complementary legislation and government agency support for FGCs with children was slow. For FGCs with adults, professional guidance and legislation has been supportive from the beginning. Advocates of FGCs welcome guidance and the introduction of key concepts – such as personalisation, wellbeing, and person-centred approaches. The involvement of the SCIE and clear encouragement to use FGCs with adults in Making Safeguarding Personal (2013a) suggests that governments want FGCs in the adult social care space, but more needs to be done by local authorities to ensure that FGCs are implemented effectively.

For this train to pick up speed and for the practice of FGCs in the UK to develop, we hope to see FGCs rolled out into a wider range of adult settings, such as adult mental health, and among more populations, including offenders, prisoners and homeless people.

The foundations are in place for FGCs to become an embedded part of adult social care policy and service delivery for vulnerable adults. The messages from research are clear: FGCs offer the potential to engage families for the benefit of vulnerable adults consistent with the underlying principles of legislation and policy.

Acknowledgements

With thanks to Daybreak Family Group Conferences, Kalm solutions and Essex mental health FGC service for adults for providing information on their services and case studies of practice.

Further Reading

De Jong, G. and Schout, G. (2013) 'Breaking through marginalisation in public mental health care with Family Group Conferencing: shame as risk and protective factor', *British Journal of Social Work*, 43(7): 1439–54.

Marsh, P. with Kent Adult FGC Service (2007) *Kent adult FGC development research*, Sheffield University and Kent Adult FGC Service.

Van Pagee, R. (n.d.) *Transforming care: the new welfare state*. Available at https://www.eigen-kracht.nl/what-we-do/

THIRTEEN

Conclusion

Deanna Edwards and Kate Parkinson

This book has given an overview of FGC practice both in the UK and in other countries across the globe in both children's and adult's services. It has outlined FGC practice and offered suggestions for good practice. It has also brought together much of the research and evidence base on FGCs, their application and efficacy. A variety of authors have contributed, representing the academic community, FGC practitioners and those who have used FGC services. FGCs have been used in numerous practice areas and this book has considered their use in specific settings within children's services. This has included their use in harmful sexual behaviour, youth justice and domestic abuse. It has also outlined a growing practice body within adult services and the use of FGCs within specific adult social care specialities which include learning disabilities, mental health and older adults. This is not exhaustive, however, and there are a number of additional areas of FGC use which the book has not explored. These include an in-depth consideration of their use with pre-birth assessments, their use in tackling gangs, homelessness, forced marriage, radicalisation and their use in prisons. The decision not to include these and other specialisms was purely from a pragmatic perspective of these being new and emerging areas of practice, with little or no research base and few services in operation. While these have been omitted from the scope of this book it is recognised that they may nonetheless constitute a valuable addition to the FGC spectrum.

The authors consider that the book has provided an exploration and a recognition of FGCs as a widely researched and applied area of social work practice which offers a culturally competent approach to working in a strengths-based manner with families. It has provided the reader with an overview of a wide range of practice areas and demonstrated that FGCs constitute a versatile tool for working with families involved with social work services.

It is clear that FGCs can be located within a strengths-based approach to social work (Burford and Hudson (eds.) 2000; Ashley and Nixon (eds.) 2007; Barnsdale and Walker, 2007; Metze, Abma and Kwekkeboom 2013) and are often linked to the concept of empowerment (Metze, Abma and Kwekkeboom 2013). In addition to this, while there is no legal mandate for FGCs in the UK other than the Justice (Northern Ireland) Act 2001, which introduced restorative conferences for young people with offending behaviour, FGCs are suggested as good practice in policy guidelines and procedures, such as the Public Law Outline (PLO, 2008). Indeed, FGCs are clearly aligned to the principles of legislation in both the fields of children's and adults social work and are an ideal approach to meeting these key principles.

FGCs are an internationally applied model originating from the 1989 Children, Young People and their Families Act in New Zealand, in response to Maori concerns about social care with Maori communities. The model is now used worldwide in over 20 countries and as such can be said to be applicable across a wide variety of cultures. It is also used in the UK with a range of service user groups including projects specifically targeting BME families and travelling communities (Barn, Das and Sawyer, 2009; Barn and Das, 2016; Haresnape, 2009; O'Shaughnessy, Fatimilehin and Collins, 2010). As FGCs are family-led it could be argued that, they are by nature culturally competent. Worship and cultural traditions can be incorporated into the FGC. The meeting can take place at a time and place to suit families and families can articulate their needs and wishes in terms of the language of the meeting, the venue and food served. Families will create their own invitation lists and to an extent can influence the agenda of the meeting.

As FGCs have grown in the UK so have calls for a process of accreditation, both of services and individual coordinators. This process has been supported by the national network of FGC services facilitated by Family Rights Group and a range of FGC qualifications for co-ordinators now exist. In addition to this, there has been a drive, supported by the Department for Education, to accredit services (Brown, 2013). It is important though to note here that accreditation is currently a voluntary process for both coordinators and services. There is no requirement to date to be either an accredited service or for coordinators to have a qualification in FGCs. As FGCs continue to grow this issue may become more pertinent.

Marsh (2009) argued that FGCs have been more widely researched than any other area of social work practice. As previous chapters have suggested, however, research has largely been short term and small in scale. As a result, several commentators suggest that longer-term, comparative studies are needed in order to create a robust evidence base for FGCs (Crampton, 2007; Fox, 2008; Frost, Abram and Burgess, 2014a,b.) It is recognised that such research is difficult, however, when working with potentially vulnerable families. Furthermore, while there is no doubt that the research generally concludes that family members who participate in FGCs are satisfied with the process, it must also be noted that those who participate in research may be those who are more positive about the process and that FGC services may be guilty of selection bias. Therefore, FGC research may also need to engage those who may not have benefited from their FGC, those who have been critical of the process and those who did not wish to have a FGC.

While FGCs are now becoming mainstream in children's social care services and are an emerging area in adult services, practice may need to guard against some pitfalls which could potentially impact on their application. With local authorities facing increasing austerity measures, FGC budgets in some areas have already been reduced and there is a danger that there will be further reductions in the future. Services are therefore at risk of being 'watered down'. Pressure to reduce staff costs may lead to services capping the number of hours taken to convene a FGC. Furthermore, budgets for food and refreshments, for transport to enable family members to attend and other essentials such as advocates that give FGCs a distinctive ability to engage families in a meaningful way may also be affected. While these may seem a realistic way of cutting costs, effective preparation and enabling families to attend their FGC with support is key to the success of the process. FGCs have consistently evidenced an ability to reduce local authority costs by reducing the need for public law proceedings and local authority care. Therefore, reducing the efficacy of the model by depriving services of resources may prove to be counterproductive (Coventry Council, 2013; Family Rights Group, 2010; Morris, 2007, Sawyer and Lohrbach, 2008; Walker, 2005).

Finally, FGC services do need to continue to work to ensure that plans made by families in their FGC are implemented. Research has suggested that in cases where family plans fail, this is largely a result of local authorities failing to provide families with resources promised to the family as part of the FGC plan (Barnsdale and Walker, 2007). Furthermore, the process will only empower families if plans are adopted by the authority as the ongoing care plan, rather than an addition to a professionally develop plan. Local authorities need to ensure that there is a sufficient mandate to enable FGC plans to be recognised as such. If local authorities do not do this, there is a danger that the FGC process becomes a tokenistic, tick box exercise.

This book has demonstrated the potential of FGCs to lead to positive outcomes for families in a diverse range of social work practice areas. The research and evidence base, while patchy, is clear on this. Policy makers, practitioners and advocates of the FGC process have a responsibility to ensure that the practice does not become marginalised by austerity measures and increasingly risk-averse practice contexts. After all FGCs not only embody the key principles of key social work legislation and policy in the UK but also the values of social work practice. Indeed, FGCs fit perfectly within the International Federation of Social Work definition of social work which states that,

> Social work is a practice-based profession and an academic discipline that promotes social change and development, social cohesion, and the empowerment and liberation of people. Principles of social justice, human rights, collective responsibility and respect for diversities are central to social work. (International Federation of Social Work, 2014)

The principles of FGCs are clearly aligned to this definition and the model provides the opportunity for local authorities to become increasingly reflective of this holistic approach to social work practice.

References

Adams, R. (2008) (4th edn) *Empowerment, participation and social work,* Basingstoke: Palgrave Macmillan.

Adams, P. and Chandler, S. (2004) 'Responsive regulation in child welfare: systemic challenges to mainstreaming the family group conference', *Journal of Sociology and Social Welfare,* 31(1): 93–116.

Adult FGC Network Survey (2017) *Online Survey of Adult FGC work conducted in 2017,* London: Family Rights Group.

Aertsen, I., Daems, T. and Robert, L. (eds) (2006) *Institutionalizing restorative justice,* Cullompton: Willan Publishing.

AIM (n.d.) Context, aimproject.org.uk/?page_id=121. Last accessed 10/04/2018.

Alderson, S., Westmarland, N. and Kelly, L. (2012) 'The need for accountability to, and support for, children of men on domestic violence perpetrator programmes', *Child Abuse Review,* 3: 182–93.

Anda, R.F., Butchart, A., Felitti, V.J. and Brown, D.W. (2010) 'Building a framework for global surveillance of the public health implications of adverse childhood experiences', *American Journal of Preventative Medicine,* 39: 93–8.

Anderson, M. and Parkinson, K. (in press) 'Balancing justice and welfare needs in Family Group Conferences for children with harmful sexual behaviour: The HSB-FGC Framework', *Journal of Child Sexual Abuse.*

Anderson, S., Bromley, C .and Given, L. (2005) *Public attitudes towards young people and youth crime in Scotland: findings from the 2004 Scottish Social Attitudes Survey,* Edinburgh: Scottish Executive.

Arney, F., McGuinness, G. and Westby, M. (2012) *Report on the implementation of family group conferences with Aboriginal families in Alice Spring,* Australia: Menzies School of Health Research.

Ashley, C. (ed.) (2006) *The family group conference toolkit: a practical guide for setting up and running an FGC service,* Department for Education and Skills, the Welsh Assembly Government and Family Rights Group.

Ashley, C. (ed.) (2011) *Working with risky fathers: fathers matter volume 3: research finding on working with domestically abusive fathers and their involvement with children's social care services,* London: Family Rights Group.

Ashley, C. and Nixon, P. (eds) (2007) *Family group conferences: where next? Policies and practices for the future,* London: Family Rights Group.

Ashley, C., Hilton, L., Horan, H. and Wiffin, J. (2006) *The family group conference toolkit*, London: Department for Education and Skills; Cardiff: The Welsh assembly and London: Family Rights Group.

Asscher, K., Dijkstra, S., Stams, G., Dekovic, M. and Creamers, H. (2014) 'Family group conferencing in youth care: characteristics of the decision making model, implementation and effectiveness of Family Group (FG) plans', *BMC Public Health*, 14: 154.

Audit commission (1996) *Misspent youth: young people and crime*, London: Audit commission, http://webarchive.nationalarchives.gov.uk/20091009065536/audit-commission.gov.uk/products/national-report/7c38f5a0-c744-4362-a6c6-90a12d52258d/archive_misyth98.pdf.

Axford, C. (2007) 'Families' experiences' in C. Ashley and P. Nixon (eds) *Family group conferences: where next? Policies and practices for the future*, London: Family Rights Group, pp 97–112.

Back, C., Gustafsson, P.A., Larsson, I. B., and Berterö, C. (2011) 'Managing the legal proceedings: an interpretative phenomenological analysis of sexually abused children's experience with the legal process', *Child Abuse and Neglect*, 35: 50–7.

Backworth, D. (2015) *Social work, poverty and social exclusion*, Milton Keynes: Open University Press.

Bagshaw, D., Brown, T., Wendt, S., Campbell, A., McInnes, E., Tinning, B., Batagol, B., Sifris, A., Tyson, D., Baker, J. and Fernandez Arias, P. (2011) 'The effect of family violence on post-separation parenting arrangements: the experiences and views of children and adults from families who separated post-1995 and post-2006', *Family Matters*, 86: 49–61.

Barn, R. and Das, C. (2016) 'Family group conferences and cultural competence in social work', *British Journal of Social Work*, 46(4): 942–59.

Barn, R., Das, C. and Sawyer, A. (2009) *Family group conferences and Black Minority Ethnic families: a study of two community-based organisations in London*, London: Family Rights Group/Royal Holloway University of London.

Barnardos, Family Rights Group and NCH (2002) *Family group conferences: principles and practice guidance*, London: Barnardos, FRG and NCH.

Barnsdale, L. and Walker, M. (2007) *Examining the use and impact of family group conferencing*, Stirling: Social Work Research Centre, University of Stirling.

Barringer, A., Hunter, B.A., Salina, D.D. and Jason, L.A., (2016) 'Empowerment and social support: implications for practice and programming among minority women with substance abuse and criminal justice histories', *The Journal of Behavioural Health Services and Research*, 44(1): 75–88.

Barter, C., McCarry, M. Berridge, D. and Evans, K. (2009) *Partner exploitation and violence in teenage intimate relationships: executive summary*, London: NSPCC.

BASW (2012) *Voices from the frontline: real comments from real social workers who responded to BASW's survey 'The State of Social Work'*, British Association of Social Workers.

Baynes, P. and Holland, S. (2012) 'Social work with violent men: a child protection file study in an English local authority', *Child Abuse Review*, 21(1): 53–65.

Beckett, R. (2006) 'Risk prediction, decision making and evaluation of adolescent sexual abusers', in M. Erooga and H. Masson (eds), *Children and young people who sexually abuse others: current developments and practice responses*, 2nd edn, London and New York: Routledge, pp 215–33.

Bell, M. and Wilson, K. (2006) 'Children's views of family group conferences', *British Journal of Social Work*, 36(4): 671–81.

Berzin, S.C., Cohen, E., Thomas, K. and Dawson, W.C. (2008) 'Does family group decision making affect child welfare outcomes? Findings from a randomized control study', *Child Welfare*, 87(4): 35–54.

Bhui, K., Stansfeld, S., Hull, S., Priebe, S., Mole, F. and Feder, G. (2003) 'Ethnic variations in pathways to and use of specialist mental health services in the UK', *The British Journal of Psychiatry*, 182(2): 105–16.

Blackburn, S. (2008) *Joint inspection of youth offending teams in England and Wales: Report on Leeds Youth Offending Service*, London: HM Inspectorate of Probation.

Blacklock, N. and Phillips, R. (2015) 'Reshaping the child protection response to domestic violence through collaborative working', in N. Stanley and C. Humphreys (eds) *Domestic violence and protecting children: new thinking and approaches*, London: Jessica Kingsley Publishers, 196–212.

Blythe, B., Heffernan, K. and Walters, B. (2010) 'Best practices for developing child protection workers' skills: domestic violence, substance abuse, and mental health training', *Revista de Asistenta Sociala*, 9(2): 51–64.

Bolitho, J. (2015) 'Putting justice needs first: a case study of best practice in restorative justice', *Restorative Justice: An International Journal*, 3(2): 256–81.

Bourdieu, P. (1977) *Outline of a theory of practice*, Cambridge: Cambridge University Press.

Boyle, D. and Harris, M. (2009) *The challenge of co-production: how equal partnerships between professionals and the public are crucial to improving public services*, London: Nesta.

Brady, B. (2006) *Facilitating family decision-making: a study of the family welfare conference service in the HSE western area (Galway, Mayo and Roscommon)*, Dublin: Health Service Executive, and Galway: National University of Ireland, Galway

Brady, B. and Miller, M. (2009) *Barnardos family welfare conference project, South Tipperary: evaluation report*, The Child and Family Research Unit, NUI Galway.

Bramley, G. and Fitzpatrick, S. (2015) *Hard edges: mapping severe and multiple disadvantage*, Lankelly Chase Foundation.

Branfield, F. and Beresford, P. (2006) *Making user involvement work: supporting service user networking and knowledge*, London: Joseph Rowntree Foundation.

Braithwaite, J. (1989) *Crime, shame and reintegration*, New York, NY: Cambridge University Press.

Braithwaite, J. (2016) *Restorative justice and responsive regulation: the question of evidence*, Regnet Australian National University: Regnet Research Papers.

Braithwaite, J. and Mugford, S. (1994) 'Conditions of successful reintegration ceremonies', *British Journal of Criminology*, 34(2): 139–71.

Brandon, M., Belderson, P., Warren, C., Howe, D., Gardner, R., Dodsworth, J. and Black, J. (2008) *Analysing child deaths and serious injury through abuse and neglect: what can we learn? A biennial analysis of serious case reviews 2003–2005*, London: Department for Children Schools and Families.

Brandon, M., Sidebotham, P., Bailey, S., Belderson, P., Hawley, C., Ellis, C. and Megson, M. (2011) *New learning from serious case reviews: a two year report for 2009–2011*, Warwick: Centre for Research on the Child and Family in the School of Social Work and Psychology, University of East Anglia and Health Sciences Research Institute, Warwick Medical School, University of Warwick.

Braye, S. and Preston-Shoot, M. (2011) (7th edn) *Empowering practice in social care*, Milton Keynes: Open University Press.

Brayne, H., Carr, H. and Goosey, D.C. (2013) *Law for social workers*, Oxford: Open University Press.

Brodsky, A.E. and Cattaneo, L.B. (2013) 'A transconceptual model of empowerment and resilience: divergence, convergence and interactions in kindred community concepts', *American Journal of Community Psychology*, 52(3–4): 333–46.

Bronfenbrenner, U. (1979) *The ecology of human development: experiments by nature and design*, Cambridge MA: Harvard University Press.

Brown, B. (2007) 'Shame and Empathy', Youtube: https://www.youtube.com/watch?v=qQiFfA7KfF0.

Brown, L. (2003) 'Mainstream or margin? The current use of family group conferences in child welfare practice in the UK', *Child and Family Social Work*, (8): 331–40.

Brown, L. (2013) *Development and trial of an accreditation framework for Family Group Conference services*, London: Family Rights Group.

Brown, L. and Walter, T. (2014) 'Towards a social model of end-of-life care', *British Journal of Social Work*, 44(8): 2375–90.

Brown, D.W., Riley, L., Butchart, A., Meddings, D.R., Kann, L. and Phinney Harvey, A. (2009) 'Exposure to physical and sexual violence and adverse health behaviours in African children: results from the Global School-based Student Health Survey', *Bulletin of the World Health Organization*, 87(6): 447–55.

Browne Olson, K. (2009) 'Family group conferencing and child protection mediation: essential tools for prioritizing family engagement in child welfare cases', *Family Court Review*, 47(1): 53–68.

Bunn, A. (2013) *Signs of safety in England: An NSPCC commissioned report on the signs of safety model in child protection*, https://www.nspcc.org.uk/globalassets/documents/research-reports/signs-safety-england.pdf. Last accessed 10/04/2018.

Burford, G. and Hudson, J. (eds) (2000) *Family group conferencing: new directions in community-centred child and family practice*, New York: Aldine de Gruyter.

Bywaters, P., Bunting, L., Davidson, G., Hanratty, J., Mason, W., McCartan, C. and Steils, N. (2016) *The relationship between poverty, child abuse and neglect: an evidence review*, York: Joseph Rowntree Foundation.

CAADA (2012) *CAADA Insights 1: 'A place of greater safety'*, Bristol: CAADA.

CAADA (2014) *In plain sight: effective help for children exposed to domestic abuse*, Bristol: CAADA.

Calder, M.C. (ed.) (2002) *Young people who sexually abuse – building the evidence base for your practice*, Lyme Regis: Russell House Publishing.

Criminal Justice and Courts Bill: Referral orders. https://www.gov.uk/government/uploads/system/uploads/attachment_data/file/322209/fact-sheet-youth-referral-orders.pdf. Caffaro, J. and Conn-Caffaro, A. (1998). *Sibling abuse trauma: Assessment and intervention strategies for children, families and adults,* New York: The Hawthorn Maltreatment and Trauma Press.

Caffaro, J.V. (2014) *Sibling abuse trauma: assessment and intervention strategies for children, families, and adults,* East Sussex: Routledge.

Cambridge Dictionary, https://dictionary.cambridge.org/dictionary/english/marginalize?q=marginalisation

Camden Family Group Conference Service (2015) *Evaluation of adult FGC work,* (unpublished).

Cameron M. (2006) *Alternate dispute resolution: Aboriginal models and practices, literature review,* Vancouver, British Columbia: Ministry of Children and Family Development.

Campbell, K.A. and Borgeson, J. (2016) *A call for radical change in child protection practice: unleashing the restorative power of relationship by authentically engaging the extended family, community and tribe,* http://familyfinding.org/assets/files/A-Call-for-Radical-Change-in-Child-Protection-Practice-1.pdf

Campbell, C., Devlin, R., O'Mahony, D., Doak, J., Jackson, J., Corrigan, T., and McEvoy, K. (2005) *Evaluation of the Northern Ireland youth conference service,* Belfast: Northern Ireland Office.

Care Act (2014) http://www.legislation.gov.uk/ukpga/2014/23/contents/enacted

Cashmore, J. (2012) 'The link between child maltreatment and adolescent offending: systems neglect of adolescents', *Family Matters,* 89: 31–41.

Cawson, P. (2002) *Child maltreatment in the family: the experience of a national sample of young people,* London: NSPCC.

Center for Social Services Research (2004) 'The California Title IV-E Child Welfare Waiver demonstration study evaluation: final report', in D. Crampton (2007) 'Research review: family group decision making: a promising practice in need of more programme theory and research', *Child and Family Social Work,* 12: 202–9.

Chaffin, M. (2008), 'Our minds are made up – don't confuse us with the facts: commentary on policies concerning children with sexual behavior problems and juvenile sex offenders', *Child Maltreatment,* 13: 110–21.

Chand, A. (2008) 'Every child matters? A critical review of child welfare reforms in the context of minority ethnic children and families', *Child Abuse Review,* 17: 6–22.

Chandler, S.M. and Giovannucci, M. (2004) 'Family group conferences, transforming traditional child welfare policy and practice', *Family Court Review: An Inter-disciplinary Journal*, 42(2): 216–31.

Chapman, T., Gellin, M., Aertsen, I. and Anderson, M. (2015a) *Protecting rights, restoring respect and strengthening relationships: A European model for restorative justice with children and young people*, Brussels: International Juvenile Justice Observatory.

Chapman, T., Gellin, M. and Anderson, M. (2015b) *Toolkit for professionals: Implementing a European model for restorative justice with children and young people*, Brussels: International Juvenile Justice Observatory.

Chen, J., Dunne, M.P. and Han, P. (2004) 'Child sexual abuse in China: a study of adolescents in four provinces', *Child Abuse and Neglect: The International Journal*, 28(11): 1171–86.

Cheon, A. and Regehr, C. (2007) 'Restorative justice models in cases of intimate partner violence: reviewing the evidence', *Victims and Offenders*, 1(4): 1–35.

Child, Youth and Family (2012) *Family recommendations on improving family group conferences to achieve better outcomes for New Zealand's most vulnerable children*, New Zealand: Ministry of Social Development.

Children 1st (2007) *Ask the family: national standards to support family-led decision making and family group conferences (FGC) in Scotland*, Edinburgh Children First.

Children 1st (n.d.) 'Family group conferencing: FAQs'.

Children Act, The, (1989), London: HMSO, https://www.legislation.gov.uk/ukpga/1989/41/contents. Last accessed 10/04/2018.

Children Act (2001), Department of Children and Youth Affairs Northern Ireland, www.dcya.gov.ie/docs/The_Children_Act_2001/166.htm. Last accessed 28/02/18.

Children and Families Act (2014), http://www.frg.org.uk/fgcsquotes-from-official-documents

Children's Commissioner (2010) *The Children's Commissioner for England's report on: family perspectives on safeguarding and on relationships with children's services*, London Office of the Children's Commissioner, http://dera.ioe.ac.uk/506/1/force_download.php%3Ffp%3D%252Fclient_assets%252Fcp%252Fpublication%252F405%252FFamily_perspectives_on_safeguarding.pdf.

Children's Commissioner for England (2015) *Protecting children from harm: a critical assessment of child sexual abuse in the family network in England and priorities for action*, London: Children's Commissioner.

The Children (Northern Ireland) Order (1995), www.legislation.gov.uk/nisi/1995/775/contents/made. Last accessed 10/04/2018.

Children, Young Persons and their Families Act (1989), New Zealand, www.legislation.govt.nz/act/public/1989/0024/112.0/DLM147088. html. Last accessed 28/02/18.

The Children (Scotland) Act (1995) www.legislation.gov.uk/ukpga/1995/36/contents

Christens, B.D. (2011) 'Toward relational empowerment', *American Journal of Community Psychology*, 50(1-2): 114–28.

Christman, J. (2004) 'Relational autonomy, liberal individualism and the social constitution of selves', *Philosophical Studies*, 117(1–2): 143–64.

Clark, H. (2010) 'What is the justice system willing to offer? Understanding sexual assault victim/survivors' criminal justice needs', *Family Matters*, 85: 28–37.

Clarke, P. and Wydall, S. (2015) 'From "rights to action": Practitioners perceptions of the needs of children experiencing domestic violence', *Child and Family Social Work*, 20: 181–190.

Cleaver, H., Nicholson, D., Tarr, S. and Cleaver, D. (2007) *Child protection, domestic violence and parental substance misuse: family experiences and effective practices*, London: Jessica Kingsley Publishers.

Coker, D. (2006) 'Restorative justice, Navajo peacemaking and domestic violence', *Theoretical Criminology*, 10(1): 67–85.

Collins Dictionary, https://www.collinsdictionary.com/dictionary/english/marginalize

Community Care (2013) 'Helping social workers resolve intractable adult safeguarding cases', www.communitycare.co.uk/2013/06/06/helping-social-workers-resolve-intractable-adult-safeguarding-cases/

Connolly, M. (1994) 'An Act of empowerment: the Children, Young Persons and their Families Act, (1989)', *British Journal of Social Work*, 24: 87–100.

Connolly, M. (2004) *Child protection and family welfare: statutory responses to children at risk*. Christchurch: Te Awatea Press.

Connolly, M. (2006) 'Up front and personal: confronting dynamics in the family group conference', *Family Process*, 45(3): 345–7.

Connolly, M. and Masson, J. (2014) 'Private and public voices: does family group conferencing privilege the voice of children and families in child welfare?' *Journal of Social Welfare and Family Law*, 36(4): 403–14.

Connolly, M. and Morris, K. (2004) *Understanding child and family welfare: Statutory responses to children at risk*, Gordonsville, VA: Palgrave Macmillan.

Connolly, M. and Morris, K. (2011) *Understanding child and family welfare: Statutory responses to children at risk,* Gordonsville, VA: Palgrave Macmillan.

Connolly, M. and Smith, R. (2010) 'Reforming child welfare: an integrated approach', *Child Welfare,* 89(3): 9–31.

Cooper, J. (2014) '"I think I've found my spiritual home": from the private sector and Ofsted to the social care director's chair': http://www.communitycare.co.uk/2014/01/06/think-ive-found-spiritual-home-private-sector-ofsted-social-care-directors-chair/

Cossins, A. (2008) 'Restorative justice and child sex offences: theory and practice', *British Journal of Criminology,* 48: 359–78.

Cottam, H. (2011) 'Relational Welfare', *Soundings,* 48: 134–44.

Coulshed, V. and Orme, J. (2012) (5th edn) *Social work practice,* Basingstoke: Palgrave.

Council of Social Work Education, (2008) *Educational policy and accreditation standards,* http://www.cswe.org/File.aspx?id=13780 (http://www.cswe.org/File.aspx?id=13780)

Coventry Council (2013) *Family group conference service annual report: April 2012 to March 2013,* Children and Young People Directorate, Coventry City Council, http://democraticservices.coventry.gov.uk/documents/s13704/Appendix%20-%20Annual%20Family%20Group%20Conference%20Service%20Report.pdf.

Crampton, D. (2007) 'Research review: family group decision-making: a promising practice in need of more programme theory and research', *Child and Family Social Work,* 12(2): 202–9.

Crampton, D. and Jackson W.L. (2007) 'Family group decision making and disproportionality in foster care: a case study', *Child Welfare,* 86(3): 51–69.

Crea, T. and Berzin, S. (2009) 'Family involvement in child welfare decision-making: strategies and research on inclusive practices', *Journal of Public Child Welfare,* 3(3): 305–27.

Criminal Justice Joint Inspection (2011) Core case inspection of youth offending work in England and wales: report on Youth Offending Work in Leeds, www.justice.gov.uk/downloads/publications/inspectorate-reports/hmiprobation/youth-inspection-reports/core-case/leeds-cci-report-rps.pdf

Criminal Justice Joint Inspection (2012) *Facing up to offending: use of restorative justice in the criminal justice system: a joint thematic inspection by HMIC, HMI Probation, HMI Prisons and the HMCPSI.* London: Criminal Justice Joint Inspection.

Crow, G. and Marsh, P. (1997) *Family group conferences, partnership and child welfare: a research report on four pilot projects in England and Wales*, Sheffield: University of Sheffield.

Crow, G., Marsh, P. and Holton, E. (2004) 'Supporting pupils, schools and families: an evaluation of the Hampshire family group conferences in education project', *Family and Welfare Findings Series* 7, University of Sheffield and Hampshire Education Department, A4: 54.

Cunning, S. and Bartlett, D. (2006) *Family group conferencing: assessing the long-term effectiveness of an alternative approach in child protection, final report*, Ottawa, Ontario: Centre of Excellence for Child Welfare: http://cwrp.ca/node/593

Dalrymple, J. (2002) 'Family group conferences and youth advocacy: the participation of children and young people in family decision making', *European Journal of Social Work*, 5(3): 287–99.

Daly, K. (2008) 'Setting the record straight and a call for radical change: a reply to Annie Cossins on "restorative justice and child sex offences"', *British Journal of Criminology*, 48: 557–66.

Daly, K. (2012) 'Conferences and gendered violence: practices, politics, and evidence', in E. Zinsstag and I. Vanfraechem (eds), *Conferences and restorative justice: international practices and perspectives*, Oxford: Oxford University Press, pp 117–135.

Daly, K., Bouhours, B., Broadhurst, R. and Loh, N. (2013) 'Youth sex offending, recidivism and restorative justice: comparing court cases and conference cases', *Australian and New Zealand Journal of Criminology*, 46(2): 241–67.

Davy, L. (2005) *The development of restorative justice in the UK: a personal perspective*, International Institute for Restorative Practices: https://www.iirp.edu/eforum-archive/4317-the-development-of-restorative-justice-in-the-uk-a-personal-perspective

Daybreak (2010) 'Family group conferences for adults', *Evaluation Report*, 2007–2010.

Daybreak (2014) 'Daybreak FGC programme for adults', *Evaluation Report*, 2013–2014.

Daybreak (2016) 'Daybreak FGC programme for adults', *Evaluation Report*, 2014–2016, www.daybreakfgc.org.uk/adult-safeguarding.

De Jong, G. and Schout, G. (2013) 'Breaking through marginalisation in public mental health care with family group conferencing: shame as risk and protective factor', *British Journal of Social Work*, 43(7): 1439–54.

De Jong, G., Schout, G. and Abma, T. (2014) 'Prevention of involuntary admission through family group conferencing: a qualitative case study in community mental health nursing', *Journal of Advanced Nursing*, 70(11): 2651–62.

De Jong, G., Schout, G., Noma, T. (2015) 'Examining the effects of family group conferencing with randomised control trials: the golden standard', *British Journal of Social Work* 45(5): 1623–29.

Department for Children, Skills and Families (2010) *The Children Act 1989 guidance and regulations Volume 2: care planning, placement and case review*, Nottingham: DCSF Publications.

Department for Education (2011a) *Family and friends care: statutory guidance for local authorities*, London: The Stationery Office.

Department for Education (2011b) *Raising the aspirations and educational outcomes of looked after children: a data tool for local authorities*, DfE.

Department for Education (2014) *Children Act 1989: court orders, volume 1*. Statutory guidance about court orders and the roles of the police and the Children and Families Court Advisory and Support Service, London: HMSO, www.gov.uk/government/publications/children-act-1989-court-orders-2. Last accessed 28/02/18.

Department for Education (2015a) *GCSE and equivalent attainment by pupil characteristics, 2013 to 2014 (revised)*, DfE: National Statistics

Department for Education (2015b) *Special guardianship review: report on findings*, London: The Stationery Office.

Department for Education (2015c) *Working together to safeguard children, a guide to inter-agency working to safeguard and promote the welfare of children*, London: The Stationery Office.

Department for Education and Skills (2006) *Working together to safeguard children: a guide to inter-agency working to safeguard and promote the welfare of children*, London: The Stationery Office.

Department of Health (1995) *Child protection: messages from research*, London: The Stationery Office.

Department of Health (1999) *Working together to safeguard children: a guide to inter-agency working to safeguard and promote the welfare of children*, London: The Stationery Office.

Department of Health (2015) 'The Care Act and Whole-Family Approaches', www.local.gov.uk/sites/default/files/documents/care-act-and-whole-family-6e1.pdf

Department of Health, Social Services and Public Safety, Northern Ireland (2004) *Northern Ireland Child Care Law: The Rough Guide*, Belfast: Department of Health, Social Services and Public Safety.

Department of Health, Social services and Public Safety and Department of Justice (2015) *Adult Safeguarding Prevention and Protection in Partnership*, Belfast: Northern Ireland Executive, https://www.health-ni.gov.uk/sites/default/files/publications/dhssps/adult-safeguarding-policy.pdf

Department of Human Services, Hawai'i (2012) *Family connections Hawai'i: final report*, Department of Human Services, Hawai'i.

Department for Work and Pensions (2015) *Households below average income: an analysis of UK income distribution 1994/95–2013/14*, DWP: National Statistics.

Department for Work and Pensions (2017) *Households below average income: an analysis of UK income distribution 1994/95–2015/16*, DWP: National Statistics.

de Shazer, S. (1988) *Clues: investigating solutions in brief therapy*, New York: WW Norton.

Dominelli, L. (2002) *Anti-oppressive social work theory and practice*, Basingstoke: Palgrave Macmillan.

Dong, M., Anda, R.F., Shanta, R.D., Giles, W.H. and Felitti, V.J. (2003) 'The relationship of exposure to childhood sexual abuse to other forms of abuse, neglect and household dysfunction during childhood', *Child Abuse and Neglect*, 27: 625–39.

Doolan, M. (1999) 'The family group conference: 10 years on', paper presented at the *Building Strong Partnerships for Restorative Practices* conference, Burlington, Vermont, 5–7 August 1999.

Doolan, M. (2002) 'Establishing an effective mandate for family group conference', *Family Group Conference Newsletter*, London: Family Rights Group.

Doolan, M. (2007) 'Working towards an effective mandate for family group conferences', in C. Ashley and P. Nixon (eds) *Family group conferences: where next? Policies and practices for the future*, London: Family Rights Group, pp 23–36.

Doolan, M. (2012) 'Creating a participation society', keynote address at Hull Centre for Restorative Practice Annual Conference, Hull, 9 November.

Early, T.J. and GlenMaye, L.F. (2000) 'Valuing families: social work practice with families from a strengths perspective', *Social Work*, 45(2): 118–30.

Eassom, E., Giacco, D., Dirik, A. and Priebe, S. (2014) 'Implementing family involvement in the treatment of patients with psychosis: a systematic review of facilitating and hindering factors', *British Medical Journal Open*, 4: e006108.

Edgar, K. and Pickford, D. (2009) *Too Little Too Late: an independent review of unmet metal health need in Prison*, London: The Prison Reform Trust.

Edwards, D. (2007) 'Family group conferences: the picture across the United Kingdom: England', in C. Ashley and P. Nixon (eds) *Family group conferences: where next? Policies and practices for the future*, London: Family Rights Group, pp 221–8.

Edwards, D, and Parkinson, K. (2016) 'Family group conferences and safeguarding children', *Seen and Heard*, 26(3): 38–53.

Edwards, M., Tinworth, K., Burford, G. and Pennell, J. (2007) *Family Team Meeting (FTM) processes, outcome and impact evaluation phase ii report*, Englewood, CO: American Humane Association.

Edwards, R., Franklin, F. and Holland, J. (2003) *Families and social capital: exploring the issues*, London: Families and Social Capital ESRC Research Group, South Bank University.

Edwards, R., Hadfield, L., Lucey, H. and Mauthner, M. (2006) *Sibling identity and relationships: sisters and brothers*, London: Routledge.

Eigen Kracht (n.d.) What We Do, www.eigen-kracht.nl/what-we-do/. Last accessed at 10/04/2018.

Erooga, M., and Masson, H. (2006) 'Children and young people with sexually harmful or abusive behaviours: underpinning knowledge, principles, approaches and service provision', in M. Erooga and H. Masson (eds), *Children and young people who sexually abuse others: current developments and practice responses*, 2nd edn, London and New York: Routledge, pp 3–17.

Evans, C.A. (2011) 'The Public Law Outline and family group conferences in childcare practice', *Child Care in Practice*, 17(1): 3–15.

Family Group Conference Northern Ireland (2016) 'Innovation in FGC Practice', Antrim, 3 March. https://www.fgcni.org/

Family Rights Group in association with University of Birmingham (2009) *Report on the impact of the Public Law Outline on Family Group Conference Services in England and Wales*, London: Family Rights Group.

Family Rights Group (2005) 'Survey of FGC Network Projects', London: Family Rights Group.

Family Rights Group (2009) *Report on the impact of the public law outline on family group conference services in England and Wales*, London: Family Rights Group.

Family Rights Group (2010) 'What is the current state of play of FGCs in the UK?' Presentation at European Network Conference, Brighton.

Family Rights Group (2011a) 'Family group conferences in the court arena: practice guidance on the use of family group conferences for children who are in, or are on the brink of, care proceedings', London: Family Rights Group.

Family Rights Group (2011b) 'FGC practice standards', available by request, London: Family Rights Group.

Family Rights Group (2011c) 'Response to proposals for the reform of legal aid in England and Wales', London: Family Rights Group.

Family Rights Group (2012) 'Education Committee – children first: The child protection system in England. Written evidence submitted by the Family Rights Group', www.publications.parliament.uk/pa/cm201213/cmselect/cmeduc/137/137vw15.htm.

Family Rights Group (2015) 'Data on the number of FGC services in the UK', unpublished, London: Family Rights Group.

Family Rights Group (2016) 'FGC accreditation scheme for FGC projects', London: Family Rights Group, http://www.frg.org.uk/accreditation-scheme-for-family-group-conference-projects.

Family Rights Group (n.d.a) Family Group Conferences and lifelong links, https://www.frg.org.uk/involving-families/family-group-conferences/lifelong-links. Last accessed 10/04/2018.

Family Rights Group (n.d.b) Family Group Conference standards and accreditation, https://www.frg.org.uk/involving-families/family-group-conferences-fgc-standards-and-accreditation.

Family Rights Group (n.d.c) Quotes from official documents, https://www.frg.org.uk/quotes-from-official-documents. Last accessed 10/04/2018.

Family Rights Group (n.d.d) The Family Group conference process, https://www.frg.org/the-family-group-conference-process. Last accessed 10/04/2018.

Family Rights Group (n.d.e) Where and how are Family Group Conferences used, https://www.frg.org.uk/where-and-how-are-family-group-conferences-used. Last accessed 10/04/2018.

Fatimilehin, I.A. and Hassan, A. (2010) 'Working with children of African heritage: the implications of extended family systems', *Clinical Psychology Forum*, 205, January: 46–50.

Fearon, P. and Morgan, C. (2006) 'Environmental factors in schizophrenia: the role of migrant studies', *Schizophrenia Bulletin*, 32(3): 405–8.

Featherstone, B. (2003) 'Taking fathers seriously', *British Journal of Social Work*, 33(2): 239–54.

Featherstone, B. and Peckover, S. (2007) 'Letting them get away with it: fathers, domestic violence and child welfare', *Critical Social Policy*, 27(2): 181–202.

Featherstone, B., White, S. and Morris, K. (2014) *Re-imagining child protection: towards humane social work with families*, Bristol: Policy Press.

FGCs and Adults Practice Network (2017) 'Using FGCs with adults', unpublished.

FGC European Network (2014), *Scottish Report*, http://www.fgcnetwork.eu/user/file/scotland_-_scottish_repor1.pdf

Field, F. (2010) 'The foundation years: preventing poor children becoming poor adults: the report of the independent review on poverty and life chances', HM Government.

Finkelhor, D. (1980) 'Sex among siblings: a survey on prevalence, variety, and effects', *Archives of sexual behavior*, 9(3): 171–94.

Finkelhor, D., Ormrod, R., and Chaffin, M. (2009) 'Juveniles who commit sex offences against minors', Office of Juvenile Justice and Delinquency Prevention: Juvenile Justice Bulletin, December 2009, http://www.unh.edu/ccrc/pdf/CV171.pdf

Fisher, T. (2013) 'What child protection can teach adult safeguarding – and vice versa', Community Care, http://www.communitycare.co.uk/2013/06/06/what-child-protection-can-teach-adult-safeguarding-and-vice-versa/

Fisher, T. (2016) 'Family group conferencing in adult services: the model', presentation at 'Using FGCs with adults' practice exchange, https://prezi.com/lxuvgplecusm/fgc-in-adults-services-short/

Flynn, R. and Ashley, C. (2007) 'Providing family group conferences to families from Black and Minority ethnic groups: the essential context', in C. Ashley, and P. Nixon (eds) *Family group conferences: where next? Policies and practices for the future*, London: Family Rights Group, pp 37–58.

Fook, J. (2008) *Social work: a critical approach to practice*, 3rd edn, London: Sage.

Forsyth, K., Górska, S., Harrison, M., Haughey, P., Irvine, L. and Prior, S. (2013) *Family group conferencing for people with dementia: evaluation of the Midlothian pilot 2012/13*, unpublished.

Forward 4 Families (n.d.) http://forward4families.co.uk/CollDecisionMaking.html

Fox, D. (2005) *An examination of the implementation of restorative justice in Canada, and family group conferencing approaches in the UK*, Birmingham: British Association of Social Workers and Venture Press.

Fox, D. (2008) 'Family Group Conferencing and evidence-based practice: what works?' *Research, Policy and Planning*, 26(3): 157–67.

FRA (European Union Agency for Fundamental Rights) (2017) *Child-friendly justice: perspectives and experiences of children involved in judicial proceedings as victims, witnesses or parties in nine EU Member States*, Vienna: FRA.

Freymond, N. and Cameron, G. (eds) (2006) *Towards positive systems of child and family welfare*, Canada: University of Toronto Press.

Frost, N., and Elmer, S. (2008) 'An Evaluation of South Leeds family group conferences', Leeds: Leeds Metropolitan University (unpublished).

Frost, N., Abbott, S. and Race, T. (2015) *Family Support: Prevention, early intervention and early help*, London: John Wiley & Sons.

Frost, N., Abram, F., and Burgess, H. (2014a) 'Family group conferences: context, process and ways forward', *Child and Family Social Work*, 19(4): 480–90.

Frost, N., Abram, F. and Burgess, H. (2014b) 'Family group conferences: evidence, outcomes and future research,' *Child and Family Social Work*, 19(4): 501–7.

Gal, T. (2011) *Child victims and restorative justice: a needs–rights model*, Oxford: Oxford University Press.

Gal, T. (2014) 'Crime victimization and child well-being', in A. Ben-Arieh, F. Casas, I. Frones and J.E. Korbin (eds), *Handbook of child well-being*, Dordrecht: Springer, pp 2617–52.

Gal, T., and Moyal, S. (2011) 'Juvenile victims in restorative justice: findings from the reintegrative shaming experiments', *British Journal of Criminology*, 51: 1014–34.

Gambrill, E. (1994) 'What's in a name? Task-centered, empirical, and behavioral practice', *Social Service Review*, 68(4): 578–99.

George Hull Centre, The (2011) *Family group conferencing/family group decision making, co-ordinator manual for Ontario*, Ontario: FGC Provincial Resource.

Gilbert, N., Parton, N. and Skivenes, M. (eds) (2011) *Child protection systems: international trends and orientations*, Oxford: Oxford University Press.

Goodman, R. (1997) 'The strengths and difficulties questionnaire', *Journal of Child Psychology*, 38(5): 581–86.

Grauwiler, P. and Mills, L.G. (2004) 'Moving beyond the criminal justice paradigm: a radical restorative justice approach to intimate abuse', *Journal of Sociology and Social Welfare,* 31(1): 49–69.

Griffin, H. (2003) 'Evaluation of the AIM framework for the assessment of adolescents who display sexually harmful behaviour: a report for the youth justice board', Greater Manchester: Youth Justice Trust.

Guy, J., Feinstein, L. and Griffiths, A. (2014) 'Early intervention in domestic violence and abuse', London: Early Intervention Foundation, http://www.eif.org.uk/wp-content/uploads/2014/03/Early-Intervention-in-Domestic-Violence-and-Abuse-Full-Report.pdf

Gxubane, T. (2016) 'Prospects of family group conferencing with youth sex offenders and their victims in South Africa', in T. Gavrielides (ed.), *Offenders no more: an interdisciplinary restorative justice dialogue*, New York: Nova Science Publishers, pp 267–287.

Hackett, S. (2006) 'The personal and professional context to work with children and young people who have sexually abused', in M. Erooga and H. Masson (eds), *Children and young people who sexually abuse others: current developments and practice responses*, 2nd edn, London and New York: Routledge, pp 237–48.

Hackett, S. (2007) 'Just how different are they? Diversity and the treatment of young people with harmful sexual behaviours', in M.C. Calder (ed.), *Working with children and young people who sexually abuse: taking the field forward*, Lyme Regis: Russell House Publishing Limited, pp 9–22.

Hackett, S. and Masson, H. (2011) 'Recidivism, desistance and life course trajectories of young sexual abusers: an in depth follow up study 10 years on', SASS research briefing no 7, Durham: Durham University.

Hackett, S., Masson, H., Balfe, M., Phillips, J. (2013) 'Individual, family and abuse characteristics of 700 British child and adolescent sexual abusers', *Child Abuse Review*, 22: 232–45.

Hackett, S., Masson, H., Balfe, M., Phillips, J. (2015) 'Community reactions to young people who have sexually abused and their families? A shotgun blast, not a rifle shot', *Children and Society*, 29(4): 243–54.

Hampshire Constabulary (2007) *Results Analysis – The daybreak dove project*, unpublished report.

Harawitz, C. (2006) 'Theoretical perspectives: conflict theory versus ecological and family systems-driven models of practice', http://www.exit0.com/cheryl/fgc/theoreticalperspectives.pdf

Harder, L. (2013) *Evaluation of Aboriginal collaborative decision-making projects*, Vancouver: The Law Foundation of British Columbia.

Haresnape, S. (2007) 'Youth justice family group conferences', in C. Ashley and P. Nixon (eds) *Family group conferences: where next? Policies and practices for the future*, London: Family Rights Group, pp 157–192.

Haresnape, S. (2009) *The use of family group conferences by Black Minority Ethnic communities*, London: Family Rights Group.

Harris, N. (2008) *Family group conferencing in Australia 15 years on*, Melbourne: Australia Institute of Family Studies.

Harrison, G. and Turner, R. (2010) 'Being a "culturally competent" social worker: making sense of a murky concept in practice', *The British Journal of Social Work*, 41(2): 333–50.

Harrison, G. and Turner, R. (2011) 'Being a "culturally competent social worker": making sense of a murky concept in practice', *British Journal of Social Work*, 41(2): 333–50.

Hayden, C. (2009) 'Family group conferences: are they an effective and viable way of working with attendance and behaviour problems in schools?' *British Journal of Educational Research*, 35(2): 205–20.

Hayden, A., Gelsthorpe, L., Kingi, V. and Morris, A. (2014) *A restorative approach to family violence*, London: Routledge.

Hayes, D. and Houston, S. (2007) '"Lifeworld", "System" and family group conferences: Habermas's contribution to discourse in child protection', *British Journal of Social Work*, 37(6): 987–1006.

Healy, K. (ed.) (2014) (2nd edn) *Social work theories in context: creating frameworks for practice*, Basingstoke: Palgrave Macmillan.

Heath, N.M., Lynch, S.M., Fritch, A.M. and Wong, M.M. (2013) 'Rape myth acceptance impacts the reporting of rape to the police', *Violence Against Women*, 19(9): 1065–78.

Heino, T. (2003) 'Using family group conferencing to protect children in Finland', *Protecting Children*, 18(1 and 2): 121–23.

Hellevik, P.M., Överlien, C., Barter, C., Wood, M., Aghtaie, N., Larkins, C. and Stanley, N. (2015) 'Traversing the generational gap: young people's views on intervention and prevention of teenage intimate partner violence', in N. Stanley, and C. Humphreys (eds), *Domestic violence and protecting children: new thinking and approaches*, London: Jessica Kingsley.

Hennessy, J., Hinton, M., Taurima, N. (2014) 'Restorative practice with family violence', in A. Hayden, L. Gelsthorpe, V, Kingi, and A. Morris (eds) *A restorative approach to family violence: changing track*, Surrey: Ashgate Publishing, pp 123–30.

Henniker, J., and Mercer, V. (2007) 'Restorative justice: can it work with young people who sexually abuse?' in M.C. Calder (ed.), *Working with children and young people who sexually abuse: taking the field forward*, Lyme Regis: Russell House Publishing Limited, pp 230–44

Herman, J.L. (2005) 'Justice from the victim's perspective', *Violence Against Women*, 11(5): 571–602.

Hester, M. (2011) 'The three planet model: towards an understanding of contradictions in approaches to women and children's safety in contexts of domestic violence', *British Journal of Social Work*, 41(5): 837–53.

Hickey, N., Vizard, E., McCrory, E. and French, L. (2006) *Links between juvenile sexually abusive behaviour and emerging severe personality disorder traits in childhood*, London: DH/Home Office/NOMS.

Higgins, D.J. and Katz, I. (2008) 'Enhancing service systems for protecting children: promoting child wellbeing and child protection reform in Australia', *Family Matters*, 80: 43–50.

Hilverdink, P., Daamen, W. and Vink, C. (2015) *Children and youth support and care in the Netherlands*, www.youthpolicy.nl/en/Publications/324549-Children-and-youth-support-and-care-in-the-Netherlands. Last accessed 28/02/18.

Hobbs, A. and Alonzi, A. (2013), 'Mediation and family group conferences in adult safeguarding', *The Journal of Adult Protection*, 15(2): 69–84.

Hodson, A. (2011) *Pre-birth assessment in social work*, Doctoral Thesis (unpublished), http://eprints.hud.ac.uk/13037/.

Holland, S. and O'Neill, S. (2006) '"We had to be there to make sure it was what we wanted": enabling children's participation in family decision making through the family group conference', *Childhood* 13: 91–111.

Holland, S. and Rivett, M. (2008) '"Everyone started shouting": making connections between the process of family group conferences and family therapy practice', *British Journal of Social Work* 38(1): 21–38.

Holland, S., Scourfield, J., O'Neill, S. Pithouse, A. (2005) 'Democratising the family and the state? The case of family group conferences in child welfare', *Journal of Social Policy*, 34(1): 59–77.

Home Office (2007) 'Cross government action plan on sexual violence and abuse', London: HM Government.

Home Office (2013) 'Guidance: domestic violence and abuse', London: HM Government.

Hoover, T. (2005) *The critical role of leadership in implementing family group decision making*, American Humane Association.

Hopkins, C.Q., Koss, M. and Bachar, K.J. (2004) 'Applying restorative justice to ongoing intimate violence: problems and possibilities', *Saint Louis University Public Law Review*, 23(1): 289–311.

Horan, H. and Dalrymple, J. (2003) 'Promoting the participation rights of children and young people in family group conferences', *Practice*, 15(2): 5–13.

Houghton, C. (2015) 'Young people's perspectives on participatory ethics: agency, power and impact in domestic abuse research and policy-making', *Child Abuse Review*, 24(4): 235–48.

House of Commons Home Affairs Select Committee (2005–06) *Draft sentencing guidelines: robbery, second report of session*, publications, parliament.uk/pa/cm200506/cmselect/cmhaff/947/947.pdf. Last accessed 28/02/18.

House of Commons Home Affairs Select Committee (2007) *Towards effective sentencing, oral and written evidence: Volume I oral and written evidence*, London: The Stationery Office, https://publications. parliament.uk/pa/cm200607/cmselect/cmconst/467/467i.pdf

House of Commons Justice Committee (2017) *The treatment of young adults in the criminal justice system: seventh report of session 2016–17*, London: The Stationery Office, https://publications.parliament.uk/ pa/cm201617/cmselect/cmjust/169/169.pdf

House of Commons Youth Justice Committee (2016) *Restorative justice: fourth report of session 2016–2017*, publications.parliament.uk/pa/ cm20167/cmselect/cmjust/164/164.pdf. Last accessed 28/02/18.

Howard, M.O., McMillen, C.J. and Polio, D.E. (2003) 'Teaching evidence-based practice: toward a new paradigm for social work education', *Research on Social Work Practice*, 13(2): 234–59.

Hoyle, C. and Noguera, S. (2008) 'Supporting young offenders through restorative justice: parents as (in)appropriate adults', *British Journal of Community Justice*, 6(3): 67–85.

Human Rights Act (1998) www.legislation.gov.uk/ukpga/1989/41/ contents. Last accessed 28/02/18.

Humphreys, C. and Thiara, R. (2003) 'Domestic violence and mental health: "I call it symptoms of abuse"', *British Journal of Social Work*, 32(2): 209–26.

Humphreys, C. and Stanley, N. (eds) (2006) *Domestic violence and child protection: directions for good practice*, London: Jessica Kingsley Publishers.

Huntsman, L. (2006) *Family group conferencing in a child welfare context*, Centre for Parenting and Research, NSW Department of Community Services

Inglis, S. (2007) 'Family decision making to plan for safety in domestic violence', in C. Ashley and P. Nixon (2007) *Family group conferences: where next? Policies and practices for the future*, London: Family Rights Group, pp 193–219.

International Federation of Social Work (2014) *Global definition of social work*, http://ifsw.org/policies/definition-of-social-work/.

Jacob, K.S. (2015) 'Recovery model of mental illness: a complementary approach to psychiatric care', *Indian Journal of Psychological Medicine*, 37(2): 117–19.

Jordan, C.E., Campbell, R. and Follingstad, D. (2010) 'Violence and women's mental health: the impact of physical, sexual and psychological aggression', *Annual Review of Clinical Psychology*, 6: 607–28.

Justice (Northern Ireland) Act 2002, www.legislation.gov.uk/ukpga/2002/26/contents. Last accessed 10/04/2018.

Kagan, C., Burton, M., Duckett, P., Lawthom, R. and Siddiquee, A. (2011) *Critical community psychology*, Oxford: BPS Blackwell.

Kanyi, T. (2013) 'Lack of outcome research on New Zealand care and protection family group conference', *Aotearoa New Zealand Social Work*, 25(1): 35–42.

Keane, M., Guest, A. and Padbury, J. (2013) 'A balancing act: a family perspective to sibling sexual abuse', *Child Abuse Review*, 22: 246–54.

Kemp, T. (2007) *Family welfare conferences: the Wexford experience: an evaluation of Barnardos family welfare conference project*, Ilford, Essex: Barnardos.

Kingi, V., Pulin, J. and Porima, L. (2008) *Review of the delivery of restorative justice in family violence cases by providers funded by the Ministry of Justice*, Victoria University of Wellington: Crime and Justice Research Centre.

Kohli, H.K., Huber, R. and Faul, A.C. (2010) 'Historical and theoretical development of culturally competent social work practice', *Journal of Teaching in Social Work*, 30(3): 252–71.

Kohn, L.S. (2010) 'What's so funny about peace, love and understanding? Restorative justice as a new paradigm for domestic violence intervention', *Sefton Hall Review*, 40: 517–40.

Laing, L. and Humphreys, C. (2013) *Social Work and domestic violence: developing critical and reflective practice: developing critical and reflective practice*, London: Sage Publications

Lamb, M.E. (1997) 'Fathers and child development: an introductory overview', in M.E. Lamb (ed.) *The role of the father in child development* (3rd edn), Chichester: Wiley, pp 1–19

Lamb, S. and Coakley, M. (1993) '"Normal" childhood sexual play and games: differentiating play from abuse', *Child Abuse and Neglect*, 17: 515–26.

Lapierre, S. (2008) 'Mothering in the context of domestic violence: the pervasiveness of a deficit model of mother', *Child and Family Social Work*, 13(4): 454–63.

Laursen, E.K. (2003) 'Frontiers in strengths based treatment', *Reclaiming Children and Youth: The Journal of Strengths Based Interventions*, 15(1): 12–17.

Laws, S. and Kirby, P. (2008) 'At the table or under the table? A comparative study of professional and informal advocacy for children in family group conferences,' in C.M. Oliver and J. Dalrympl, *Developing Advocacy for Children and Young People: Current Issues in Research, Policy and Practice*, London: Jessica Kingsley Publishing.

Leeds Youth Offending Service (n.d.) *Youth justice plan 2016–17*, http://217.35.77.12/CB/england/papers/pdfs/2008/Leeds_YOS_report.pdf

Letourneau, E.J. and Miner, M.H. (2005) 'Juvenile sex offenders: A case against the legal and clinical status quo', *Sex abuse*, 17(3): 293–312.

Levitas, R., Pantazis, C., Fahmy, E., Gordon, D., Lloyd, E. and Patsios, D. (2007) *The Multi-dimensional analysis of social exclusion*, Bristol: University of Bristol.

Liebmann, M. (2015) 'Building the restorative city', in T. Gavrilides (ed.) *Offenders no more: an interdisciplinary dialogue*, Hauppauge, New York: Nova Science, pp 289–311.

Leibmann, M. and McGeorge, N. (2015) Presentation at 13th United Nations Congress on Crime Prevention and Criminal Justice, 15 April

Liebmann, M. and Wootton, L. (2010) *Restorative justice and domestic violence/abuse*, Cardiff: HMP Cardiff.

Litchfield, M., Gatowski, S. and Dobbin, S. (2003) 'Improving outcomes for families: results from an evaluation of Miami's family decision making program', *Protecting Children* 18(1–2): 48–51.

Local Government Association (LGA) (2013) *Making safeguarding personal*, http://www.local.gov.uk/topics/social-care-health-and-integration/adult-social-care/making-safeguarding-personal.

Local Government Association (LGA) (2015) *Adult safeguarding improvement tool*, http://www.local.gov.uk/sites/default/files/documents/adult-safeguarding-improv-c15.pdf.

Lupton, C. and Nixon, P. (1999) *Empowering practice? A critical appraisal of the family group conference approach*, Bristol: Policy Press.

Luthar, S.S. and Cicchetti, D. (2000) 'The construct of resilience: implications for interventions and social policies', *Developmental Psychopathology* 12(4): 857–85.

MacFarlane, A.H. and Anglem, J. (2014) *Evaluation of family group conference practice and outcomes*, Christchurch New Zealand: University of Canterbury.

Machura, S. (2016) 'Inter- and intra-agency co-operation in safeguarding children: a staff survey', *British Journal of Social Work*, 46 (3): 652–68.

Malmberg-Heimonen, I. (2011) 'The effects of family group conferences on social support and mental health for longer-term social assistance recipients in Norway', *British Journal of Social Work*, 41(5), 949–67.

Malone, D. and Banks, J. (2016) 'FGCs in Scotland: new approaches', Conference Presentation, *Making research count*, University of Salford, http://hub.salford.ac.uk/mrc/mrcevents/innovative-uses-family-group-conferences-social-work/.

Marmot, M. (2010) *Fair society, healthy lives*, The Marmot Review.

Marsh, P. (2009) 'Library and information service: highlight no 248', North West Institute for Children and Families, London: National Children's Bureau.

Marsh, P. and Crow, G. (1998) *Family group conferences in child welfare*, Oxford: Blackwell.

Marsh, P. with Kent Adult FGC Service (2007) *Kent adult FGC development research*, Sheffield University and Kent Adult FGC Service.

Marsh, P. and Walsh, D. (2007) *Family group conference plans: a study of planning and outcomes in Kent family group conferences service*, University of Sheffield.

Mason, P., Ferguson, H., Morris, K., Monton, T. and Sen, R. (2017) *Leeds family values, evaluation report, July 2017*, London: Department for Education.

Maxwell, G. and Morris, A. (2006) 'Youth justice in New Zealand: Restorative justice in practice?' *Journal of Social Issues*, 62(2): 239–58.

Maxwell, G.M., and Robertson, J.P. (1991) *Statistics on the first year of the Children, Young Persons and Their Families Act 1989*, Wellington: The Commissioner for Children.

McCold, P. and Wachtel, T. (2003) 'In pursuit of paradigm: a theory of restorative justice', *Restorative Practices eForum*, 1–3, https://www.scribd.com/document/251715408/Ted-Wachtel-In-Pursuit-of-Paradig.

McKillop, L. (n.d.) *Practitioner research summary life changing decisions: the relevance of family group conferences in permanence planning*, Children 1st, http://lx.iriss.org.uk/sites/default/files/resources/Life%20changing%20decisions.pdf.

McMorris, B.J., Beckman, K., Shea, G., Baumgartner, J. and Eggert, R.C. (2013) *Applying restorative practices to Minneapolis Public Schools Students recommended for possible expulsion: a pilot program evaluation of the Family Youth Restorative Conference program. Final report*, Minneapolis, MN: School of Nursing and the Healthy Youth Development Prevention Research Center, Department of Pediatrics, University of Minnesota.

McNevin, E. (2010) 'Applied restorative justice as a complement to systemic family therapy: theory and practice implications for families experiencing intra-familial adolescent sibling incest', *The Australian and New Zealand Journal of Family Therapy*, 31(1), 60–72.

Mental Capacity Act 2005, London: HMSO, www.scie.org.uk/mca/introduction/mental-capacity-act-2005-at-a-glance. Last accessed 10/04/2018.

Mercer, V. (2009) *Victim contact and sexually harmful behaviour*, Manchester: AIM Project.

Mercer, V., Sten Madsen, K., Keenan, M. and Zinsstag, E (2015) *Doing restorative justice in cases of sexual violence: a practice guide*, Leuven: Leuven Institute of Criminology.

Merkel-Holguin, L (2004) 'Sharing power with the people: family group conferencing as a democratic experiment', *Journal of Sociology and Social Welfare*, 31: 155–73.

Merkel-Holguin, L., Nixon, P. and Burford, G. (2003) 'Learning with families: a synopsis of FGDM research and evaluation in child welfare', *Protecting Children*, 18(1–2): 2–11.

Metze, R.N., Abma, T.A. and Kwekkeboom, R.H. (2013) 'Family group conferencing: a theoretical underpinning', *Health Care Analysis*, 23: 165–80.

Metze, R.N., Kwekkeboom, R.H., Abma, T.A., (2015) 'The potential of family group conferencing for the resilience and relational autonomy of older adults', *Journal of Aging Studies*, 34: 68–81

Meunch, K., Diaz, C. and Wright, R. (2016) 'Children and parent participation in child protection conferences: a study in one English local authority', *Child Care in Practice*, 23: 1–15.

Miller, S. L. and Hefner, M. K. (2015) 'Procedural justice for victims and offenders? Exploring restorative justice processes in Australia and the US', *Justice Quarterly*, 32(1): 142–67.

Mills, L.G., Grauwiler, P. and Pezold, N. (2006) 'Enhancing safety and rehabilitation in intimate violence treatments: new perspectives', *Public Health Reports*, 121(4): 363–8.

Minieri, A.M., Staton-Tindall, M., Leukefeld, C., Clarke, J.G., Surratt, H.L. and Frisman, L.K. (2014) 'Relationship power as a mediator of intimate partner violence and mental health issues among incarcerated women', *International Journal of Offender Therapy and Comparative Criminology*, 58(3): 303–19.

Ministerial Advisory Committee (1988) *Puao-te-ata-tu: The report of the Ministerial Advisory Committee on a Maori perspective for the Department of Social Welfare*, www.msd.govt.nz/documents/about-msd-and-our-work/publications-resources/archive/1988-puaoteatatu.pdf. Last accessed 28/02/18.

Ministerial Advisory Committee on a Maori perspective for the Department of Social Welfare in New Zealand (1990) *Puao-te-ata-tu*, Wellington: New Zealand Government.

Ministry of Civil Affairs (2014) *Notice about further developing the work on piloting the appropriate universal system of child welfare (in Chinese)*. http://www.fujian.gov.cn/ggfwpt/shazer/shel/etfl/etfl/201408/t20140822_769524.htm.

Ministry of Justice (2008) *The Public Law Outline: guide to case management in public law proceedings*, London: Ministry of Justice.

Ministry of Justice (2010) *Family Procedures Rules*, https://www.justice.gov.uk/courts/procedure-rules/family.

Ministry of Justice (2011) *Family justice review: final report*, London: Ministry of Justice.

Ministry of Justice (2012) *Family justice review: government response*, London: Ministry of Justice, www.gov.uk/government/publications/family-justice-review-government-response. Last accessed 28/02/18.

Ministry of Justice (2013) *Statistics on race and the criminal justice system 2012*, London: Ministry of Justice.

Ministry of Justice (2015) *Statistics on race and the criminal justice system 2014*, A Ministry of Justice publication under Section 95 of the Criminal Justice Act 1991, London: Ministry of Justice.

Ministry of Justice and Department for Education (2012) *The Government response to the family justice review: a system with children and families at its heart*, London: The Stationery Office.

Mirsky, L. (2003) 'Family Group Conferencing Worldwide: Part 1 in a series', *Restorative Practices eForum*, (February 20, 2003), 1–8, www.iirp.edu/eforum-archive/family-group-conferencing-worldwide-part-one-in-a-series

Morgan, A., Boxall, H., Kerer, T. and Harris, N. (2012) *Evaluation of alternative dispute resolution initiatives in the care and protection jurisdiction of the NSW Children's Court*, Canberra: Australian Institute of Criminology.

Moriarty, J., Baginsky, M. and Manthorpe, J. (2015) *Literature review of roles and issues within the social work profession in England*, Kings College London: Social Care Workforce Research Unit.

Morris, K. (2007) *Camden FGC service: an evaluation of service use and outcomes*, London: Camden FGC Service.

Morris, K. and Connolly, M. (2012) 'Family decision making in child welfare: challenges in developing a knowledge base for practice', *Child Abuse Review*, 21(1): 41–52.

Morrison, T., and Henniker, J. (2006) 'Building a comprehensive inter-agency assessment and intervention system for young people who sexually harm: the AIM project', in M. Erooga and H. Masson (eds), *Children and young people who sexually abuse others: Current developments and practice responses*, 2nd edn, London and New York: Routledge, pp 31–50.

Moulding, N.T., Buchanan, F. and Wendt, S. (2015) 'Untangling self-blame and mother-blame in women's and children's perspectives on maternal protectiveness in domestic violence: implications for practice', *Child Abuse Review*, 24(4): 249–60.

Mowlam, A., Tennant, R., Dixon, J. and McCreadie, C. (2007) 'UK study of abuse and neglect of older people: qualitative findings', http://assets.comicrelief.com/cr09/docs/older_people_abuse_report.pdf

Moyle, P. (2013) *From family group conferencing to Whanau Ora: social workers talk about their experiences* (unpublished), Palmerston North: Massey University.

Moyle, P. (2014) 'Maori social workers experiences of care and protection: a selection of findings', *Te Komako, Social Work Review*, 26(1): 55–64.

Munro, E. (2011) *The Munro Review of child protection, final report: a child-centred system*, London: Department for Education.

Murphy, M. and Rogers, M. (in press) 'Working with adult-oriented issues: parental substance misuse, mental ill-health and domestic violence', in J. Horwath and D. Platt (eds) *The child's world: the comprehensive guide to assessing children in need* (3rd edn), London: Jessica Kingsley Publishers.

Mutter, R., Judge, N., Flynn, L. and Hennessy, J. (2002) *Supporting people together: family group conference in mental health services – research findings and practice developments*, Chelmsford: North Essex Mental Health Partnership NHS Trust.

Mutter, R., Shemmings, D., Dugmore, P. and Hyare, M. (2008) 'Family group conferences in Youth Justice', *Health and Social Care in the Community*, 16(3): 262–70.

Myers, S. (2007) *Solution-focused approaches*, Lyme Regis, Dorset: Russell House Publishing Ltd.

Naslund, E. (2013) *Family group conferences in Sweden 2013*, http://www.fgcnetwork.eu/user/file/country_report_sweden_2013.pdf.

National Audit Office (2016) *Personalised commissioning in Adult Social Care*, London: National Audit Office, https://www.nao.org.uk/wp-content/uploads/2016/03/Personalised-commissioning-in-adult-social-care-update.pdf.

Nazroo, J. and Kapadia, D. (2013a) *Have ethnic inequalities in employment persisted between 1991 and 2011?* Briefing Paper: The Dynamics of Diversity: evidence from the 2011 census. The University of Manchester: Centre on Dynamics of Ethnicity

Nazroo, J. and Kapadia, D. (2013b) *Ethnic inequalities in labour market participation?* University of Manchester and Joseph Rowntree Foundation: Centre on Dynamics of Ethnicity.

New South Wales Government, Family and Community Services (2016) FGC Caseworkers encouraged to use Family Group Conferencing, https://www.facs.nsw.gov.au/about_us/news/facs-caseworkers-encouraged-to-use-family-group-conferencing. Last accessed 10/04/18.

Ney, T., Stoltz, J. and Maloney, M. (2011) 'Voice, power and discourse: experiences of participants in family group conferences in the context of child protection', *Journal of Social Work*, 13(2): 184–202.

Nissen, L.B., Mackin, J.R., Weller, J.M. and Tarte, J.M. (2005) 'Identifying strengths as fuel for change: a theoretical framework for the youth competency assessment', *Juvenile and Family Court Journal*, 1–15.

Oak, J. and Campling, E. (2008) *Social work and social work perspectives*, Basingstoke: Palgrave.

O'Brien, M.J. (1991) 'Taking sibling incest seriously', in M.Q. Patton (ed.), *Family sexual abuse: frontline research and evaluation*, London: Sage Publications, pp 75–92.

O'Brien, V. and Alohen, H. (2015) *Pathways and outcomes: a study of 335 referrals to the Family Welfare Conference (FWC) service in Dublin, 2011–2013*, Dublin: University College.

O'Driscoll, S.J. (2006) *Youth justice in New Zealand: a restorative approach to reducing youth offending*, http://www.unafei.or.jp/english/pdf/RS_No75/No75_10VE_O'Driscoll.pdf.

Office for National Statistics (2001) 'Social capital: a review of the literature', Social Analysis and Reporting Division Office for National Statistics, October 2001, London: ONS.

Office for National Statistics (2014) *Inequality in healthy life expectancy at birth by national deciles of area deprivation: England, 2009–11*, Statistical Bulletin: Office for National Statistics.

Office for National Statistics (2016) *Focus on violent crime and sexual offences: year ending March 2015. Violent crime and sexual offences from the year ending March 2015 Crime Survey for England and Wales and crimes recorded by police*, London: ONS.

Office for National Statistics; National Records of Scotland; Northern Ireland Statistics and Research Agency (2017): *2011 Census aggregate data*, UK Data Service (Edition: February 2017), DOI: http://dx.doi.org/10.5257/census/aggregate-2011-2

Ogilvie, K. and Williams, C. (2010) *Making safeguarding personal: a toolkit for responses*, London: Local Government Association.

Olson, K.B. (2009) 'Family group conferencing and child protection mediation: essential tools for prioritising family engagement in child welfare cases', *Family Court Review*, 47 (1): 53–68.

Oosterkamp-Swajcer, E.M. and de Swart, J.J.W. (2012), *Op Eigen Kracht voonit 2012 een onder zoek naar de resultan van Eigen Kracht conferenties*, Netherlands: University of Saxion.

O'Shaughnessy, R., Fatimilehin, I. and Collins, C. (2010) 'Building bridges in Liverpool: exploring the use of family group conferences for Black and Minority Ethnic children and their families', *British Journal of Social Work*, 40 (7): 2034–49.

Oudshoorn, J., Jackett, M. and Stutzman Amstutz, L. (2015) *The little book of restorative justice for sexual abuse: hope through trauma*, New York: Good Books.

Ozbay, F., H. Fitterling, D. Charney, and S. Southwick (2008) 'Social support and resilience to stress across the life span: a neurobiologic framework', *Current Psychiatry Reports* 10: 304–10.

Pakura, S. (2003) 'A review of the family group conference 13 years on', *Social Work Review*, 15(3): 3–7.

Papadopoulos, I. (2006) *Transcultural health and social care: development of culturally competent practitioners*, Edinburgh: Churchill Livingstone Elsevier.

Parton, N. (2012) *The politics of child protection: contemporary developments and future directions*, Basingstoke: Palgrave Macmillan.

Pattoni, L. (2012) 'Strengths-based approaches for working with individuals', Insight 16, IRISS, https://www.iriss.org.uk/resources/insights/strengths-based-approaches-working-individuals.

Payne, B., Conway, V., Bell, C., Falk, A., Flynn, H., McNeil, C. and Rice, F. (2009) *Restorative practices in Northern Ireland: a mapping exercise*, Belfast: School of Law, Queen's University.

Pease, B. (2002) 'Rethinking empowerment: a postmodern reappraisal for emancipatory practice', *British Journal Social Work*, 32(2): 135–147.

Peckover, S. (2014) 'Domestic abuse, safeguarding children and public health: towards an analysis of discursive forms and surveillant techniques in contemporary UK policy and practice', *British Journal of Social Work*, 44(7): 1770–87.

Peled, E. (2000) 'Parenting by men who abuse women: issues and dilemmas', *British Journal of Social Work*, 30: 25–36.

Pence, E. and McMahon, M. (1999) 'Duluth: a coordinated community response to domestic violence', in N. Harwin, G. Hague, and E. Malos (eds) *From the multi-agency approach to domestic violence: new opportunities, old challenges?* London: Whiting and Birch, pp 150–68.

Pennell, J. (2003) 'Are we following key FGC practices? Views of conference participants', in Merkel-Holguin, L. (ed), *Promising results, potential new directions: international FGDM research and evaluation in child welfare*, Englewood: American Humane Association.

Pennell, J. (2006) 'Restorative practices and child welfare: towards an inclusive civil society', *Journal of Social Issues*, 62(2): 257–77.

Pennell, J. and Burford, G. (2000) 'Family group decision making: protecting children and women', *Child Welfare*, 79(2): 131–58.

Pennell, J. and Francis, S. (2005) 'Safety conferencing: towards a co-ordinated and inclusive response to safeguard women and children', *Violence Against Women*, 11(5): 666–92.

Pennell, J., Edwards, M. and Burford, G. (2010) 'Expedited family group engagement and child permanency', *Children and Youth Services Review*, 32: 1012–19.

Pennell, J., Shapiro, C. and Spigner, W. (2011) *Safety, fairness, stability: repositioning juvenile justice and child welfare to engage families and communities*, Georgetown: Center for Juvenile Justice Reform, http://jbcc.harvard.edu/sites/default/files/safety_fairness_stability_ repositioning_juvenile_justice_and_child_welfare_to_engage_ families_and_communities.pdf.

Percy-Smith, B. and Thomas, N. (eds) (2010) *A handbook of children and young people's participation: perspectives from theory and practice*, London and New York: Routledge.

Preferred Futures (n.d.) Information for professionals, http:// preferredfuturesfs.co.uk/information-for-professionals/. Last accessed 10/04/2018.

Radford, L., Corral, S., Bradley, C., Fisher, H., Bassett, C., Howat, N., and Collishaw, S. (2011) *Child abuse and neglect in the UK today*, London: NSPCC.

Rapp, C., Saleebey, D. and Sullivan, P.W. (2008) 'The future of strengths-based social work practice', in D. Saleebey (ed) The strengths perspective in social work practice, (4th edn), Boston: Pearson Education.

Reid, W.J. and L. Epstein (1972) Task-centered casework, New York: Columbia University Press.

Richards, R. (2003) Findings from the multi-agency domestic violence murder reviews in London, London: Metropolitan Police.

Ricks, J.M. and DiClemente, R.J. (2015) 'Adolescent sex offenders', in T.P. Gullotta, R.W. Plant and M.A. Evans (eds), Handbook of adolescent behavioral problems: evidence-based approaches to prevention and treatment, New York: Springer, pp 577–93.

Robbins, R., McLaughlin, H., Banks, C., Bellamy, C., and Thackray, D. (2014) 'Domestic violence and multi-agency risk assessment conferences (MARACs): a scoping review', The Journal of Adult Protection, 16(6): 389–98.

Robertson, J. (1996) 'Research on Family Group Conferences on child welfare in New Zealand', in J. Hudson, G. Morris, G. Maxwell and B. Galaway (eds) Family Group Conferences: perspectives on practice and policy, Monsey, New York: Willow Tree Press, pp 49–64.

Robinson, L.J., Schmid, A.A., and Siles, M.E. (2002) 'Is social capital really capital?', Review of Social Economy, 60: 1–24.

Rogers, E.S., Ralph, R.O. and Salzer, M.S. (2010) 'Validating the empowerment scale with a multisite sample of consumers of mental health services', Psychiatric Services, 61(9): 933–6.

Rogers, M. and Parkinson, K. (2018) 'Exploring approaches to child welfare in contexts of domestic violence and abuse: family group conferences', Child and Family Social Work, 23(1): 105–12.

Rossner, M. (2011) 'Emotions and interaction ritual, a micro analysis of restorative justice', British Journal of Criminology, 51: 95–119.

Rutter, M. (1980) 'The long-term effects of early experience', Developmental Medicine and Child Neurology, 22(6): 800–15.

Ryan, G. (2010) 'Sexually abusive youth: Defining the problem and the population', in G. Ryan, T. F. Leversee and S. Lane (eds) Juvenile sexual offending: causes, consequences, and correction, 3rd edition, New Jersey: Wiley, pp 3–8.

Salcido Carter, L. (2003) Family team conferences in domestic violence cases: guidelines for practice. San Francisco: Family Violence Prevention Fund.

Saleebey, D. (1996) 'The strengths perspective in social work practice: extensions and cautions', Social Work, 41(3): 296–305.

Samuel, M. (2012) 'Resources on using mediation/family group conferencing as safeguarding tools', *Adult Care Blog: Community Care*, http://www.communitycare.co.uk/2013/04/22/family-group-conferencing-can-transform-social-work-with-adults/

Sawyer, R.Q., and Lohrbach, S. (2008) *Olmsted County child and family services: family involvement strategies*, Rochester, MN: Olmsted County Child and Family Services.

Schuurman, M. (2011) 'Opbrengsten en effect en van Eigen Kracht-conferenties', *Jeugbeleid*, 4: 227–32.

SCIE (Social Care Institute for Excellence), (2012a) 'Safeguarding adults: mediation and family group conferences: working with adults, the Mental Capacity Act', http://www.scie.org.uk/publications/mediation/workingwithadults/mentalcapacityact.asp

SCIE (Social Care Institute for Excellence), (2012b) 'Safeguarding adults: mediation and family group conferences: information for directors and senior managers', http://www.scie.org.uk/publications/mediation/files/informationfordirectorsandseniormanagers.pdf?res=true

SCIE (Social Care Institute for Excellence), (2013a) 'Royal Greenwich: social work practice pioneer project', http://www.scie.org.uk/workforce/socialworkpractice/files/pioneers/RoyalGreenwich.pdf?res=true

SCIE (Social Care Institute for Excellence), (2013b) 'Central Bedfordshire Council: final evaluation report', http://www.scie.org.uk/workforce/socialworkpractice/files/pioneers/centralbedfordshire.pdf?res=true

SCIE (Social Care Institute for Excellence), (2015) 'Strengths based approaches', http://www.scie.org.uk/care-act-2014/assessment-and-eligibility/strengths-based-approach/

SCIE (Social Care Institute for Excellence), (2016) 'Lack of communication between children's and adults' social care: practice issues from serious case reviews: learning into practice', http://www.scie.org.uk/children/safeguarding/case-reviews/learning-from-case-reviews/14.asp

Scott, K. and Crooks, C. (2004) 'Effecting change in maltreating fathers: critical principles for intervention planning', *Clinical psychology: science and practice*, 11(1): 95–111.

Scottish Executive (2002) *National Standards for Scotland's Youth Justice Services: A report by the Improving the Effectiveness of the Youth Justice System Working Group*, Edinburgh: The Stationery Office.

Scottish Government (2002) *National standards for Scotland's Youth Justice Services: a report by the Improving the Effectiveness of the Youth Justice System Working Group*, www.gov.scot/Resource/Doc/46932/0025195.pdf. Last accessed 28/02/18.

Scottish Government (2014) *Self-directed Support: my support, my choice: your guide to social care*, Edinburgh: Scottish Government, http://www.gov.scot/Publications/2014/07/2758

Scottish Government (2016) *Getting it right for every child*, Edinburgh: Scottish Government, http://www.gov.scot/Topics/People/Young-People/gettingitright

Scourfield, J. (2006) 'The challenge of engaging fathers in the child protection process', *Critical Social Policy, special issue on gender and child welfare*, 26(2): 440–9.

Shang, X.-Y. (2012) 'Looking for best practice in caring for disabled children: a case of socialized foster care in China', *Asia Pacific Journal of Social Work and Development*, 22(1–2): 127–38.

Shapland, J., Atkinson, A., Chapman, B., Dignan, J., Howes, M., Johnstone, J., Robinson, G. and Sorsby, A. (2007) *Restorative justice: the views of victims and offenders; the third report from the evaluation of three schemes*, University of Sheffield: Centre for Criminological Research.

Sheets, J., Wittenstrom, K., Fong, R., James, J., Tecci, M., Baumann, D.J. and Rodriguez, C. (2009) 'Evidence-based practice in family group decision-making for Anglo, African American and Hispanic families', *Children and Youth Services Review*, 31: 1187–91.

Shennan, G. (2014) *Solution-focused practice: effective communication to facilitate change*, Basingstoke: Palgrave Macmillan.

Sherman, L. H. and Strang, H. (2007) *Restorative Justice: the evidence*. London: The Smith Institute.

Signs of Safety (n.d.) www.signsofsafety.net.

Simmons, C.A. and Lehmann, P. (2013) *Tools for strengths based assessment and evaluation*. New York: Springer.

Skaale Havnen, K. and Christiansen, O. (2014) *Knowledge review on family group conferencing, experiences and outcomes*, Norway: Regional Centre for Child and Youth Mental Health and Child Welfare (RKBU West), Uni Research Health.

Slater, C., McDowell, H. and Lambie, I. (2015) 'Youth Justice Co-ordinators' perspectives on New Zealand's youth justice family group conference process', *Journal of Social Work*, 15(6): 621–43.

Smith, L. and Hennessey, J. (1998) *Making a difference: Essex family group conference project; research findings and practice issues*, Chelmsford, Essex County Council Social Services Department.

Snow, P.C. and Sanger, D.D. (2011) 'Restorative justice conferencing and the youth offender: exploring the role of language competence', *International Journal of Language and Communication Disorders*, 46(3): 324–33.

Snow, P.C., Powell, M.B. and Sanger, D.D. (2012) 'Oral language competence, young speakers and the law', *Language, Speech and Hearing Services in Schools*, 43: 496–506.

Social Care (Self Directed Support) (Scotland) Act 2013, www. legislation.gov.uk/asp/2013/contents/enacted. Last accessed 10/04/2018.

Social Services and Research Information Unit (SSRIU), University of Portsmouth (2003) *The Dove project: the Basingstoke domestic violence family group conference project*, Hampshire: unpublished.

Spring consortium (n.d.) 'Learning and evaluation', http:// springconsortium.com/learn-to-innovate

Stahlkopf, C. (2009) 'Restorative justice, rhetoric, or reality? Conferencing with young offenders', *Contemporary Justice Review: Issues in Criminal, Social and Restorative Justice*, 12(3): 231–51.

Stanley, T. (2016) 'A practice framework to support the Care Act 2014', *The Journal of Adult Protection*, 18(2): 53–64.

Stanley, N. and Flood, S. (2011) 'Children experiencing domestic violence: a research review', Research in Practice/Dartington.

Stanley, N. and Humphreys, C. (eds) (2015) *Domestic violence and protecting children: new thinking and approaches*, London: Jessica Kingsley Publishers.

Stanley, N., Cleaver, H. and Hart, D. (2010) 'The impact of domestic violence, parental mental health problems, substance misuse and learning disability on parenting capacity', in J. Horwath (ed.) *The child's world: the comprehensive guide to assessing children in need* (2nd edn), London: Jessica Kingsley Publishers.

Stanley, N., Miller, P. and Richardson Foster, H. (2012) 'Engaging with children's and parents' perspectives on domestic violence', *Child and Family Social Work*, 17: 192–201.

Stanley, N., Miller, P., Richardson Foster, H. and Thompson, G. (2010) 'Children's experiences of domestic violence: developing an integrated response from police and child protection services', *Journal of Interpersonal Violence*, 26(12): 2372–91.

Stark, E. (2007) *Coercive control: how men entrap women in personal life*, New York: Oxford University Press.

Strang, H. and Braithwaite, J. (eds) (2002) *Restorative justice and family violence*, Cambridge: Cambridge University Press.

Stubbs, J. (2007) 'Beyond apology? Domestic violence and critical questions for restorative justice', *Criminology and Criminal Justice*, 7(2): 169–87.

Sundell, K. and Vinnerljung, B. (2004) 'Outcomes of family group conferencing in Sweden: a 3-year follow up', *Child Abuse and Neglect*, 28: 267–87.

Swisher, L.M. and Pierce, K. (2014) 'Sexualized behaviors among siblings', Webinar: www.wcsap.org/sexualized-behaviours-among-siblings-0.

Tapper, (2010) 'Using family group conferences in safeguarding adults', *The Journal of Adult Protection*, 12(1): 27–31.

Tapper, L. (2010) 'Using family group conferences in safeguarding adults', *The Journal of Adult Protection*, 2(1): 27–31.

Tapsfield, R. (2003) *FGCs: family led decision making*, London: Family Rights Group.

Te Awatea Violence Research Centre (2014) 'Evaluation of family group conference practice and outcomes: a review of the literature', *The Journal of Te Awatea Violence Research Centre*, 11(1): 12–16.

Tengland, P.A. (2008) 'Empowerment: a conceptual discussion', *Health Care Analysis*, 16(2): 77–96.

Tew, J. (2015) *Family minded practice and family group conferencing in adult services and mental health*, conference presentation, slideplayer. com/6065217

Thompson, C. (2013) 'Mental health bulletin: annual report from MHMDS returns: England 2011-12, initial national figures', Health and Social Care Information Centre.

Thompson, N. (2016) *Anti-discriminatory practice: equality, diversity and social justice*, Basingstoke: Palgrave Macmillan.

Thornton, C. (1993) *Family group conferences: a literature review*, Lower Hutt, New Zealand: Practitioner's Publishing.

Tidefors, I., Arvidsson, H., Ingevaldson, S., and Larsson, M. (2010) 'Sibling incest: a literature review and clinical study', *Journal of Sexual Aggression*, 16: 347–60.

Tilley, S. and Pollock, L. (1999) 'Discourses on empowerment', *Journal of Psychiatric and Mental Health Nursing*, 6: 63–70.

Tinworth, K. and Merkel-Holguin, L. (2006) 'Reviewing a Swedish outcome study on FGCs', *FGDM Issues in Brief*, American Humane.

Titcomb, A. and LeCroy, C. (2003) 'Evaluation of Arizona's family group decision making program: protecting children, promising results, potential new directions', *International FGDM Research and Evaluation in Child Welfare*, 18(1–2): 58–64.

Treseder, P. (1997) *Empowering children and young people: promoting involvement and decision making*, London: Save the Children.

Turnell, A. and Edwards, S. (1999) *Signs of safety: a safety and solution oriented approach to child protection casework*, New York: WW Norton.

Turney, D., Selwyn, J., Farmer, E. and Platt, D. (2012) *Improving child and family assessments: turning research into practice*, London: Jessica Kingsley Publishing.

Uglow, S., Hale, C., Crawford, A.J. and Newburn, T. (2002) *The introduction of Referral Orders into the youth justice system: final report*, London: Home Office, https://kar.kent.ac.uk/308/1/Uglow_Introduction_of_referral_2002.pdf.

Umbreit, M. and Peterson Armour, M. (2011) *Restorative justice dialogue: an essential guide for research and practice*, Springer Publishing Company.

UN General Assembly (1989) *Convention on the Rights of the Child*, 20 November 1989, United Nations, Treaty Series, vol. 1577.

University of Salford (2016) *Innovative uses of Family Group Conferences in social work*, http://hub.salford.ac.uk/mrc/mrcevents/innovative-uses-family-group-conferences-social-work/. Last accessed 10/04/2018.

van Ness, D.W. (2005) *An overview of restorative justice around the world*, Washington DC: Centre for Justice and Reconciliation at Prison Fellowship International.

Veneski, W. and Kemp, S. (2000) 'Families as resources: the Washington State family group conference project', in G. Burford and J. Hudson (eds), *Family group conferences: new directions in community-centered child and family practice*, Hawthorne, NY: Aldine de Gruyter, pp 312–23.

Wachtel, J. (2015) New Dutch law outs family power first, https://www.iirp.edu/news-from-iirp/new-dutch-law-puts-family-power-first. Last accessed 10/04/18.

Wager, N. (2013) 'The experience and insight of survivors who have engaged in a justice meeting with their assailant', *Temida* 16(1): 11–32.

Waites, C., Macgowan, M., Pennell, J., Carlton-LaNey, I. and Weil, M. (2004) 'Increasing the cultural responsiveness of family group conferencing', *Social Work*, 49(2): 291–300

Walby, S. and Allen, J. (2004) 'Domestic violence, sexual assault and stalking: findings from the British Crime Survey', *Home Office Research Study* 276, London: Home Office.

Walker, L. (1979) *The battered woman*, New York: Harper and Row.

Walker, L. (2005) 'A cohort study of Ohana conferencing in child abuse and neglect cases', *Protecting Children* 19(4): 36–46.

Wallcraft, J. and Sweeney, A. (2011) *SCIE report 47: user involvement in adult safeguarding*, Social Care Institute for Excellence, www.scie.org.uk/publications/reports/report47/files/report47.pdf.

Wang, E.W., Lambert, M.C., Johnson, L.E., Boudreau, B., Breidenbach, R. and Baumann, D. (2012) 'Expediting permanent placement from foster care systems: the role of family group decision making', *Children and Youth Services Review*, 34(4): 845–50.

Weaver, H.N. (1997) 'Training culturally competent social workers: what students should know about native people', *Journal of Teaching in Social Work*, 15(2): 97–111.

Weaver, H.N. (2004) 'The elements of cultural competence: applications with Native American clients', *Journal of Ethnic and Cultural Diversity in Social Work*, 13(1): 19–35.

Webb, J., Schirato, T. and Danaher, G. (2002) *Understanding Bourdieu*, London: Sage.

Weigensberg, E., Barth, R. and Guo, S. (2009) 'Family group decision making: a propensity score analysis to evaluate child and family services at baseline and after 36 months', *Children and Youth Services Review*, 31(3): 383–90.

Weijers, I. (2002) 'Restoration and the family: a pedagogical point of view', in L. Walgrave (ed.), *Restorative justice and the law*, Devon and Oregon: Willan Publishing, pp 68–81.

Weld, N. and Greening, M. (2004) 'The three houses tool: building safety and positive change', in M. Calder (ed.) *Contemporary risk assessment in safeguarding children*, Lyme Regis: Russell House Publishing, pp 224–31.

Whaley, A.L. and Davis, K.E. (2007) 'Cultural competence and evidence-based practice in mental health services: a complementary perspective', *American Psychologist*, 62: 563–74.

WHO (World Health Organisation) (2013) *Violence against women: a 'global health problem of epidemic proportions'*, http://www.who.int/mediacentre/news/releases/2013/violence_against_women_20130620/en/.

WHO (World Health Organisation) (2016) *Violence and Injury Prevention: prevention of Intimate partner and sexual violence (violence against women), Intimate partner and Sexual violence factsheet*, http://www.who.int/mediacentre/factsheets/fs239/en/

Williams, B. (2000) 'Youth offending teams and partnerships', *British Criminology Conference: Selected Proceedings*, Volume 3, www.britsoccrim.org/volume3/016.pdf

Wilson, D.M., Ratajewicz, S. E., Els, C. and Asirifi, M.A. (2011) 'Evidence-based approaches to remedy and also to prevent abuse of community-dwelling older persons', *Nursing Research and Practice*, 861484.

Worling, J.R., and Långström, N. (2006) 'Risk of sexual recidivism in adolescents who offend sexually: correlates and assessment', in H.E. Barbaree and W.L. Marshall (eds), *The juvenile sex offender*, New York and London: The Guilford Press, pp 219–47.

Yokley, J., LaCortiglia, J. and Bulanda, B. (2007) 'An overview of social responsibility therapy for preteen children with sexual behaviour problems', in M.C. Calder (ed.), *Working with children and young people who sexually abuse: taking the field forward*, Lyme Regis: Russell House Publishing Limited, pp 262–75.

Zayed, Y. and Harker, R. (2015) *Children in care in England: statistics*, Briefing Paper No. 04470, 5th October, London: House of Commons Library.

Zehr, H. (2015) *The little book of restorative justice: revised and updated (justice and peacebuilding)*, Brattleboro, VT: Good Books.

Zinsstag, E. and Keenan, M. (2017) 'Restorative responses to sexual violence: legal, social and therapeutic dimensions', London: Routledge.

Zweig, J. and Dank, M. (2013) *Teen dating, violence and harassment in the digital world: implications for prevention and intervention*, Washington, DC: The Urban Institute.

Index